CHARLES HADFIELD

CANAL MAN AND MORE

Dedicated with respect to

Brenda M. Boughey
My own Alice Mary

and the memory of

Joseph Pemberton Jepson Boughey (1922–1986)
for whom my respect continues to grow

and Ellis Charles Raymond Hadfield (1909–1996)
il meglio artigiano

CHARLES HADFIELD

CANAL MAN AND MORE

Joseph Boughey

with autobiographical writings by
Charles Hadfield

SUTTON PUBLISHING
in association with
THE INLAND WATERWAYS ASSOCIATION

First published in 1998 by
Sutton Publishing Limited · Phoenix Mill
Thrupp · Stroud · Gloucestershire · GL5 2BU
in association with
The Inland Waterways Association

British Library Cataloguing in Publication Data
A catalogue record for this book is available from the British Library.

ISBN 0-7509-1052-6

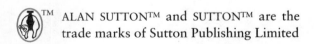TM ALAN SUTTONTM and SUTTONTM are the
trade marks of Sutton Publishing Limited

Typeset in 10/13pt Sabon.
Typesetting and origination by
Sutton Publishing Limited.
Printed in Great Britain by
Biddles Limited, Guildford and King's Lynn

CONTENTS

FOREWORD

It sounds trite, not to speak a truism, to say that I am honoured, more than honoured, to be asked to write a foreword to this book. I knew and loved Charles over about fifty years. I think we both found ourselves involved in canals at roughly the same time. I have also always thought that *he* loved my husband Tom, in spite of their disagreements in a number of ways. It seems necessary to say this; how else to justify one's presence on pages preceding this remarkable book?

It is remarkable in that it not only sets the man Charles Hadfield before us by the careful weaving of documents, reflection and recollections, but also ventures forth, on academic and historical grounds, towards stabilising those uncertain tides of reputation and happening, historical status and the fluctuating viability of canals themselves over a similar period and of Charles's position in this field. Charles as history. Of course, Charles can never be history to me, entwined as some of the memories of him and Alice Mary are with my own memories.

In the latter half of the volume the subject of it speaks out on his own, enlivening us with the wry and dry humour remembered, in recollections of the strong vigour of early and middle life, and rending us somewhat with the mild and straightforward telling of latter-day loss and declared sustained love.

I suppose that it was after Eily Gayford brought him to our own boats that I first found myself sitting on what I recollect was a packing case, to have supper (later referred to by Tom as the Hadfield plain-living high-thinking period) and enveloped by the particular warmth and friendship which was to last so long. It was surely lucky that this should be so. Looking back, Charles cannot have approved of much of what I was doing or thinking at that time, and we continued a fairly impassioned argument thereafter. The point I was trying to make was that there was an equal truth in the expressed feelings and emotions *of the time*, such as Clare's poems of rural loss, as there could be in extracted records of withdrawing shareholders: both the inheritance on which to build and think.

Did he finally think he had completed his life? I think he did. He was certainly very ordered in completions at the end, alone at South Cerney. We shared intimacies and confidences of a fireside kind at this time. I know he suffered in thinking of Alice Mary, ordering her papers and correspondences. He once said that he believed the rejection of his potential contribution to the awakening canal interest through the Inland Waterways Association after the war (and he implied Tom's as well) had driven the course of his life to show activity could be as effective and of another sort to that they both had had to leave behind.

Charles's public life, his writings, his monumental foundation history in the canal volumes show this life effective indeed.

Sonia Rolt
June 1998

AUTHOR'S NOTE AND ACKNOWLEDGEMENTS

Part Two of this book is based on drafts by Charles Hadfield; when Charles died on 6 August 1996, he had spent much of the preceding week cutting and moving text. Although the drafts were not quite finalised, it proved possible to present these for publication. He left instructions that no aspects should be added which an editor might feel should be committed to print. I have edited these so as to keep as far as possible to Charles's words. Where explanatory words or sentences needed to be added, I have enclosed these in square brackets [ ]. In the few places where I have incorporated material from other accounts by Charles, this is indicated in endnotes. I hope that the result conveys the spirit of what Charles intended, almost entirely in his own words.

I have attempted to avoid language which is gender-specific, but it has to be recorded that posts were called 'chairmen', and that many of those quoted herein, including Charles, assumed that their audience would be male. Although I am young enough for these assumptions to grate, I have been unable to adopt gender-neutral language throughout.

I have adopted the practice that those few who were Charles's enemies should be referred to by surname, those closest to him by forename. So it is 'Aickman', but 'Tom Rolt' or 'Tom'. One exception is Charles Clinker: almost everybody who knew him refers to him as 'Clinker'. In academic writings everyone is referred to by surname, but it would be inappropriate to use this for people whom Charles knew intimately.

Metrication is a perennial problem; I have used metric and Imperial equivalents for more recent times, but left measurements in earlier periods undisturbed.

The illustrations are mainly photographs from Charles's own, rather disorganised, collection. He was emphatically not a photographer, but took snapshots to provide reminders to himself. Nevertheless, they are of some historic interest, and this will, it is hoped, outweigh their limited quality.

Some waterways have alternative names; I have called what some call the 'Caldon Canal' the 'Caldon Branch' of the Trent & Mersey Canal throughout, while what some call the 'Brecon & Abergavenny Canal' I have called by its original name of 'Brecknock & Abergavenny Canal'. My apologies if anyone is offended.

Very many people have helped me in the research for Part One, and in explaining points which assisted in the editing of Part Two. I should first thank colleagues in the School of the Built Environment, especially Professor David Jagger, Deputy Director, who approved leave towards the completion of what seemed an unusual study, and Paul Hodgkinson, who drew the maps with his usual skill. My wife Brenda, who urged me not to carry out this project, nevertheless provided much practical assistance, and bore with evenings, weekends and much annual leave demolished in the cause of research.

So many have helped in diverse ways that I can only list them here: Arnold Allen; Professor Theo Barker; Gordon Biddle; Raymond Bowen; Grahame Boyes; John Boyes; Allan Brackenbury; Kenneth R. Clew; Dr Edwin Course; Richard Dean; John Horsley Denton; David Edwards-May; Alan Faulkner; Pamela Griffiths; Alec Hadfield; the late Alfred Hayman; Dr David Hilling; Tony Hirst and Lynn Doylerush of the Boat Museum, Ellesmere Port; Stanley Holland; John Humphries; Dr Guy Johnson; Roger Kidner; David Kinnersley; Dr Jean Lindsay; Dr Alan McCutcheon; John Miller; Ian Moss; John Norris; Ron Oakley; Martin Palmer; the late Neil Pitts; Dr Angela Raspin and staff at the British Library of Political and Economic Science; staff at the Public Record Office; Ronald Russell; Malcolm Sadler; Kenneth Seaward; Robert Shopland; Paul Sillitoe; Professor Jack Simmons; Professor Alec Skempton; Peter Stevenson; Jackie Stratford; John Taunton; David Tew; David St John Thomas; David Tomlinson; Paul Vine; Alan Voce; Philip and Rodney Weaver; and Ian L. Wright. My account of 1960s events was enhanced by earlier researches, assisted by the late Pauline Dower, the late Christopher Marsh and the late Admiral Sir Frederick Parham.

It may be invidious to single out anyone, but two people must be specially mentioned. Dr Mark Baldwin, Charles's literary executor, gave me a free hand to move and use numerous papers from Charles's house, answered many questions and allowed me to use his bibliography of Charles's writings. Sonia Rolt has not only written the Foreword, but offered me hospitality at Stanley Pontlarge and provided many insights into Charles's life; she is one of those rare people through whom history seems to flow.

Needless to say, none of those who helped is responsible for any errors or misconceptions in this book, or for my interpretations.

INTRODUCTION

This book contains elements of both biography and autobiography, in two distinct parts. The second comprises a collection of personal reminiscences by Charles Hadfield, best known for the serious study of history and contemporary events in the canal world. Those who have assumed, given his prolific writings about transport and transport history, that he had no other major concerns in his life, will be surprised.

The first part, for which I have been entirely responsible, is a study of Charles's canal work, largely based on named primary sources, analytical, and attempting assessment. This includes some unpublished reminiscences and contemporary writings from Charles Hadfield, but presented within a framework which seeks to explain and assess his developing contribution to the transport field in which he was involved. It is possible to follow elements of a chronological biography, but one set within a wider context of events and developments than 'straight' biographies usually attempt.

This book takes this form partly because of the initial division of interest between Charles and myself, and partly because of the way in which my concerns have predominated, especially since Charles's death in August 1996. It is thus very much my study of Charles, and reflects my deepening interest in the detailed development of literature, personalities and events, alongside a more academic drive to analyse and explain.

I am both a university lecturer and an enthusiast for inland waterways and their history, and my account reflects this dual background. I was, however, an enthusiast long before I completed a postgraduate research thesis and subsequently became an academic. The research processes involved in my thesis made me re-examine what had earlier seemed a parochial enthusiasm and perceive its connections to academic concerns. I hope that the first part can thus be read in two ways: as a study by an academic whose mission is to analyse and explain, and as a study by an enthusiast who wanted to know more about his subject.

I grew up with Charles Hadfield's work; at the age of sixteen I bought the last of his volumes in the 'British Isles' series. Like Charles, I grew up with transport and travel; on numerous journeys with my mother in the early 1960s along the railways from New Brighton to Wrexham Central and Chester Northgate, my fascination lay in the journey, not in the destination. I grew up also with canals and their history, on family boat holidays between 1963 and 1974. Only now that I too am in middle age do I realise what a pestilential nuisance it must have been for my father to spend his well-earned annual holiday with a son who wanted to stop to photograph every derelict canal, and who argued with him even over the names of canals, so that the 'Llangollen Canal' had to be called the 'Ellesmere Canal', 'because it says that in *Hadfield*'. I shared with Charles a further circumstance: we both had sociable and popular fathers who did not seem to understand their solitary and unsociable only sons, for whom collections of books and artefacts were much better companions than other boys. Perhaps for the same reason, reading and writing have been overwhelmingly important in my life too.

I first met Charles (and his wife Alice Mary) on 21 September 1985, when I interviewed him as a source for a proposed book which was, despite Charles's encouragement, never to appear. He was not as I had expected: he proved to be very tall, with a fairly high-pitched voice, very welcoming, kindly, and self-effacing. He lived in a very ordinary modern semi-detached house, which manifested no air of history beyond the contents of his bookshelves. Behind his thick spectacles, his faintly hooded eyes indicated a toughness (but not a hardness); I felt that anyone who came to talk nonsense to him would not last long. He seemed impressed by my insatiable curiosity about canal history, and even more by my enthusiasm for serious transport history which would both meet his own exacting standards of accuracy and develop new approaches to explanation.

I met him once more before Alice Mary died; she had appeared a little eccentric before, but by now was distressingly confused. He mentioned that a new edition of *British Canals* was needed. I wrote to him to express my sympathy, and suggested that I might be able to help with a new edition of *British Canals*, perhaps by checking the occasional fact. To my astonishment, he wrote back to suggest that I should rewrite the entire book. I duly did so, writing a completely reshaped and reoriented book, which Charles steadfastly declined to read until Sutton Publishing delivered a copy to him. We called it *Hadfield's British Canals* to reflect the change in authorship, and in the hope that it could outlive Charles (as indeed it has).

On numerous visits to archives to research articles for various waterways journals, I had become aware of the way in which sources for history could disappear when files were destroyed, evidence on the ground was swept away, and witnesses' memories removed with every obituary. Aware that Charles's memories could die with Charles, I sought to recover the way in which he had fashioned his canal history work through the rendering of primary sources, field explorations and the writing and editing process itself. He agreed to discuss this with me, along with his role in waterways developments since the 1940s, in which I was already deeply interested. At the time, I envisaged scholarly articles rather than a book.

To provide me with some background, Charles forwarded two manuscripts of private autobiographical writings, the first of which, the 'family autobiography' *Youth Shows But Half*, he had produced in 1974 for his children. He told me that while he had completed this in 1974, some events had been written up shortly after they took place, before his own memories would fade. Parts of Charles's reminiscences in Part Two, notably on his Fire Service work, thus date, in edited form, from the mid-1940s. He also mentioned that he was attempting to write an 'autobiography' of Alice Mary, using her words where possible from her published and unpublished writings and letters, amid his own recollections, apparently as a form of recovery.

Charles had declined to write a full autobiography, but in 1991 agreed that Harry Arnold, the prominent waterways journalist and photographer, should write a full but 'canal-angled' biography. Charles insisted that it was not to appear as a 'ghosted' autobiography, and that, subject to factual accuracy, Harry was to express any opinions he wished about Charles's work. When other pressures made it difficult for Harry to proceed, it became possible to expand my own researches towards a book, corresponding to the material in Part One.

When the latter proposal was put forward, it was met with a counter-proposal that Charles should write a full-scale autobiography himself, expanding his private writings. He declined this, but then saw an opportunity to publish an edited version of his earlier work alongside my study of his canal work; this was soon agreed. He worked on successive selected drafts of Part Two, and was still working on these, almost to completion, in the last week of his life. Since his death I have had the difficult task of moulding these into more coherent form. Charles had envisaged this necessity, and left instructions (to which I have, with minor exceptions, adhered) that I should not add to this account.

I should stress that some of the apparent omissions from, and emphases in, Charles's account relate to the manner in which his drafts were written. For instance, while he tells us little about his children, this is not surprising, as he wrote *Youth Shows But Half* for them. The last chapter concentrates more on Alice Mary than on Charles, but it is drawn from a very much larger account in which his feelings for her were paramount. The 'Scenes' in Part Two record what was important to Charles outside the world of inland waterways with which his name will always be associated.

I must also stress further points about my own account in Part One. First, it was not planned, directed, detailed or approved by Charles; it is my work entirely. Where Charles's opinions are given, they are sourced; otherwise any editorial opinions, about Charles or about the world which he influenced, are mine, or are quoted from named sources. Where controversies (and there were a number) are discussed, I try to distinguish between my views and those of Charles and others. This is not a study in hagiography, and our views were not synonymous.

Second, I do not know how much of Part One would have been endorsed by Charles; I have a vision of him being somewhat bemused, but it is a matter of obvious regret that he did not survive to see it. The opportunity for him to discuss his contribution to a much wider field has been lost, although I suspect that he would have insisted that this was a matter for others to decide. I should stress that some of the matters upon which I focus attention reflect my own interests. For instance, I enjoyed reading about his canal exploration visits on foot and by boat, and I was fascinated by some of his experiences searching records in archives, so these are shared with readers. I doubt if Charles would share my somewhat sentimental interest in places which have since, inevitably, greatly changed, but I have tried to bring these to life. He might also, perhaps, be dubious about the more academic emphasis of parts of my study, especially the concluding chapter.

Third, and oddly, most of this book has been written since Charles's death, and it is macabre to speculate about what would have emerged had he survived. It is sadly true that people are more keen to discuss a person after they have died than while they are still alive. Despite Charles's insistence that I would have to garner other participants' views of him, many more were forthcoming once they were aware that I could no longer consult him. His death, sadly, thus brought me into contact with many new sources, which have enabled me to quote from numerous letters which I had not seen. I had the unpleasant task of clearing from his house papers about which he was probably only dimly aware, and these have provided me with many observations and much information about the progress of events. Charles was surprisingly unforthcoming about sources which would have helped; perhaps he feared shaping my study too much and inhibiting the production of a reasonably objective account. On occasions, when my questions to him grew more obscure and detailed, he seemed to indicate that a brief summary of matters upon which I spent much time (the early IWA, for instance) would surely suffice.

I have thus had to piece together evidence for my account from widely scattered sources. These have included several thousand private letters, Charles's research files at the LSE and Boat Museum, and materials at the Public Record Office, as well as gleanings from his own literature and my own correspondence with his surviving contemporaries. The main deficiency, however, has been my inability to seek corroboration from him of some of my discoveries and interpretations. That, rather than any practical assistance over drafting or structure, is the collaboration which has been lost – and lost irrevocably.

Finally, during my researches I have become increasingly aware that postwar research into canal history, seen in some quarters as a parochial pursuit for eccentrics, has formed a component of wider postwar developments in the study of industrial archaeology and transport history. In the absence of any comprehensive account of this movement, I have had to sketch parts in order to attempt to set Charles's contribution against a wider background, along with other figures in transport history. I hope that rigorous studies will eventually appear of the postwar development of transport literature, of transport history and industrial archaeology, and of individuals influential in these fields, which will enable a more detailed assessment of Charles's contribution.

Charles's funeral on 14 August 1996, at which I had to deliver an appreciation of his life, proved a strange if moving affair. After I had spoken, rather shakily as grief took hold, the vicar announced that Charles had left a self-composed obituary with strict instructions to read this out. This reflected Charles's concern for the accuracy of information to the very end. After the funeral, I found myself to be a temporary celebrity, hearing many tributes to Charles. One gentleman, though, came up to ask me why I had not mentioned (in a very short appreciation) events in which he and Charles had been involved, and he showed me an extract from an account which Charles had sent him, part of which appears in Part Two. I have been haunted by this gentleman, and the feeling that I had somehow written him out of Charles's life. I have had to select, and Charles made his own selection, but we should both apologise if anyone feels that they have been omitted unfairly.

While working on this book, I have become increasingly aware of the barriers which exist between the serious academic study of transport history and that produced by enthusiasts or those professionally involved in transport. Charles's work sought to breach these barriers, for whose existence there seems to be no rational justification; I hope that his example will be followed by others. Transport and engineering history are among the fields in which some have reduced the height of the barriers both between academic disciplines and inside and outside academia. I would here pay tribute to my own university colleagues in civil engineering who view inland waterways as a serious subject for academic study.

The conclusion should not be drawn that with the loss of Charles, there is a limited future for inland waterways history in Britain. I hope instead that study of his example may assist the modest revival in such history which now seems to be beginning. I hope that this book achieves the dual aims of contributing to the serious study of wider movements in the history of the built environment, and detailing the life and work, serious and light, of one of its principal contributors.

Joseph Boughey
January 1998

PART ONE

Charles Hadfield's Contribution to Canal History

JOSEPH BOUGHEY

CHAPTER ONE

BEGINNINGS TO 1950

Today Charles Hadfield's name is synonymous with canal history, but for someone who was to contribute so much to the development of canals and canal history in Britain, his early background was an unlikely one. Born in South Africa on 5 August 1909, he lived there until the age of thirteen. While South Africa has no canals or river navigations, Charles travelled a great deal by rail and ship, and attributed to this his general interest in transport and later in both the history and future of canals. He subsequently felt that the intense interest of most South Africans in politics, and his lack of feeling for the status divisions inherent in British society, also provided him with the motive and confidence to become actively involved in the development of policy.

Probably the fact that he was an only child, outstandingly tall and disliked for it, meant that he spent much time in private study, in reading and with his collections, rather than spending it with other children. Much must lie behind his later comment that 'I did not like most other boys, and most certainly they did not like me, whereas my collections were good friends.'[1] Many writers lead lives marked by solitary periods; Charles would prove no exception.

THE GRAND WESTERN TO WILLAN

Charles's mother came from Devon, and when his father retired they moved there, arriving in Plymouth in 1923. They soon moved to Halberton, in rural mid-Devon, so that Charles could attend Blundells School near Tiverton. There, on walks, he soon encountered what he later described as 'perhaps the most extraordinary canal in England'.[2] The Grand Western Canal was mysterious: an isolated length of canal built to barge dimensions, with extensive engineering works, which 'began at Tiverton at a basin high above the town, ran past Blundells School and then in a long curve, the Swan's Neck, round Halberton to Sampford Peverell and its apparent end at nowhere in particular beyond Burlescombe quarries by the Somerset border'.[3] When he first saw it, the final minor traffic in quarried roadstone to Elsworthy's Wharf was just ending. Charles had seen no other canals, nor any part of the extensive network in lowland England, with its surviving traffics, some by narrow boat, and its potential for development.

Today, enquiry in one of Charles's volumes in the 'Canals of the British Isles' series would reveal the essential history of this or any other canal, but there were few readily available sources in the 1920s, and his researches only began after a chance encounter. In September 1925 Charles's father invited the family solicitor, who practised in Tiverton, to dinner, over which Charles casually asked him if he knew anything about the Grand Western. The solicitor replied that his firm had acted for the Grand Western Canal Company, before it was taken over by the Great Western Railway, and it still had a tin box of records relating to it. Charles agreed to examine these with care, and so, 'Sixteen, I now handled for the first time original documents and records dating from the eighteenth century.'[4] The tin box proved to contain two types of record. Charles transcribed and returned the printed documents, but was allowed to retain handwritten correspondence for further study. Much later these were deposited with the other records at Tiverton Museum.

The death of Charles's father in 1926 was devastating, emotionally and financially; probably Charles's researches helped him retreat from these cares. His interests deepened when he moved with his widowed mother to Rock Cottage in Halberton, directly alongside the canal; then, in the spring of 1927, his mother moved to Plymouth, leaving him to lodge in the village with the family of Violet Marshall, so that he could continue to attend Blundells School. Although she was twenty years his senior, he became unofficially engaged to Violet at the age of eighteen.

Courting Violet involved explorations along the Grand Western towpath at Halberton, which heightened his interest in the canal. Further and wider researches followed visits to the library in Exeter, some 15 miles away, to explore successive files of the *Exeter Flying Post*. Only four sides of each issue of the newspaper needed to be examined, and he soon began to learn about other canals, both in the West Country and (more briefly) elsewhere. Still at school, he wrote an account of the Grand Western Canal for himself; methodically compiled and set out, the manuscript survived for many years. This early work seems to have followed the same methodical approach as those which he later expounded.

From these further researches, Charles learned that some canals were the result of over-ambitious schemes, like the canal he knew, which formed a branch from a main line that was never built; that the barge canal had been later extended by a small tub-boat canal to Taunton which employed some of the world's earliest boat lifts; and that some canals were taken over by railway companies, either by lease, like the Grand Western at first, or by outright purchase, both to reduce competition and to enable their lines to be built. He would not apply these insights to general transport history for another seventeen years.

His interests at Blundells School lay mainly in the humanities, studying English, history and economics in the sixth form. Economic history as such was then very much in its infancy, even at universities, and even economics was rarely taught in schools. In 1928 he won an exhibition in English at Oxford, but moved to read Economics in the new School of Philosophy, Politics and Economics. Charles has left few clues as to his motivations, but he fully intended to marry Violet on his return from Oxford. This relationship certainly removed a major source of distraction for a studious youth.

Charles's studies at Oxford between 1928 and 1932 enhanced his general intellectual abilities, but did not involve further investigations into canal history. He did briefly attempt further research into the Grand Western at the Bodleian Library in Oxford, but found himself defeated by the Bodleian's index system. He encountered canals on visits into the surrounding countryside; for instance, he cycled alongside parts of the Wilts & Berks Canal, much of which was still in water although it had closed in 1914.

He was reading economics as the early 1930s Depression began, and this made him develop a practical interest in politics; he became an instinctive reformer, seeking practical solutions soundly based on the detailed knowledge of problems. Thirty years later this would characterise his approach when he joined the first British Waterways Board.

His interest in transport – he took the periodical *Modern Transport* between 1931 and its final issue in 1968 – lay at first in railways, where employment and future development might lie. Having failed to ensure employment with the London & North Eastern Railway Company, and newly married to Violet, he became involved with a second-hand bookshop between 1932 and 1936.

The bookshop did not excite interest in the few books which were related to transport history, almost all out of print. He did buy, for 6d each, three volumes of Samuel Smiles's *Lives of the Engineers*, which presented somewhat romanticised Victorian biographies of canal, road and railway engineers, including people such as Telford, Brindley and Rennie. Smiles laid the foundations of what would later be termed engineering biography, although this was rare until the 1950s.

Charles also bought, from other second-hand bookshops, H.R. De Salis's *Bradshaw's Canals and Navigable Rivers* of 1904, which detailed the ownership, dimensions and lengths of all operational navigations in England and Wales in 1901. *Priestley*, a not altogether accurate contemporary handbook from 1830, cost him 30s in 1938, when, as he put it, 30s was the price of 30 dinners. These books were professional and contemporary, rather than histories; much later, Charles's copies would be used for reprints by the publishers David & Charles. These books would eventually provide part of the backbone for a general history of canals, but he would only conceive this later.

He joined the Labour Party while living in Maida Vale, and was unexpectedly elected to Paddington Borough Council in 1934. Although Paddington's refuse was boated away to tips in Middlesex, Charles took only a councillor's interest in this activity. His engagement with waterways and their history was revived after 1936, when he went to work for Oxford University Press, and encountered his first new books on waterways history.

It may be difficult today, when there is so much enthusiasm for Britain's canals and river navigations, and even more for railways, to envisage a period when interest in their history and development was very limited. Charles's own work has since helped to create and foster interest among serious readers and researchers into transport history.

Charles's work would bridge three often different types of transport history, which may be loosely termed academic, professional and enthusiast. The authors of the few studies in British transport history up to the mid-1930s reflected these varied perspectives. The Canadian academic transport economist William Jackman had published *The Development of Transportation in Modern England* in 1916, much of it based on research between 1906 and 1915 into legislative and manuscript sources. Jackman regarded his study as a contribution to general history rather than as a study of transport; even so, it was 820 pages long. He stressed that

> it has required much self-constraint to keep from branching out farther into a discussion of the relation of transportation to the progress of agriculture, the growth of markets, the advance of industry, the increase of wealth, and many other economic and social factors which have affected the welfare of different classes of the people and of the nation as a whole.[5]

Jackman's 'modern' period ended around 1850, with one exception: 'the history of the canals has been sketched to date, in order to give a proper basis for judging of the merits of the existing agitation for the resuscitation of the inland waterways.'[6]

The pressure after 1900 for the improvement of waterway transport in lowland England brought forward a number of books by those who might be termed 'enthusiasts'. Edwin Pratt's *A History of Inland Transport and Communication in England* of 1912 was one of several books from this journalist; he also wrote two detailed polemics against the Royal Commission of 1906–12, which recommended the public ownership and enlargement of many English canals. Many investigators into British canal history would, like Charles at first, be enthusiasts without academic or professional involvement.

Other investigators might be classed as 'professional', being involved in and employed by, transport concerns. One example was C.E. Sherrington, head of the Railway Research Service of the Railway Companies Association, who produced the slighter *A Hundred Years of Inland Transport 1830–1933* in 1934. His 'chronicle of achievement' presented a Whiggish view of historical progress, and his introduction referred to the 'common cry that transport should be regarded as a coherent whole, not divided into the watertight compartments of rail, road and water movement; in practice, it is doubtful if transport has ever been regarded other than in its co-ordinated form'.[7]

Although Sherrington devoted most of his study to railways, he did acknowledge that railway development had not brought about the 'supposed extinction' of canals, and that some routes remained useful for freight transport. Later canal enthusiasts would follow the largely false assumption that the railway companies had deliberately stifled canal traffic, and that their release from railway control would thus bring forward new traffics and commercial viability.

By the 1930s, however, twenty years (and a world war) after the Royal Commission's final report, British canals were seen to belong in the past. Popular interest in railways, including, increasingly, their history, had grown since the completion of the last main lines in the 1890s. The four main interwar railway companies began to produce magazines which developed some interest in their history. However, waterways had only attracted studies of operations like that by Cadbury and Dobbs in 1929, policy discussions related to the Royal Commission of 1906–12, or popular boating handbooks and accounts of cruises. Interest in the history of British canals was at a nadir. Even in the *Transactions* of the Newcomen Society, formed in 1920 to foster the historical study of engineering and technology, there were more studies of the horse tramroads which often served canals, and of overseas canals, than in the canals of Britain, about which the first major papers would only appear in 1950.

After Charles joined Oxford University Press (henceforth OUP) in 1936, he acquired the firm's only canal books, beginning with the canals volume of Vernon-Harcourt's *Rivers and Canals*, a professional study by a Victorian engineer which was now of historical interest. Later he would buy Christopher Roberts's *The Middlesex Canal* of 1938; this academic history of an American canal, which Charles found dull, reflected the availability of extensive, well-organised archives in the United States. As Charles would discover, until the 1950s much British canal history could not be based upon primary sources in public archives.

A much more significant purchase was that of Thomas S. Willan's *River Navigation in England 1600–1750*, which inspired an interest in the general history of English waterways. Dr Willan was an academic historian, even younger than Charles, but his study, published in 1936, laid the foundations for Charles's work.

River Navigation in England was strictly an academic study, reflecting the concerns of economic history. In Britain, this was a young discipline which had only really developed after the 1890s; the London School of Economics had been founded only in 1895, with the first full-time lecturer in economic history appointed in 1904. One notable centre was the University of Manchester, where the first professor of economic history was appointed in 1910; Dr Willan would become the third such professor, in 1961. In 1926 the Economic History Society was founded, to publish a journal, the *Economic History Review*, and to hold an annual meeting.

Dr Willan's study established that river navigations had been a much more significant part of English internal transport than most historians, following Macaulay, had thought; they had assumed that before the development of canals, inadequate turnpike roads formed the principal form of inland transport. Willan's book, taken from a larger D.Phil thesis which also examined the coasting trade, provided the first comprehensive study of English waterways history. It detailed the history, mainly but not wholly legislative, of most river navigations, together with aspects of traffic and engineering. Willan made comparisons with canal-building in mainland Europe, which pre-dated that in England, but stressed that

The Dutch, French and Germans might provide concrete examples for the English pamphleteers and engineers, but none of them was strong enough to influence the public mind in the direction of canal building. The English preferred to direct what energy they had for navigable waterways towards their rivers, and it was only when they had exhausted what appeared to be the possibilities of these that they turned to canals as the connecting links of a system the foundations of which they had already laid.[8]

He proceeded to demonstrate this through detailed empirical research and examples, and to point out that the canal network from the late eighteenth century completed, but did not supersede, the water transport possibilities opened up by river navigations.

Charles would become the chronicler of that canal network, and there were other similarities with Willan, whose obituarist stressed that 'Willan's scholarship was innovatory, and was characterised by close attention to manuscript sources . . . not for him the broad generalisation, nor the thrust of current debate.'[9] This bias towards a neutral detailing of the factual partly reflected the approach of colleagues in what has been termed the Manchester School, which then included T.S. Ashton, or Willan's D.Phil supervisor, Professor George Clark of Oxford. The latter's approach has been criticised as 'Not analysing, not using economics, not posing economic questions, not demanding to know how long, how much, or how representative: but tracing. This was indeed the historian's route to the neutralist position.'[10]

This would tend to epitomise Charles's approach to the writing of history, but not his approach to modern policies towards waterways. Dr Willan's work, supplemented by various specialised studies of individual rivers which appeared elsewhere up to the 1950s, would be a major influence upon Charles's later attempts to establish a factual basis for canal history in England and Wales.

After reading his book, Charles contacted Willan, who suggested that he join the Economic History Society. Charles probably attended its annual meeting of 1939 and there met Willan, whom he found less memorable than his work, but helpful. Charles felt daunted by the academics there, thinking that they might look down on amateur enthusiasts like him. The war would curtail further contact, but provide opportunities for practical research.

WARTIME RESEARCH

Charles's relationship with his first wife Violet began to deteriorate in the late 1930s, and from 1938 he began to develop a strong attachment to Alice Mary Miller, who also worked at OUP. Together, on visits to Ludlow, he and Alice Mary explored the remains of long-forgotten waterways like the Leominster Canal. Just before war broke out in 1939, realising that it might part them for good, they hired a camping punt on the Thames at Kingston for a fortnight, taking it to Shillingford and back. Two months later Charles was preparing to fight fires on wartime service on the Thames in London, while Alice Mary was to leave for the safety of Bermuda in August 1940.

During 1939 and 1940, during visits to Alice Mary in Oxford, Charles carried out some research at the offices of the Oxford Canal Company, in what he later recalled as 'the lovely eighteenth-century Canal House at Oxford'.[11] With no particular view to their future use, he copied entries from ledgers which summarised the tonnages handled at various wharves. Later, while the Oxford company retained its minute books, it sold the ledgers for scrap; Charles's notes now provide the only surviving records.

Detailed research into primary sources began during wartime service, and accelerated after Alice Mary left for Bermuda. He then had one day in every three free, an uncertain future in the Blitz, and few other distractions. He and a companion, Geoffrey Charles, known as 'Chas', explored London's second-hand bookshops, searching for old waterways books, and entertained ideas of buying a narrow boat for pleasure use, to explore the waterways detailed in De Salis's book. They were considering the purchase of a surplus Grand Union Canal Carrying Company narrow boat, converting a car engine in the basement of the fire station, when 'Chas' joined the RAF after the invasion of Norway in April 1940.

They found books in Charing Cross Road (including the celebrated no. 84), and a specialist transport bookshop, Graftons, in Museum Street, opposite the British Museum. Prices were then very low, and Charles built up a large collection – probably then the largest library of its kind. One bizarre feature of pre-war publishing was that any Act of Parliament could be acquired from HMSO at its original price, so long as copies were in stock. Charles was thus able to acquire all four Grand Western Canal Acts. After the Blitz, such documents became rare.

He also began research in libraries and archives. At the outbreak of war, he was still interested in the Grand Western Canal. He contacted the editor of *Great Western Railway Magazine*, who, in turn, put him in contact with the curator of the GWR Collection, Ted Atkinson, who would later become archivist to British Transport Historical Records. Records there included those of other GWR-owned canals such as the Kennet & Avon Navigation, and the Swansea, Monmouthshire and Brecknock & Abergavenny Canals in South Wales.

Dr Willan introduced a further source; like Jackman, he had used the pamphlet collections in the Goldsmiths Library of the University of London. Charles found this library up in Senate House; it included a good catalogue of canal material. Charles made so many requests for documents that the librarian eventually allowed him to look through the book stacks himself. One bound collection of reports, *Somerset Canals*, proved directly useful for his first publication.

He spent most of his time in the Institution of Civil Engineers (henceforth ICE) Library, then behind sandbagged walls; assent to research was quickly given. He discovered a vast collection of books on waterways engineering, daunting in size and number, and sixty bound volumes of pamphlets and booklets. He began to read the latter, which were disordered and unclassified, then listed each one, and read laboriously all those which seemed of interest, focusing mainly on waterways in southern England. Much of the material related to the Thames and associated canals, which he would use for his second publication. Some notes, like those on Brazilian waterways, would be used forty years later for *World Canals*.

Leave days also provided the opportunity to get away from London and the noise of the Blitz, and to search for records. He discovered that Smallpeice and Merriman, the former solicitors to the Wey & Arun Junction Canal Company, which had closed in 1868, still had an office in Guildford, where he arranged to see their records. He spent a series of leave days taking extracts from minute books and other records, and found a plate used to print share certificates. The solicitors allowed him to borrow this; he had it cleaned, at unexpectedly high expense, and a series of blank certificates printed. One of these would later be used to illustrate *British Canals*, along with items from his collection of company seals. The Wey & Arun records were later saved from destruction and placed in the Surrey Record Office.

He spent his longer annual leave in 1942 with his mother near Tavistock. There he explored the small Tavistock Canal, which had long been disused. Explorations included the long tunnel and inclined plane leading down to Morwellham, then very overgrown. He visited the Tavistock estate offices of the canal's owner, where he met the insistence that he could only take notes from records of the canal in pencil, then an unfamiliar practice. He would put these notes to good use five years later.

Risks which would be unacceptable today were taken with original documents then, despite the Blitz. Charles learned that a museum in Basingstoke held documents relating to the Basingstoke Canal, and the curator posted the actual original documents to him at his fire station in Putney. He dutifully typed out extracts from minutes and reports at his desk in the station and in its air-raid shelter, and then posted them back. Later he learned that, at the height of the Blitz, a Bristol solicitor had sent records of two Somerset waterways, the Bridgwater & Taunton and Chard Canals, to a London office, which was destroyed by incendiaries.

Charles had not visited many waterways except the Tavistock, but when he moved to work on the *Manual of Firemanship*, between 1942 and 1945, this involved much travel to various points in Britain, and he took the opportunity to visit waterways which were strictly *en route*. On one memorable day, travelling from York to Hull, he succeeded in viewing the Yorkshire Derwent at Stamford Bridge, the Pocklington Canal at Canal Head, the Market Weighton Canal and Beverley Beck. He also visited waterways in Scotland, including both ends of the Forth & Clyde Canal.

WARTIME WRITING

While his gathering enquiries had no particular aim, Charles was uncovering haphazard but detailed historical materials, which he could link to Willan's work, and older, out of print books like *Phillips* and *De Salis*, which detailed the waterways system of England and Wales at particular dates. He needed to shape these materials to fit the available means of publication. Charles was familiar with publishing from his work with OUP, and had growing experience of writing on other subjects (detailed in Chapter 9). His first short book had been published in 1940, but his first canal work was to appear in an academic journal, which is still being published.

This was the *Economic History Review*, in which Charles's first article, 'Canals between the English and the Bristol Channels', appeared in 1942. This incorporated Charles's schoolday researches, along with material from primary sources and a 1914 article from the *Great Western Railway Magazine*. A further source was E.T. MacDermot's *History of the Great Western Railway*, published in 1927 and 1931, one of the few serious volumes of railway history produced by this time; Charles would later meet Charles Clinker, one of MacDermot's assistants. The article ranged beyond the more parochial story of the Grand Western Canal to consider other waterways which had been built, including the Bridgwater & Taunton Canal, and several schemes which had not materialised. It also considered canal lifts and inclined planes; the Grand Western featured both, but only one example, at Anderton in Cheshire, was then in use. More briefly, it considered railway company ownership and schemes for ship canals; while their inclusion was probably essential in a learned journal, these were subjects to which Charles would return.

A further paper in this journal would be published late in 1944, by which time Charles's abilities and writing experience had greatly advanced through much non-canal work on the *Manual*. This covered the Thames Navigation and associated canals, which had especially featured in the ICE records and the Goldsmiths pamphlets. Charles's meticulous notes, recorded in tiny handwriting, proved useful in assembling material from these diverse sources.

Wartime brought a further publication, more impressive in appearance but slighter in content. Charles had written *The Fire Service Today* with his colleague on the *Manual*, Frank Eyre. His pre-war experiences had included working as an editor and researcher, and racing at Brooklands. In 1943 he had begun to write a book about rivers, reflecting his leisure interests as a sea and river yachtsman and wild-water canoeist. In January 1944 Charles sought a copy of *Salters Guide to the Thames*, to help with what was then Frank Eyre's book, but on 10 May 1944 both he and Eyre signed a contract for a volume in Collins's 'Britain in Pictures' series, entitled *English Rivers and Canals*. While Charles's part was probably completed in 1944, illness delayed Eyre's contribution, and the book was not published until the end of 1945.

Frank Eyre's descriptive and over-lyrical material (he had published a volume of poetry in 1935) dominated part of the book. Charles contributed Chapter II, the only one not written in the first person. It mainly comprised stock elements from published works like Edwin Pratt's *British Canals*, enlivened with items such as one from the *Exeter Flying Post* about the Worcester & Birmingham Canal. One assertion reflects his contact with economic history: 'It is an interesting fact, and one seldom recorded, that it was inland waterways which first made possible the industrial revolution, and that a small stretch of canal between Worsley and Manchester is the cradle of England's modern industrial strength.'[12]

Later researches would qualify the latter assertion, but Charles's interest in modern waterways is reflected in his commendation of the then recent improvements to the Grand Union Canal, Trent, Aire & Calder, and Nene. The latter derived from contact with George Dallas, a former Labour MP who chaired the Nene Catchment Board. This book was a minor one, but in any event was overshadowed by the publication of another canal book, L.T.C. Rolt's *Narrow Boat*.

Charles's concerns in the latter part of the war centred around Alice Mary; she returned with her daughter Laura from Bermuda early in 1944, and they were to marry once he had divorced Violet. While they were to settle in Paddington, during 1944 they considered living in rural Wales or Gloucestershire. He did find time to pursue some research in Gloucester in 1945, into Severn Commission, and Gloucester & Berkeley Canal records.

Although most work was suspended in wartime, Charles remained a member of Paddington Borough Council and, with a general election inevitable, a career in politics was possible. Two surviving letters reveal his capacity to make fixed decisions about his own future. On 14 September 1944 he wrote: 'I do not yet know the lines of my life – whether books or politics or even writing of books or plays.' By 26 September his views had changed: 'Politics I need not regret – I have come to the end of an era in that. I feel that my future life lies in books – in publishing them, and writing them, and finding other people to write them. I have the experience now within me.'[13]

Nevertheless, he was to seek, unsuccessfully, nomination as Labour Prospective Parliamentary Candidate for Paddington North; as this would prove to be a Labour seat until reorganisation in 1979, his career might thus have been starkly different. He did not stand again for Paddington Council, and would later direct his political experience towards practical ends, including the future development of inland waterways.

NARROW BOAT AND THE IWA

December 1944 brought the publication of *Narrow Boat*, by L.T.C. Rolt; Charles bought a copy, from The Ken Bookshop at 84 Victoria Street, the jacket having caught his eye, and, 'I read it through at a sitting, and felt like Stanley meeting Livingstone. Here was a man who had done the voyaging, made the discoveries, that I had planned.'[14]

Narrow Boat described a journey in 1939 and 1940, in which Tom Rolt and his then wife Angela had explored many of the smaller English canals in *Cressy*, a narrow boat converted to form their home. His quest, however, was not leisure but to seek out an alternative way of life, connected to the rural past:

I felt certain that there could be no better way of approaching what is left to us of that older England of tradition which is fast disappearing. . . . Because they have been outpaced and forgotten in the headlong flight of modern progress, many old traditions and customs survive on the canals.[15]

The style of the resulting book, completed in 1940 but only published in 1944 after many rejections, resembled the country books from the 1920s and 1930s produced by publishers like Batsford. It described, as Charles discerned, 'with accuracy and insight, things which were already gone or were going'.[16] It was full of regret for the past: Tom Rolt felt that

> if the canals are left to the mercies of economists and scientific planners, before many years are past the last of them will become a weedy, stagnant ditch, and the bright boats will rot at the wharves, to live on only in old men's memories. It is because I fear that this may happen that I have made this record of them.[17]

Charles did not sympathise with this sentiment, but he was very impressed with *Narrow Boat*. He wrote later of his own writing career that 'little of it, except maybe one or two canal histories, would have happened had *Narrow Boat* not been written. The time, the need and the man came together to produce the book.'[18] Charles felt that the book demonstrated the possibilities of using canals for pleasure boating, a pursuit then mainly confined to the Norfolk Broads or rivers like the Thames. While it provided limited direct history, it recorded a world which had partly survived, and whose history needed to be investigated. Although Charles would come to see this as a precarious survival, it also provided some details of commercial traffic by narrow boat on canals.

Much more importantly, *Narrow Boat* drew public attention to canals; numerous letters followed its publication, and it enabled the formation of a campaigning body, publicity for waterways, and consequent interest in their history and future which would provide a market for publications.

In May 1945 Charles sent a letter of appreciation to Tom Rolt, suggesting that after the war some sort of society to encourage interest in waterways should be founded. Tom Rolt had not written the book with any campaigning purpose, but he received another letter, from Robert Aickman, which suggested the formation of a society to seek the preservation and development of waterways. Contact between these three men was to lead to the formation of the Inland Waterways Association (henceforth IWA).

While Charles had located others who shared an interest in waterways, it was a meeting of minds which differed in both aims and methods. Charles was interested in learning more about the canals, especially their history, but any concern for their future related mainly to their modernisation, including new waterways and craft, which he had already commended in *English Rivers and Canals*. Tom Rolt's perspective was almost the opposite. He primarily sought the survival of the narrow boat and the way of life of working boatpeople, who 'unconsciously applied that subtle traditional patina of constant use. . . . an essential part of that blend of utility and beauty which used to compound the particular magic of canals.'[19] His views emanated from a distrust of industrialism, and a type of romantic individualism, developed by his experiences on *Cressy*.

While Robert Aickman had very limited experience of canals, he saw this as a cause in which he could be influential. He was a supporter of Social Credit, a movement for financial reform which, while critical of the entertainment industry, fostered the view that leisure was a primary aim of human endeavour. This fitted well with his disdain for industry, his love of opera and theatre, and his disinclination to work for a living; it underlay his interest in pleasure-boating, for which the smaller waterways would eventually be retained.

These views diverged even further from Charles's views of the future, which were then optimistically left-wing. A Labour Government had been elected in July 1945 with a clear majority and a programme of nationalisation, which would include canals, railways and much road transport. He viewed work as a life-long pursuit, and he saw government and planning as a potentially benevolent force. He disagreed with the suspicion of nationalisation and of postwar planning inherent in Tom Rolt's press announcement of November 1945, which blamed the decline of the canals on 'the influence of centralised trade and transport monopolies', and objected to its attacks on 'collective planning' – 'Personally, I am in favour of it', he responded.

Charles's life during 1945 and 1946 was dominated by his second wedding, setting up home, his return to OUP, and commercial writing of 'potboilers' for magazines. He could therefore play only a limited part in the formation of the IWA, in which the driving force was Tom Rolt, who drafted the initial manifesto and press announcements. By January 1946 Rolt was urging Aickman that they must hold a public meeting, 'otherwise we would talk and write about it forever and get nowhere, whereas, in view of impending nationalisation, we ought to move soon or not at all'. He correctly saw the stumbling block as 'how the routine work of the Society can be done'.[20]

Charles laid out his own views of the proposed Society on 28 January 1946. He advocated the encouragement of waterborne trade on waterways where they were useful for this purpose, and pleasure traffic where they were not. Above all, he sought the gathering of information and publicity: 'The more we know, the more press publicity we can get.'[21] He was to develop his knowledge for other purposes, but would make his library and researches available to the early IWA.

A small group first met on 15 February 1946; Charles brought Frank Eyre along to lend him moral support. This meeting simply confirmed the intention to form an Inland Waterways Association, based on Tom Rolt's manifesto, and agreed to make Aickman chairman, Rolt secretary, Eyre treasurer and Charles vice-chairman. Charles took to Tom Rolt, with whom he had been corresponding, but was less impressed by Robert Aickman. The winter intervened, and at the first formal meeting on 8 May, a formal Council was appointed, and rules, based on those of the Richmond Canoe Club, were approved.

This meeting transacted very little business. Charles suggested a letter of protest to the Oldham Town Planning Committee, expressing regret at its postwar plans which included the proposed destruction of part of the Rochdale Canal; nobody knew at the time that this canal was unnavigable, and little more could be done.

Very much later, Charles would lend support to the restoration of this canal.

Tom Rolt was away exploring the Irish waterways during the spring and summer of 1946, and by the time of his return in September, Charles had resigned from the IWA Council. While Charles's evenings were mainly taken up by non-canal writing, much more had been expected from him by Robert Aickman, with whom Charles had two disturbing encounters. At one meeting, Aickman carefully read out a letter which he had written, and then said that he thought it so good that he should read it out again; to Charles's astonishment, he proceeded to do just that. On 11 July 1946 the Aickmans invited him for tea; Aickman complained that while 300 invitations to join the IWA had been sent out, only 13 responses had been received. Aickman wrote that 'Hadfield, however, professed himself quite undisturbed by it, and blandly remarked that we must expect to have to follow up most people with at least two personal letters.'[22] At this, much to Charles's surprise, Aickman burst into tears, and declared that the whole cause was lost.

In the event, Charles was correct, and membership did climb steadily; within twelve days, there were 65 members. His resignation coincided with his appointment in the Central Office of Information (henceforth COI), which precluded him from remaining an officer. Tom Rolt, however, perceived one of the real reasons for his withdrawal:

> I am sorry that you could not see eye to eye with Aickman. . . . Aickman has not, I know, an easily likeable personality, and is apt, on this account to antagonise people unreasonably. But he is remarkably enthusiastic and efficient, he has devoted an immense amount of time and labour to the IWA, and without his efforts it is extremely doubtful whether the Association would ever have been born at all.[23]

Charles also felt that Tom Rolt's draft of the IWA booklet *The Future of the Waterways* set out a future too far rooted in the past, seeking to preserve the way of life of traditional boating, rather than the development of leisure and, especially, modern freight waterways.

Charles had little further involvement with the IWA until 1950. However, his notes from the GWR Collection enabled him to help with queries about navigation rights over the GWR's Stratford Canal and its Kennet & Avon Navigation. In December 1946 Aickman heard rumours that the GWR company proposed to close the Kennet & Avon; Charles furnished him with a 'private history', based on his wartime researches. While Aickman urged Charles to 'rouse your many influential political friends to the enormity of this proposed abandonment',[24] by now Charles had no such friends.

Charles also submitted a canal bibliography for an IWA *Bulletin* in 1948. It was not then at all clear what had been published about canals, nor indeed what their precise history had been.

EXPLORING BRITISH CANALS

English Rivers and Canals brought another contact, with Eily ('Kit') Gayford, who had taught wartime female trainees to crew narrow boats out of London. She would be the Hadfields' first guest at their new home, late in 1945. As Charles recalled later, she 'talked as only Kit can, putting all of herself into every sentence. I don't think she realised how small she was making me feel, for after her five years of life on the boats she knew so much more about canals than I did.'[25]

She introduced Charles to narrow boat crews; her main contact was Sonia Smith, who had stayed on the boats when the other trainees left, and married a boatman. Charles first boarded a canal boat in October 1946, when Kit alerted him that Sonia and George Smith, on the narrow boats *Cairo* and *Warwick*, were in Regents Canal Dock, in Limehouse. Charles arrived in the dark, and 'Kit and Sonia and I sat in the cabin and talked . . . about Rolt and boaters' rations and all sorts of things.'[26] On another visit to the dock in August 1947, Charles took the Smiths some books; they sat and talked on the boat, and then went to the Grapes nearby, further downstream than the better-known Prospect of Whitby. They talked on the balcony there until 10.30, when Charles crossed the dock to return home. On another occasion Kit Gayford took him to Brentford Depot.

In autumn 1947 Charles spent a night with the Rolts on board *Cressy*, then moored at Gayton Junction. It was Charles's first night on board a canal boat, and his first visit to *Cressy*, and he recalled:

In one way I was full of admiration for what Tom had achieved, in another clear that such a life, in such a house, even without our children, was not for Alice Mary and me.

In early morning, drowsy, I heard the sound of a Bolinder approaching. It was strange and evocative. *Cressy* rocked gently once or twice in the wash of the pair that passed.[27]

On that weekend, as Charles later recalled, Tom and he argued 'all the length of the Northampton flight about the likely shape of the postwar world'.[28]

He had been impressed by Tom Rolt since their first meeting, and they assisted each other's researches. When they began to correspond in July 1945, Tom was working on *Worcestershire*, which would not be published until 1949; Charles sent him some details about the Southnet Tunnel on the Leominster Canal. Tom offered to find a narrow boat hull for Charles to convert and explore the canals, using *De Salis* as his guide; he soon relinquished this ambition, perhaps because his son Alec was born in 1946.

In January 1946 Tom noted some minor discrepancies in *English Rivers and Canals*, which he otherwise found 'admirable'. By this time Charles, still writing potboilers most evenings, planned to compile an anthology of canals, with Frank Eyre, for publication by OUP. On 6 February 1946 Tom sent him an unpublished piece for the anthology, but with Frank Eyre departing for Australia, Tom agreed to Charles's suggestion that they might collaborate in the anthology. Their writing commitments delayed this project, although they were still referring to it in August 1949; it never appeared, although Charles considered it further in the 1960s.

Charles was making plans for other books, some on religious and political subjects. In October 1946 Charles proposed a joint book with Alice Mary: 'I have a few notes in a file (as I have for innumerable books).'[29] Although Alice Mary was also a writer, no work would emerge until the 1960s. Charles was to complete or plan a number of books on non-canal subjects into the 1950s.

A review of *English Rivers and Canals* in *Time and Tide* of May 1946, suggested the need for a detailed history of canals:

> Mr Hadfield . . . has something valuable to offer us; indeed, his section on the canals could hardly, within its small compass, be bettered. Here is someone who knows what he is talking about and is not afraid, even in a brief popular sketch, to quote a few figures in support of his argument. We may hope that he will one day write a history of English canals for the general reader: it is much needed.[30]

The reviewer was Jack Simmons of University College Leicester (later Leicester University), who from 1947 would become Professor of History there, a position from which he would be a major influence on the growth and development of transport history. Unusually, Leicester University would develop both transport and urban history and provide bridges between academic and more popular history. His review inspired Charles, then at work with James MacColl MP on a book about local government, to consider a general history of canals.

A further influence was his appointment to the COI, which reduced some of the pressure to earn cash through writing. Once the book with James MacColl was finished, at the end of 1946, Charles turned to a canal history. The provisional title, *The Story of the Canals*, suggests a more superficial history than the careful synthesis from secondary sources which emerged.

Most of the research for the book was carried out in 1947; letters to Alice Mary demonstrate its progress during August. Charles spent the evening of 7 August copying extracts from library books, 'ploughing slowly and sorrowfully through the nineteenth century'. He commented that the second half of the book would be dull, as 'it records a decline with almost no relief'.[31] On the 10th he wrote that he had 'more or less finished the 1840–1900 chapter, though with yawning gaps in it' which would have to be filled. His interest in the twentieth century lay in the future rather than the past; one reason, ironically, was the dearth of available sources: 'the worst is ahead, for between 1900 and the war I know precious little, and worse, I'm not very sure where to go for the information. However, I shall find out.'[32]

This gap in twentieth-century coverage was rectified by a memorandum of 12 September 1947, which Charles obtained through COI; unusually for a civil servant, this contained much angry comment on the failure of governments to secure modernisation since the Royal Commission recommended it in 1910.

Charles continued to explore canals; in the same August, he explored the Thames & Medway Canal, catching a train between Gravesend and Rochester which ran alongside the canal, now out of use, and through Strood Tunnel, built for the canal until the railway was constructed along this part of its route. It had been the second longest canal tunnel in Britain before closure; at its far end he found the Strood Basin, still used by its owners, the Southern Railway.

The later research for this new book coincided with Tom Rolt's own waterways study, *The Inland Waterways of England*, commissioned late in 1947. They agreed that this should have limited historical coverage and be illustrated by photographs rather than line illustrations; Tom was concerned when the draft of Charles's new book was illustrated by photographs, and they had to make hurried comparisons in April 1949 to avoid any duplication of views or quotations.

By November 1948 Charles's book was complete. Promotion in June 1948, which removed the financial pressure on him, came after much of *British Canals* had been drafted, and he later deemed *British Canals* to be little more than a potboiler.

That summer saw a tragedy which caused tremendous grief to Charles and Alice Mary; their second son, Henry, was born but died five weeks later, on 15 June 1948. Charles seems to have continued writing, perhaps again as a solace, but the delays to the new book can be imagined.

For much of *British Canals*, Charles leaned heavily on existing writings, including Edwin Pratt's book *British Canals*, and Smiles's *Lives of the Engineers*, from which many illustrations were taken, along with his wartime researches. The first parts of the book to be written, on pages 104 and 105, came almost directly from his wartime notes on the Tavistock Canal.

While he carried out very little original research for the book, one exception came from a holiday in the late spring of 1948 to the Four Swans at Sudbury in Suffolk. Charles's earlier researches had scarcely covered waterways in eastern England. Seeking the records of the Suffolk (or Essex) Stour, he consulted the 1928 edition of *De Salis*, which gave the address of the navigation company as a timber yard in Sudbury, where Charles enquired of the manager:

'Old records?' . . . A pause; then he led us forth through a haze of sawdust to seek George, who led us to a large tin trunk deep in sawdust, in which, George assured us, old papers were kept. But how to open it? More cogitation and enquiries suggested Bill, who arrived with a huge key. Some oil, and it indeed opened the trunk. My eyes goggled. It was full of old papers and right on top were 18th century leather-bound books, clearly minute books, labelled 'River Stour Navigation', oldest on the top. I turned pages dating back to 1704, and quickly saw the names of Constable and Gainsborough.

The manager allowed Charles and Alice Mary to take the first two books back to the Four Swans,

. . . and back we went to our sitting room. So began Alice Mary's introduction to the joys of canal research, for I don't suppose she had ever handled such original manuscript material before. For that and our few succeeding evenings, I skimmed through those books and others for which they exchanged them, that opened a new world to me, then picked out quotations, statistics and whatever for my dazed but willing wife to note down.[33]

During the days they explored the navigation, paddling in a canoe from the disused warehouse at its head to the highest derelict lock at Great Cornard. The records would later be deposited at the Essex Record Office.

The resulting account appeared on pages 195 and 196 of *British Canals*. In July 1949 Charles read the proofs of Tom Rolt's *The Inland Waterways of England*, but three publishers declined *British Canals*, and it was not until February 1950 that Tom Rolt could reciprocate. Tom objected to the title – 'its dull and its been used before'.[34] It would indeed produce problems much later when *British Canals* formed the central volume in a series of studies of British Isles canals, including Ireland.

The book was published in the summer of 1950 by John Baker of Phoenix House (a branch of Dents). John Baker was an unusual publisher, who saw publishing as a vocation, helping to disseminate knowledge. He stated that his aim was 'to sell books to the non book-buying public', and he encouraged this through the book club Readers' Union in the 1930s; Charles's new book was placed in this club's list in 1952.

British Canals, despite its limited origins, became a classic work, as, in Tom Rolt's words, 'the first comprehensive and readable history of the canal period that has ever been written'.[35] In the first edition the vagaries of Charles's previous research produced a strong bias towards Southern England, with no coverage of Ireland, and very limited mention of the canals of Scotland or Wales. Discussion of events in the twentieth century was limited, despite Charles's interest in the development of traffic.

One problem was the uncertain market for a factual history in a field which was unfamiliar to many; Tom Rolt's book had the advantage that its author was already well known. There was increasing public interest in waterways, much fostered by the growth of the IWA and the publicity which it generated up to the Market Harborough Rally of 1950. There were also the first stirrings towards extensive pleasure-boating on canals.

Charles was co-opted on to a sub-committee of the IWA, which included Sonia Smith, formed in October 1949 to investigate the working conditions of boat crews, and the means by which they could be improved. This committee reported in June 1950, with a number of practical proposals for the education of boat children. By then, as the next chapter explains, the IWA was in no position to act.

The capriciousness and haphazardness of events in Charles's life to 1950 do not indicate any linear and orderly progress towards a spare-time writing career as a canal historian. Charles still intended to write about various other subjects, and the problems in placing *British Canals* did not suggest a ready demand for any successor.

He was, however, in a stronger position in 1950 from which to launch further writing. He had a secure income, and a growing interest in canals; his interest in politics had diminished, certainly on an everyday party level; he was less committed to publishing in areas other than canal history; and it was clear that any involvement in canal politics would lie outside the IWA which he had helped to found. Significantly, nationalisation had both brought the waterways to public attention, and gathered the records of acquired concerns into a central archive, British Transport Historical Records, which would open in 1951. It was the response to *British Canals* which would raise the possibility of further research into canals.

CHAPTER TWO

WIDENING ENQUIRIES:
THE EARLY 1950S

The 1950s was a period of growing interest in the history of transport, engineering and industry, to which Charles increasingly contributed, finding that his interests began to coincide with those of others. Once it became clear that the COI would not be abolished by the Conservative Government which took office in 1951, Charles's life became more settled, with two young children, including a new daughter, Molly, and a stable financial base. He could now afford to write books whose revenues might do little more than defray the cost of research.

He was able to concentrate attention on canal history, although after *British Canals* it was by no means clear that there was a steady market for canal books; this would develop only slowly in the 1950s. This chapter will attempt to set Charles's work in context, examining his next canal history, sketching the broad context of transport history in the 1950s, before considering his first popular book and the founding of the Railway and Canal Historical Society. Curiously, his interest in canals was heightened by his exclusion from the IWA which he had helped to found.

IWA EXPULSIONS AND ISSUES

Charles had taken no part in IWA attempts to influence policy towards canals, bar his membership of the short-lived Working Boaters sub-committee. The IWA was to dissipate the goodwill built up in the late 1940s, including that of the British Transport Commission (henceforth BTC), the new owners of the nationalised waterways, and to spend much of the 1950s developing and defending a position of intransigence.

By 1951 it was clear that the BTC, which had been formed to own and plan the development of most freight and passenger transport, did not intend to preserve many smaller historic waterways which had little traffic potential, and whose nationalisation had been inadvertent. The BTC's approach was to focus support and investment on a limited group of larger waterways with a reasonably viable future for transport; it had no remit to foster pleasure-boating, and it was unclear whether this would develop significantly. Having reviewed its newly acquired assets, one clear option was to dispose of the smaller canals as traffics ended. A similar approach was adopted by private owners, like that of the Bridgewater Canal.

As traffics continued to decline and the condition of waterways like the Kennet & Avon worsened, unease grew among some IWA members over the effectiveness of a London-based leadership which seemed to prioritise activities like the staging of plays at the Market Harborough Rally over more local campaigning. The IWA could respond to the declining position in two ways: either to campaign for the retention of all waterways, or to concentrate support upon waterways with traffics, even if these were by narrow boat, and with clear potential for the development of pleasure-boating. Support for the latter position seems to have grown among those who had practical knowledge of carrying, including the Working Boaters sub-committee, and those with knowledge of pleasure-boating, including the IWA Kennet & Avon Branch and Rendel Wyatt, the owner of one of the few canal boat hire firms.

Charles unequivocally supported the latter stance; as he put it later: 'I am a priorities man – I always have been, and I am now. I see *no* contradiction between an ideal of what one would like the whole system to become and the priorities list of what should be done first.'[1] His researches had revealed that some waterways had never been viable and ought perhaps never to have been built. Any future seemed to lie in the enlargement and modernisation of significant routes, retaining some of the smaller waterways for pleasure-boating. His concerns, though, were that without factual investigation and analysis, little could be done, and that governments and the BTC needed to be convinced rather than pressurised by ridicule or by sentimental regret.

The controversies surrounding the IWA disruption of the early 1950s have been related elsewhere, from contrasting perspectives: a general summary must suffice here. The unease over policy was intermingled with personality clashes with Robert Aickman. By 1950 these had extended to Tom Rolt, who explained to Charles his concern at 'the, to me, distasteful way in which the Aickmans and their particular little clique have always tried to use the IWA as a vehicle for self-aggrandisement'.[2] Tom Rolt also felt that Aickman's approach to organisation – dictatorial, and intolerant of dissent – was counter-productive, while it also rankled that Aickman's own pursuits so often coincided with activities at the IWA's expense. All this detracted from Aickman's considerable ability to inspire and build support and publicity for what was then often seen as an eccentric minority cause.

Tom Rolt found his unpaid voluntary work as IWA secretary overwhelming, and decided to resign early in 1950. He anticipated that this could cause a rift with Aickman, and, when he wrote to Charles that the IWA might have to be reorganised, Charles offered his support. After unpleasant exchanges with Aickman, Tom resigned from the IWA Council in June 1950. At a subsequent meeting in November, Aickman forced through a resolution which sought to amend the aims of the Association both to promote the future of every waterway equally, and for every waterway to be restored and maintained for both pleasure-boating and commercial traffic. Presumably he intended the IWA to campaign to revive commercial carrying on canals like the Grand Western, whose final traffic had ended twenty-seven years before. In many respects, this was a pretext for Aickman to rid the council of people who could oppose his dominance.

Charles had no qualms about supporting and signing a memorandum, promoted by Rendel Wyatt and signed by Tom Rolt, opposing this change in aims, and advocating support for commercial traffic only on routes where it could be developed. A small group of dissenters, led by Lord Lucan (father of the Lord Lucan who disappeared in the 1970s), planned to form an alternative society if the Aickman leadership would not compromise. These dissenters, including Charles, perceived that they had a reasonable level of support among the IWA membership, and hoped that Aickman, shaken by evidence of this, might compromise. However, this group was itself divided over tactics, some, including Tom Rolt, favouring resignation, others, including Charles, preferring to seek Aickman's defeat from within.

Charles was not involved in the successive IWA meetings which resulted in moves to expel the signatories to this memorandum. On his return from Africa on COI business (related in Chapter 12), however, he was met by a letter from the new IWA honorary secretary, seeking his 'expression of regret' at the memorandum, and requiring him to appear before a special sub-committee formed to deal with the 'rebels'. Charles replied mildly that 'I do not desire to resign from the Association, and as I helped to found it, I am naturally in agreement with the purposes for which it was founded.'[3]

When a further letter required him to resign or recant his support for the Wyatt memorandum, he repeated that he had no intention of resigning, while 'the fact that the Council has not accepted my assurance that I am in agreement with the purposes for which the Association was founded demonstrates, of course, my thesis that the Association, as at present constituted, has departed from these purposes'.[4]

His subscription cheque was eventually returned, on 4 July 1951, on the grounds that he had not met the special sub-committee. No alternative society was to emerge, but he did join the Kennet & Avon Canal Association, which was formed from the dissolved IWA Kennet & Avon Branch. At its second meeting on 27 October 1951, he gave a lecture on the canal's history, and also speculated about its future.

Later, Charles attributed his affront at this correspondence, and the manner in which Tom Rolt had been removed from the organisation which he had founded, to his increased interest in waterways. In a sense, Aickman's high-handed behaviour, and his developing personal enmity towards Charles, made the latter more determined to find out the true position, an opportunity which would arise in 1954 with *Introducing Canals*. Twelve years later, it would help him to join the British Waterways Board.

THE CANALS OF SOUTHERN ENGLAND

A further spur to Charles's interest in canals followed the publication of *British Canals*. Since the war, he had considered the possibility of working his researches into some sort of publication on waterways in southern England, although he seems to have envisaged a subsidised academic monograph rather than a book.

Among the letters which followed the appearance of *British Canals*, a number contained queries relating mostly to waterways in the south of England, towards which the book's coverage leaned. One such came from Roger Sellman, who had drawn the maps for *British Canals*. As an undergraduate between 1933 and 1935, he had explored the Sussex rivers and other waterways in central southern England, and had published articles on Sussex waterways in a county magazine in 1935. He had no further use for the photographs and other materials which he had amassed, and offered these to Charles. Charles then decided to lay aside work which he had begun with James MacColl on a history of Victorian local government, and to embark on a regional study which would become *The Canals of Southern England*.

He was able to draw on his wartime researches, and upon (then) unpublished studies of the Exeter Canal by Arthur Clark, and Humphrey Household's partly published MA study, based on the extensive Gloucestershire County papers, of the Thames & Severn Canal. Humphrey Household had already detailed its early history in articles in the *Railway Magazine* and the Newcomen Society *Transactions* early in 1950, and he was to check Charles's account of the Thames & Severn in April 1953.

Charles could also draw upon Paul Vine's developing work on the Wey & Arun Junction Canal. Paul Vine had explored this canal since boyhood in 1942, had researched the same records that Charles had seen at Guildford, and many others, and was to publish the first results in *Country Life* in 1953. He had been impressed by Tom Rolt's *Inland Waterways of England*; Tom had introduced him to Charles in 1951. This provided an early example of the kind of networks of researchers that were developing on a much larger scale among railway historians.

With exceptions, most of the sources involved for *Southern England* were within reach of either London or South Cerney. After her mother died on 17 October 1949, Alice Mary inherited her house in South Cerney; they renamed it Silver Street House, and arranged to let it every year for all but a fortnight in August, when they would use it as a holiday home. During August 1950 they began to visit canals in the West Country. At the time it was not clear how canals like the Chard Canal had been completed, and the Hadfields had to trace, on maps and then on the ground, its precise line and works along the route. There was no initial outline of the history of canals like the Chard which had been built after the publication of *Priestley* in 1830, and closed before they could be recorded in the Board of Trade Canal Returns in 1888. He was unable to establish whether the Radstock line of the Somersetshire Coal Canal, and their connecting tramroad, had ever been used.

Manuscript sources included further work on those consulted during his wartime researches, while a smaller number used records released as a result of nationalisation. The BTC had inherited very large collections of railway and canal company archives and artefact collections (including a small museum at York), and decided to create a single public archive, British Transport Historical Records (henceforth BTHR). This did not open until 1951, when Charles received its first reader's ticket. Before this time Charles had arranged for records of railway-owned canals to be sent up to a former GWR parcels office, next to an enquiry office, at Bishops Bridge Road. He had begun work on the Ashby Canal, but soon transferred to the Kennet & Avon Navigation. For many others, it was necessary to examine records deposited at county record offices, and, for some river navigations such as the Wey, to rely heavily on T.S. Willan's work. Dr Sellman read and commented upon the whole draft.

Charles faced problems in arranging the text; one alternative was to write short separate histories of each waterway, but this was difficult when the histories of individually owned canals were intertwined and when there were common themes. He therefore split his account of each canal's history into several sections with cross-referencing, so that the book could either be read through from beginning to end or in separate sections. He would use a modified version of this, where necessary, in later studies.

An opening chapter attempted to sketch some of the background to the region's general economic and transport history. Appendices carefully classified and tabulated the main feature of each waterway, although at this stage he did not record dates of formal legal closure. Later volumes of regional history would, with this exception, follow the pattern laid down here, although space and time precluded the sketch of general transport history. Charles's conclusions were also related to general transport history and its influence:

> Transport . . . should not be looked at in terms of one mode alone. . . . As we look today at derelict river locks or canal beds, as those interested in other transport forms look at disused coach roads or railless branch lines or little ports without ships, we must remember that they were the foundations; that in most cases they created a traffic which, many times bigger to-day, still exists, even if it be carried by rail or lorry. Moreover, though the waterways of the south have mostly ended their useful lives there are others in Britain which not only survive, but meet present needs efficiently and are capable of fulfilling those of to-morrow. There is a future as well as a past for British inland navigation.[5]

Charles avoided issues of current controversy. Thus, he merely reported that traffic on the Kennet & Avon Canal had declined to a minimum by 1906; by early 1955, when the book was published, this waterway was the focus of controversy for the IWA and the K&ACA, as the BTC proposed closure. Charles favoured restoration, but offered no comment.

TRANSPORT HISTORY AND RELATED FIELDS

The letters which followed *British Canals* also brought Charles into contact with historians of railways, and encounters with engineering history, along with what would later be termed industrial archaeology. Perhaps owing to the experience of rail passenger transport, and the large numbers of railway staff, railways had attracted greater numbers of enthusiasts than other forms of freight transport. Since 1899 there had been a Railway Club in London, which included many railway staff, and a number of railway magazines and journals were published from the early twentieth century. Some of these studied current rail operations, but increasingly articles appeared on historical subjects. The four main companies all produced magazines, partly to foster interest among their employees and the travelling public; the *Great Western Railway Magazine*, the oldest, dated back to 1888. Historical pieces began to appear in these; sometimes these were based on anecdotal sources or had scant regard for historical accuracy.

The Grouping process of the early 1920s brought together the records of predecessor companies, and archives were created to sort and house these, partly for operational purposes. While records of their canals were limited, especially for the period of railway ownership, the pre-1923 railway records proved useful to researchers of railway history. However, the dominance of popular accounts fostered amateur approaches dominated by secondary sources, and sometimes by hearsay and myth. Specialist publishers, such as Oakwood Press, from 1936, and Ian Allan, founded in 1943, had appeared, but these tended to concentrate on detailed studies of individual lines or locomotives.

Twenty years later Professor Derek Aldcroft characterised, somewhat caustically, a field which had expanded partly on the interwar foundations:

> There is no shortage of writers on transport history. Each branch of transport spouts a large following of enthusiasts whose pens toil ceaselessly, judging by the large number of items that appear in print each year. Much of the writing reflects a certain amount of nostalgia and personal reminiscence which, to use Kellett's words, has given rise to books 'intended to be wallowed in rather than read, and certainly not to be studied, to be used for convenient reference, or to serve as the basis for further work'. However, though many such writings lack the substance and documentation that appeal to the academic mind, many of them do contain useful material which can serve to illustrate or support a particular thesis.[6]

At the start of the 1950s, no such development could be predicted. The growth of enthusiast societies and suitable publications were important to its development, as was the opening up of new sources. One factor was perhaps the greater availability of the private car and the advent of cheaper cameras and film processing, essential to much field recording.

The early 1950s began a period of exceptional advance in general industrial and transport history. The term 'industrial archaeology' was introduced in print by Michael Rix in 1955, and reflected a growing interest in field studies into Britain's industrial past. Defined by Kenneth Hudson as 'the discovery, recording and study of the physical remains of yesterday's industries and communications',[7] industrial archaeology also focused the interest of amateurs and volunteers in the discovery and recording of canals and other transport routes, encouraging explorations on (or under) the ground as well as in written sources. Some local historians could develop interests away from the recording of local personalities or churches to the explanation of historical elements of landscapes; Robin Atthill's *The Curious Past* of 1955 (and later *Old Mendip*) was a significant example. Extramural adult education courses, sometimes involving field studies, were to proliferate during the 1950s. All encouraged the expert investigation, recording and interpretation of the industrial past.

The Newcomen Society for the study of the history of engineering and technology had been founded in 1920. While Charles would join this in 1953, he did not play any major part. However, its annual *Transactions* increasingly included articles on transport engineering, such as 'Canal Inclines and Lifts', presented on 19 December 1951 by David Tew; the ensuing paper drew on an article in the *Journal of Transport History* – Charles's later article on the engineer James Green.

A very significant paper was that presented by Alec W. Skempton on English river navigation engineers in December 1953. His academic specialism was in soil mechanics, but after reading Tom Rolt's *The Inland Waterways of England*, he was alerted to T.S. Willan's work, which continued to appear in the 1940s in various journals. As with Charles's, this work was seminal, and from around 1950 inspired Professor Skempton (as he became in 1957) to investigate the engineering of the early river navigations. Although his background was civil engineering and Dr Willan's was in economic history, Professor Skempton found Willan very willing to help. The history of engineers, rather than engineering works, had advanced very little since Samuel Smiles's somewhat hagiographical work, and its advance was partly due to the work of non-academics, including Charles, and especially Tom Rolt.

The *Journal of Transport History* would provide one means of bringing together academics and non-academics, with the prospect that the latter might produce research to high standards. It was founded by Michael Robbins and Jack Simmons in May 1953; while both had long been interested in the history of railways, they sought the wider expansion of transport history. They formed part of a trio of school contemporaries, all interested in railways, who between them bridged the gaps between academic, enthusiast and professional approaches to transport history. Roger Kidner, the third in the trio, had founded Oakwood Press in 1936, to publish monographs on railway lines, with Michael Robbins, who would later become a transport professional, joining the board of London Transport in 1957. Professor Jack Simmons, already mentioned, had broad interests beyond his specialism in transport history, including an interest in English. Charles was inspired by his reflections on history published in 1952 in *Parish and Empire*, in which he also detailed all that he could find about William Jessop, who had engineered many of the canals of the English East Midlands. Yet he, like Michael Robbins (and Roger Kidner), had written straightforward popular railway histories for Oakwood Press. The rigid divisions between academic and enthusiast history, notable elsewhere, were absent from his work.

The new journal partly addressed the need to publish scholarly work which could be expected to follow the opening of the BTHR archive in 1951. Its opening editorial noted the growing interest in transport history and in the 'history of transport technology', and sought studies which would view transport as a whole, a need noted by Charles in *Southern England*. They hoped that the journal could

> offer common ground to historians both in the academic world and in the actual world of transport, who will in turn be writing for readers of both kinds. Both parties should gain valuable advantage: practical knowledge and understanding by the one, the discipline of academic standards by the other.[8]

They also noted the neglect of bibliographies and of book reviews, and warned that there were some topics 'which are misunderstood, or where the myth-making faculties of former writers have planted unsound conceptions even in the respectable history-books'.[9]

Charles contributed a long article to the first issue, 'James Green as Canal Engineer', which reflected his researches into West Country waterways, including the Grand Western, and the development of inclined planes and lifts. He would write only two further articles for the journal, both in the 1950s, after which he concentrated his efforts on books. The most significant was one in a series of sources for transport history: 'Sources for the History of British Canals', which also reflected some of his developing views on canal history. He identified less with historians who studied a single canal in great detail, than with others who

> prefer to set out on paper as best they can the broad lines of development of a bigger subject. In doing so they make as much use as possible of the researches of the local historians, and seek the help of interested people who live where they seek information, or who are willing to do local work. For the rest, they have to do quick and far-ranging research which is bound not to be complete until the day comes when each day has more than twenty-four hours. They in turn will, if they are good historians, be reasonably accurate in the generalizations they make and the conclusions they draw; but they are bound to make mistakes in detail, because they have not completely covered their local sources.[10]

He somewhat prophetically asserted that: 'No one has yet had the temerity to write a world history of inland water transport, but he who does will find many interactions between British and other waterways which will give a different shade to much of our national writing.'[11] It is unclear whether he envisaged that he would one day have the required temerity, but he was already collecting press cuttings about waterways in mainland Europe and North America.

Charles saw his work, and that of other transport historians, as a contribution to economic history. He stressed that

> a canal is part of the economic history of a region, with relationships to other forms of transport, to local government, and to every kind of agricultural and industrial enterprise within the region. Again, a canal is part of the economic history, sometimes also of the political or military history, of the nation itself. Economic history would have been different without the Duke of Bridgewater's, the Trent & Mersey, or the Birmingham canals; political history was affected, for instance, by the opportunities for employing the out-of-work in canal construction that followed the passing of the Poor Employment Act of 1817 and the establishment of the Exchequer Bill Loan Commissioners, and military history was affected by the building of the Royal Military and the Caledonian canals.[12]

A second assumption was that the main historical period for canals was what he termed the 'Canal Age', between 1760 and 1840, 'when so many of the foundations of the modern world were laid, a period from which no student, once committed, ever returns'.[13] One reason for this emphasis was that this was indeed the period when canals were most influential in shaping economic development in Britain, although Charles would discover that this was not the case in continental Europe and North America, in which he would develop an equal interest in twentieth-century history. Another reason was that, with exceptions, the available sources were at their most useful for this period. Parliamentary activity was at its height in respect of canal development, newspapers and other local sources showed their greatest interest when canals were newly developed, and the minute books of canal companies more fully recorded events when they were a leading form of transport, and before railway companies either took over companies or dominated their affairs. Finally, in 1955 BTHR and other archives operated a fifty-year rule, which meant that records which (then) included material later than 1905 could not be examined. Not until 1967 would the replacement of this rule by a thirty-year rule release a large block of sources from the interwar years.

The kind of academic history promoted by the new journal was not one in which Charles would strictly engage, but he would follow its standards and aims. He would encounter quite different kinds of investigators of history in researches which underpinned his first popular book, *Introducing Canals*.

ENTHUSIAST HISTORIANS, WATERWAYS OFFICIALS AND *INTRODUCING CANALS*

In 1951 Charles was contacted by an investigator of railway history, Charles Clinker. He had begun to work for the GWR in 1923, and was soon involved in 'helping the late E.T. MacDermot to sort an unwieldy and very dusty collection of Bristol & Exeter Railway books and papers stacked away, long forgotten, in a building which was formerly that Company's head office'.[14] MacDermot, an historian from Somerset, had agreed in 1924 to write an official history of the GWR, at the General Manager's behest; this in turn drew on careful notes taken by a GWR audit clerk before 1908. Clinker later used these notes and documents; he felt that MacDermot's researches encouraged, if not actually engendered, the development of soundly based accurate railway history. MacDermot's study, published in two volumes in 1927 and 1931, provided what was seen as a model of accurate railway history, although even it later needed correction.

Clinker noted that early railway histories tended towards inaccuracy and myth, partly because of a dearth of accurate information, and this led him to concentrate on obtaining precise factual details, drawn, wherever possible, from primary sources. His interest in railway history grew; convinced that much evidence of railway history was being lost, he left the GWR staff in 1945 to collect materials and to write about railway history.

In *British Canals* Charles had noted that the authorised line of the Ashby Canal had been completed by the use of tramroads (horse railways), and Clinker, who lived nearby in Rugby, wrote to request further information. Charles could not supply this, but, having arranged to read minutes of various former railway-owned canal companies at Bishops Bridge Road, began with the Ashby Canal. These records were not yet in BTHR.

Clinker's approach to research resembled Charles's in its reliance on primary sources. Unlike Charles, he was more interested in producing aids to research, such as chronologies, than actual detailed histories. Charles and he were very different; Charles found him

> . . . essentially uncreative, a man who loved detail. He never wrote books of his own. . . . The nearest he got was when he revised MacDermot's *History of the GWR* for a new edition. He loved pointing out other people's mistakes, but was very slow at parting with information, even to close friends like I was – he would take months to check a paragraph.[15]

Clinker, however, was often plagued with requests for trivial information.

As Charles had never seen the Ashby Canal tramroads, Clinker offered to guide him to various sites, from his house in Rugby, where he 'had a large study in a front room lined floor to ceiling with books with periodicals in piles on the floor. He smoked heavily, and the windows were *never* opened to my knowledge. You can imagine the atmosphere!'[16] They worked together on a short account entitled 'The Ashby-de-la-Zouch Canal and its Railways', which appeared in *Modern Transport* on 7 August 1954, and in enlarged form in 1958. In turn, Clinker found details of the Par Canal and discerned the closure date of the Haytor Granite Tramway, which served the Stover Canal, for *Southern England*, and read the manuscript of the book. Clinker's influence led Charles to be invited to write the 'Canal' entries for the *Victoria County History of Wiltshire* in 1959, but not for the Gloucestershire volume.

Clinker claimed to have put on Britain's first full-length course in transport history, of extramural lectures for the University of Birmingham in 1953. These and later classes recruited a number of people, many of them youthful, into the field of railway history. As Clinker's interest in canals grew in the early 1950s, he organised visits by car with Charles to waterways near Rugby, usually accompanied by Ray Cook of Coventry, one of his recruits. Places visited in 1953 included the loops created by the shortening of the Oxford Canal, and the termini of the Peak Forest and Cromford Canals. These visits helped Charles consider an idea for a further regional study, *The Canals of the Midlands and Wales.*

The contract for *Midlands and Wales* was dated 12 January 1954, but by then Charles had agreed to write another, shorter, book. At a COI party he had met Keon Hughes, a director of the publisher Ernest Benn, and agreed to produce another book, to

> set down the things I myself would like to have known twenty years ago: something about the commercial side of canals and about their history, something of what is to be seen on and near them and what they are for, something about holidays on the water and about exploring those that are derelict and often difficult to find.[17]

No such popular book existed at this time, although Aickman would produce his guide, *Know Your Waterways*, in 1955. In *Introducing Canals* Charles used historical materials from his earlier work and from work in progress, but also developed further explorations. He also returned to the contemporary position of canals, at a time when this was controversial; he was keen to set out what he saw as the true position in contrast to the emotional orientation of Aickman and his IWA supporters, and to enlarge his interest in modern freight waterways. The book, and his COI connections, enabled him to meet waterways officials who might not otherwise have been willing to talk; he later recalled another factor:

> It dawned on me then that Aickman had done me a very good turn, for each interview began with: 'Are you anything to do with that man Aickman?' 'No', I would reply, 'I've been expelled from the IWA.'
> 'Then come right in, Mr Hadfield, and sit down.'[18]

The IWA had become seen as a vociferous and unconstructive body since the expulsions.

One of the officials, later to prove a useful contact, was Christopher Marsh, the Divisional Waterways Officer for the North West. He arranged an itinerary for Charles's visit to northern waterways which he only knew through books and maps. One feature which Charles knew through engravings was the tall aqueduct at Pontcysyllte on the Shropshire Union Canal, over which he walked with Marsh for the first time in May 1954. Charles commended readers to

> Stand in the centre on a windy day, and pay tribute to Thomas Telford, whose work it was. He chose to build his aqueducts not with a puddled bed enclosed

in masonry, but with a cast-iron trough. His first, at Longdon-upon-Tern on the Shrewsbury Canal, still stands . . . but Pontcysyllte is the perfection of his art.[19]

While he would later cast doubt on Telford's involvement, Charles's interest in engineering works is manifest. Parts of his book covered practical details such as hire-boating firms and pleasure-cruising, of which Charles had no real practical experience. Rendel Wyatt, one of the IWA dissenters, who had started the Canal Cruising Company at Stone in 1948, provided much help here.

Two chapters which remain of interest are those covering future policy and the last chapter, on 'looking for the past'. In that on policy, described as 'a condensation of the views of many interested and informed people',[20] Charles devoted much attention to canals still used for commercial transport, which were increasingly affected by competition with road and rail. He discerned that their problem was that they were 'believed to be dying by those who matter: the men who buy transport. No amount of "traffic-mindedness" by canal officials and canal carriers can get over this hurdle.'[21] He suggested that if certain routes were safeguarded and developed, if carrying upon them was subsidised and new traffic diverted to them from other modes, canalside industries and carriers could be encouraged to make long-term investments in craft and handling equipment. He advocated the enlargement of the Weaver–Wolverhampton route to a 100-ton standard, and suggested that the route upstream of Nottingham to Leicester might follow. The Board of Survey which was to report to the government in April 1955 drew similar conclusions to Charles's. Its most controversial proposals, however, involved the closure and disposal of much of the system upon which there was little or no traffic.

Charles's views on this would vary from those which he put to use in the 1960s. In 1949 the Lower Avon Navigation Trust had been formed to acquire the declining Warwickshire Avon Navigation, primarily to preserve and restore it for pleasure-boating with the aid of voluntary labour. Charles had joined this Trust in 1950, along with the Kennet & Avon Canal Association, and noted the pioneering voluntary preservation work by the Talyllyn Railway Preservation Society, co-founded in 1950 by Tom Rolt. He now suggested that a Trust (or series of trusts) be formed to take over the non-commercial waterways, using grants from central government, local authority contributions, and voluntary involvement to run these waterways for pleasure-cruising. Limited government funding would bridge the inevitable gap between revenue and expenditure for a number of years. He concluded that

Whether these proposals be the right ones or not, it is clear that something on these lines must be done if the Kennet & Avon, the southern part of the Oxford, the Lancaster, and other lovely canals are not to go the way of the Thames & Severn, the Wilts & Berks, and the Huddersfield Narrow. It is not impossible; it is only difficult.[22]

Charles devoted the final chapter of *Introducing Canals* to the exploration of disused canals, prefacing it by an unusual profession of interest:

> I confess that such derelict canals have a fascination for me. I am not one of those who would rather have lived a hundred or two hundred years ago, who rail at the worst things of to-day and compare them with the best of yesterday, and who see the past through the double lenses of make-believe and ignorance of what the past was really like. I have read too many canal records for that.[23]

His coverage included short notes on the Pocklington and Market Weighton Canals, presumably recalled from wartime visits; Sapperton Tunnel – 'my own first favourite'; the Leominster Canal, which he had visited again in February 1954; the Oxford Canal curves; several southern waterways, such as the Grand Western; and the longest section, on the canals of East Shropshire, 'a most fascinating part of England for the stranger'.[24] Many visitors to the Ironbridge and Coalbrookdale area may endorse this today, but in the 1950s, before the foundation of Telford (previously Dawley) New Town, it was an area of major industrial dereliction.

The latter section owed much to the assistance of W. Howard Williams of Trench. The area had long been of interest to students of history; one of the Newcomen Society's earliest visits was to the Trench inclined plane in 1924, when it had been disused for three years but remained intact. David Tew, who had joined the Society in 1947, visited the area in 1948 to view local tramroads, and had become interested in inclined planes there; he then began researches into canal lifts and planes, giving a lecture to the Society in December 1951, in which he listed and discussed every known example of these devices.

He had been assisted by Howard Williams, who had been interested in local history since the 1920s, and spent much time exploring the complex and extensive networks of tramroads and canal remains in East Shropshire. After 1951 Tew and Williams corresponded further, and Williams made a photographic survey of canals in the area in 1952 and 1953; parts of his work were published in the newly founded *Shropshire Magazine* in 1951 and 1954. He could himself recall, as a boy, the Trench plane working, and his sources included canal workers like the last operator of the incline from the 1880s to 1921; these provided links through oral evidence with the mid-nineteenth century, well before oral history was formally developed.

Charles seems to have first contacted Howard Williams in April 1954, and he helped to arrange a trip for Charles, Clinker and Cook in late May. The first day included the Newport branch of the Shropshire Union Canal, the Donnington Wood Canal, the Trench Locks and the Trench incline; and the remains of the Shropshire Canal, including the Windmill and Hay inclined planes.

In *Introducing Canals* Charles suggested a day visit by car, beginning with the Wrockwardine Wood inclined plane, and moving on to the Oakengates Tunnel, the Windmill plane and then along the canal towpath to the top of the Hay inclined plane. The former length has since disappeared under Telford New Town, but the latter length, within Blist's Hill Open Air Museum (renamed Blist's Hill Victorian Town in 1997), has been restored visually and the canal re-watered. He suggested next a visit to the Iron Bridge, and then up Coalbrookdale to the Brierley Hill incline. Then it was north to Trench, where Trench Top Lock had been partly demolished in September 1954, and to the foot of Trench plane, where remains of the winding gantries could be seen; all of this has since been destroyed. Then to places on the Shrewsbury Canal, which were later altered and the canal drained; the bottom lock and buildings at Wappenshall Junction, 'the whole making as pretty a canal picture as can be found', and the early iron aqueduct at Longdon, and then on towards Shrewsbury. As well as transport remains, Charles also noted

two herons, a curlew, and two moorhen's nests full of speckled eggs on the canal at Marsh Green, where the towpath was thick with buttercups, cuckoo-flower and clover; at Longdon the cuckoo was calling, and a pair of swans were taking their cygnets beneath the aqueduct. Canal hunting regards the living as well as the dead.[25]

So much for the present pleasures of exploring what lay unequivocally in the past. Charles's book also provided a portrait of the canals as they then existed, including details of main traffics passing, derived from various publications and meetings with officials; and a gazetteer of every known pleasure-boat operator, based on hundreds of letters to local authorities and others.

Howard Williams's researches continued, and proved to be a useful source for *Midlands and Wales*. They were also put to good use in an extramural course in June 1956 at Attingham Park in Shropshire, where Charles spoke on canals and tramroads in East Shropshire, Michael Rix on the early history of industrial Coalbrookdale, and Charles Clinker on railway history. This was one of many courses from this period; Charles would take part in several until 1963. One catalyst, among several, was the founding of a specialist society in transport history.

THE RAILWAY AND CANAL HISTORICAL SOCIETY

The founding of what became the Railway and Canal Historical Society began with a letter to the magazine *Railway World* in July 1954 by Kenneth Seaward of Norton-on-Tees. A geography graduate, he was interested in researching the South Durham & Lancashire Union Railway, but found publications dominated by interest in locomotives rather than in the history of railways themselves. In his letter he noted that while there were many railway enthusiast societies, there was 'a need for a society specializing in the serious study of railway history, with a view to the regular publication of a journal on this subject'.[26]

Specific societies to study transport history, as opposed to those gathering enthusiasts in locomotives or rail travel, were rare; even in the United States the earliest such organisation, the Railroad and Locomotive Historical Society, was founded in Massachusetts only in 1921. In Ireland the Irish Rail Record Society, publishing a serious journal of railway history, had been founded in 1946; although one long-standing member of the IRRS, Walter McGrath of Cork, was to join the RCHS, contact was to be limited. Other societies, like the Railway Travel and Correspondence Society, founded in 1928, tended to visit railways rather than to systematically research history, while the title of the Historical Railway Model Society, founded in 1950, is no doubt self-explanatory.

A number of people interested in railway history were already in regular contact, but Kenneth Seaward's letter seems to have convinced several of the need for more formal links; around sixty people seemed to be interested. Several letters to *Railway World* followed, and at an informal meeting in Preston station it was decided to call a further formal meeting to form a Railway History Society. Clinker then spent a weekend in August 1954 with the Hadfields at South Cerney, and, when he mentioned the decision to form a new society, Charles suggested that canal history be added to its title. Clinker agreed, although Charles was at the time the only canal historian, and he was duly deemed to be a founder member at the first meeting of the Railway and Canal Historical Society (henceforth RCHS) in Preston on 4 September 1954. Clinker was then made president.

The other founders were interested mainly in railways, and most were of a similar age to Charles. Maurice Greville of Okehampton, the oldest at sixty-eight, and also the first subscriber, had been interested in railways since boyhood, when he had seen railways being built in their final major phase in the 1890s. He had been a committee member of the Railway Club, which he had joined in 1904, and which Clinker had addressed in 1953, and probably earlier. Another fellow Club member, Hugh A. Vallance of Godalming, was on the staff of the *Railway Magazine*; his paper on the London & Greenwich Railway, the first delivered to the new Society, was a new version of one given to the Railway Club in 1927. The second oldest founder, Bertram Baxter, had long been interested in exploring tramroads, and had published a paper in 1929 on the Peak Forest Tramway, which connected with the Peak Forest Canal.

Other members were much younger, like Gordon Biddle, born in 1928, who became secretary. He was the only other founder with an interest in canals, which had begun in wartime. Having cycled towpaths in the Midlands, since moving to Blackburn in 1951 he had developed an interest in waterways in northern England. He had been at school with Ray Cook, and had known both him and Clinker for some time.

The prospectus of September 1954 was addressed mainly to the need to develop railway history, but guardedly included canal history, 'not only for its own importance, but because the history of canals was very much interwoven with that of railways in their early days, and indeed, also in latter times'.[27] The formal object of the RCHS was to 'promote, encourage, foster and co-ordinate the study of the history of railways and canals in Great Britain and to implement this object by all possible means'. Other objects included to bring together those with a 'serious interest', to 'raise the standard of original research', stressing 'the accuracy of published data', to disseminate historical information, and to act as a channel of communication between researchers and to indicate where information might be found. It attempted to deal systematically with the kind of problems which Charles's researches in the 1950s would encounter and surmount: the need to track down sources, to develop and draw upon contact with other researchers with whom notes and data could be exchanged, and to publish the results of research. The early progress of the new Society, to the end of 1955, will be considered in this chapter, with later developments sketched in later chapters.

An early move was the launch of a quarterly *Journal*; Charles declined to be its first editor. The first four issues contained short articles and notes, lists of Railway Acts of Parliament (by Clinker) and book reviews. The opening issue set the tone with a blistering review, by Gordon Biddle, of a popular railway history book by C. Hamilton Ellis, Charles's one-time collaborator on his first (non-canal) book. The breadth of coverage and readable style was welcomed, but the numerous factual inaccuracies in this book were condemned.

Very little appeared about canal history, although a number of railway pieces appeared by an author who was also investigating the Ellesmere Canal, Edward Wilson; in August 1955 he reviewed favourably *The Canals of Southern England*, confessing that 'I was lost in admiration for his thoroughness and scrupulous accuracy, although this very thoroughness makes it more difficult to read the book as a continuous narrative'.[28]

The main canal contribution came from Charles himself, in one of three papers presented to the first AGM in Leicester on 30 April 1955, which addressed problems involved in researching history. In Charles's paper, 'An approach to canal research', he stressed the difficulties in his own task:

> canal history is as nearly an unexplored subject as one is likely to find, except perhaps for the history of roads. I am myself working on books that try to give the broad picture of canal development in this country, but that picture has to be built up without the help of detailed local studies, because hardly any exist.

He also stressed the problems of choosing a period of time for study since the beginning of river navigation began (railways had a more clearly defined inception), and the need to place canal research within a broad frame of economic history, with a warning:

> against the dangers of short-sightedness, of conducting a piece of research not as a part, however small, of the great sweep of history, but as something in itself. To study the history of a canal or a navigable river is to study a small bit of the economic history of the country, and I suggest you never forget the background because of your interest in the thing itself.[29]

This view contrasted with that of some railway members, who tended to regard minute but accurate details about railways as an important goal. There may have been more agreement with Charles's view that the first task was to visit the waterway on the ground before examining the documentary sources, although this often reversed his own experience.

Among the initiatives launched were measures to secure a detailed bibliography of railway history, and the systematic collecting of details about the availability of sources in record offices, archives and libraries. It was clearly established that the Society would not engage in controversies about current transport issues, but it seemed appropriate to campaign for extended opening hours for the BTHR archive. Charles arranged a visit in October 1955 to this archive and its opening hours were later extended.

An early suggestion, from Geoffrey Holt of Cumbria, was to celebrate centenaries by such activities as staging exhibitions and special lectures and by running trips; it was felt that by drawing attention to such events, the Society would become regarded as an authority. He suggested the 200th anniversary of the Sankey Navigation, while Charles suggested the 150th anniversary of the opening of Blisworth Tunnel, and agreed to report on possible events.

The latter became the occasion of the Society's first outing, on 26 March 1955, which included the Blisworth and Northampton Tramroads, Wolverton Aqueduct, and an optional boat trip through Blisworth Tunnel. The celebration was run in conjunction with local people who put on an exhibition there. After the exhibition, 'but with historical enthusiasm undiminished we went on to look at Blisworth wharf, and the site of the Northampton tramroad which connected that town to the canal until the canal branch was built. Finally, we climbed into a boat kindly provided by British Transport Waterways, and went through the Blisworth tunnel to Stoke Bruerne.'[30] It turned out to be almost as wet inside the tunnel as in the pouring rain outside, and the passage was enlivened by having to pass a narrow boat pair inside: 'Dawning horror spread over the faces of my boatload of railwaymen as they realised we were not on rails. However, they survived to take many other waterway cruises.'[31] Further entertainment was provided when their coach grounded on a humped-back bridge over the canal.

The second trip, on 17 September, along the Sankey Canal from Widnes to Winwick, was preceded by an exhibition in Widnes, and lunch with the Mayor and the local MP, James MacColl. The Leeds & Liverpool Canal short boat *Leo* was then boarded for the trip to Winwick, some 8 miles away. At Sankey Bridges, both the railway and road bridges were opening ones; the road bridge, which carried the main road from Liverpool to Manchester, was opened long before *Leo* arrived, which did not please motorists travelling on a Saturday afternoon. The day ended with a tour of the Winwick Depot by Christopher Marsh, and then a reception by St Helens Corporation, with a talk by Dr T.C. Barker, then a local expert on the canal's history, but later Professor of Economic and Social History and RCHS President. Gordon Biddle was interviewed on BBC radio about the trip. Later trips would be less elaborate, and attract less publicity, although one on the Ellesmere Canal in 1956 would involve a television crew. Interestingly, railway trips were less popular, perhaps because other societies also organised them; a Liverpool & Manchester Railway trip on 18 September had to be cancelled for lack of support.

By the end of 1955 the new Society was on a stable footing, with an expanding membership, and drawing in others who would develop enthusiasm for both railway and canal history. The extent to which it would succeed in raising awareness of transport history and in developing standards of accuracy will be outlined in the next chapter. Charles would benefit from the mutual support of members over the next twenty years. Kenneth Seaward did not regret sending his letter; the RCHS brought him into contact with informed fellow members which helped his researches.

By the mid-1950s Charles was established as an historian of canals, in a gradually expanding field which encompassed a wide range of studies. He had also established an interest in the current position of inland waterways, outside the IWA whose approach was mainly confined to protest. While he would write on other subjects from time to time, his work was now firmly focused on waterways. This would bear fruit later.

CHAPTER THREE

EXPLORATIONS AND PUBLICATIONS: 1955–62

The mid-1950s began a period in which Charles's explorations of waterways increased, and in which the writing and publishing of waterways history became paramount. His writing commitments elsewhere largely ended, and he concentrated upon canal history. His life was now in a position of stability, developing his division of COI, and his children were steadily growing up; a new adopted son, John Gardiner, born at the same time as their lost son Henry, joined the family in 1959.

VISITING SOUTH WALES AND THE BORDER

The Canals of Southern England did not sell well after 1955, perhaps because few people could identify with a region known as 'Southern England', and hence purchasers were limited. The same probably applied to *Midlands and Wales*, so that, having begun to write this book in 1954, after about 1956 Charles broke off the South Wales coverage, combining it with studies of three isolated Border waterways which had limited connections with the canals of the Midlands and North Wales. He had expected the combined book to take a long time – 'I shall be working on the new book for years yet, so there is absolutely no hurry,' he wrote in July 1955.[1]

This section will focus in greater detail upon the way in which Charles researched *The Canals of South Wales and the Border* (henceforth *South Wales*), the regional book which he most enjoyed writing. Before 1954 he had explored none of the South Wales canals, although he had looked at parts of the Leominster and Herefordshire & Gloucestershire Canals in 1944, when he and Alice Mary stayed in Ludlow, and again with Clinker in February 1954. One visit to the Herefordshire & Gloucestershire Canal, with Alice Mary, involved the discovery of the canal's route, unclear from the Ordnance Survey map:

I did not know whether the canal had ever reached Hereford until we ordered tea from a menu surrounded by advertisements. One named a firm at 'The Wharf'. I could hardly finish my tea before dragging her off to find the old basins. There they were much as they had been left long before.[2]

He also met a man whose father had been a boatman on the canal, disused since 1882, but no record of their conversation has survived.

Unlike some transport historians, Charles saw familiarisation with canals on the ground as essential, and explored canals in South Wales during parts of his summer leave. In August 1954 he and Alice Mary returned to cycle alongside the Monmouthshire and Brecknock & Abergavenny Canals, then navigable only by small boats between locks. At Pontypool Road they found the towpath too overgrown, and proceeded by road to view a plan of the Brecknock & Abergavenny at Brecon Museum. In the following August they returned to explore on foot the remains of the Kidwelly & Llanelly Canal, scrambling over the remains of two of its inclined planes; they found that the middle one at Capel Ifan was under a slag heap. Then in September 1956 they walked the towpath of the Swansea, Tennant, Neath, and Llansamlet Canals. They also walked along the top section of the Glamorganshire Canal, south from Merthyr Tydfil:

> along the hilltop on the western side of the steep valley of the Taff, its bed empty but still showing items of canal furniture such as footbridges, all, as one would expect in this country of ironworks, made of iron. The canal level dropped steadily by single locks or, more usually, staircase pairs, until we reached the head of Lock 17 and Abercynon, where the Aberdare Canal, also long disused, had come in from the west.
>
> We followed the line of the last staircase pair towards Abercynon, our tongues hanging out for a drink, until we reached the lower lock. This puzzled me, for the lock chamber was covered with a semi-circular concrete roof. I had developed a few wild theories to account for it, none, of course, at all credible (I remember one, that it had been a shelter for disembarking boat passengers), before we moved to the New Inn. I asked the landlord if he knew anything about the semi-circular structure. 'Oh yes,' he replied, 'it was built as an air-raid shelter during the war.' My ego sagged.[3]

With the exception of Harold Pollins, a university lecturer from Swansea whose study of the Swansea Canal had appeared in the *Journal of Transport History* in May 1954, very little of these canals' history had been explored, and few of the increasing numbers of boating enthusiasts knew them. Charles found, however, that local librarians proved exceptionally public-spirited: the one at Llanelly advised him in July 1955 that the library held twenty maps and the Kidwelly & Llanelly Canal Acts. Charles would retain contact with him until he retired; one discovery at Llanelly was the Earl of Ashburnham's Canal, which was previously forgotten. The Pontypridd librarian sent useful extracts from two local history books, and put him in contact with the manager of the council's transport department, who was especially interested in the Doctor's Canal in Pontypridd. The Neath Antiquarian Society let him explore a large cupboard full of rolled-up plans and other documents, from which he discovered that the Tennant Canal had old branches, of which no traces remained on the ground.

In June 1956 he discovered that most of the records of the Tennant Canal had been destroyed by air raids on Swansea in 1943. However, he contacted the canal's owner, A.J. Coombe-Tennant, in London, and discovered that there were some surviving records in the basement of Cadoxton Lodge. He was also allowed to examine records at the offices of the Neath Canal Company, which would later be placed in Glamorgan Record Office.

For the first time, Charles paid a researcher, H.D. Emmanuel, to carry out research into collections, some of them of private papers, at the National Library of Wales at Aberystwyth. In December 1957 Emmanuel reported that he had been through various collections but 'the harvest, as you can see, is disappointing. There is no continuous body of material, no bundles of accounts or tonnages, and there is no sign of the minute-books of the Aberdare Canal.'[4] He did, however, locate the minute books of the Glamorganshire Canal Company, whose last entry stated that they were to be destroyed one year after the canal was sold to Cardiff Corporation; no doubt the Corporation thought better of it. He later discovered, by accident, records of the Aberdare Canal, which had been bought by the Marquess of Bute; the Bute Estates allowed him to examine these records in their office at Queen Anne's Gate in London.

In early May 1958 Charles decided to spend a week in Wales to 'walk as many towpaths as I can'.[5] After spending his first day in Newport, researching in the County Record Office and Public Library, he walked from Newport along the Monmouthshire Canal branch to Crumlin, some 11 miles away. It drizzled the whole day, but 'it didn't really matter except that I couldn't take many photos'.[6] As the canal beyond Crosskeys would later be destroyed to construct a road, it is unfortunate that few photographs survive. After stopping for lunch, soaked through, at 'a very gloomy looking hotel' in Crosskeys, he returned into the rain to find the scenery

> More industrial now as the canal ran nearer the valley floor – passed three collieries, and then got to Crumlin, under the large railway viaduct. There was a nice looking Navigation Hotel, but inside Messrs Simmonds had decorated the saloon bar with naked ladies drawn all round the saloon bar. So they only got ½ pint from me for spoiling a good pub.

The pub was actually the Navigation Inn, which survives, unlike the viaduct (then the tallest in Britain), the canal in Crumlin, or the diesel train service which took Charles back to Newport. From there he took a train to Abergavenny.

The next day was largely spent exploring tramroads; unusually, the Brecknock & Abergavenny Canal Company had built a tramroad before it began to build its canal. He first noted the remains of the tramroad, which came from Blaenavon, at Llanfoist, where it crossed the canal to join the tramroad to Hereford. Walking 7 miles north along the towpath, he passed wharves at Govilon, Gilwern, Clydach and Llanelly, before reaching Llangattock Wharf; in the later stages, 'All along it was very pretty, quiet, birds everywhere, trees arching over, the canal set along the side of the hill, steep up on the inside, high embankment and views over the valley on the outside.' Lunching at the Horse Shoe at Llangattock, he asked the landlord about the Llangattock tramroad, which was built to the canal from quarries at the summit end, and later joined up to Nantyglo through Brynmawr by Crawshay Bailey. He said it could be found, so I found it – a green track leading away from the wharf (I found a stone sleeper with a hole in it!). After a mile of green track I reached the bottom of an incline – about 1 in 2, and very rough. I scrambled up, puffing and resting, about 500 ft, and discovered another one going up about another 500 ft to about the 1400 ft contour. I puffed and rested up that. Most lovely views on top – right above Crickhowell. A few small hill farms below – little white house, one ploughed field, and a lot of sheep on the moor, which the farmer rounded up on horseback.

Bailey's tramroad led off as a green track to the left along the side of the mountain, and soon turned into a road serving the local farms. . . . I walked along this beautifully engineered road, almost flat, carried on embankment and through cutting and round the shoulders of hills, for miles – about 8 above Llangattock. I came around high above the Clydach valley to meet it at Brynmawr, where my tramroad became a street running across the town to Nantyglo. Grand views, very windy, no noise, birds and sheep noises, and met hardly anyone.

From here he caught a bus back to Abergavenny, after a walk of some 15 miles.

The next day he walked south along the canal from Llanfoist to Pontymoile, some 13 miles away. It was

A lovely walk, the first part very lonely, along the side of the mountain through the trees, and the later part out in the open most of the time, and more like an English canal. . . . on to Pontymoile, which we saw but didn't appreciate because I didn't know the detail, where the Brecon & Abergavenny and the Monmouthshire meet. Very nice junction house, partly circular, and the bottom of the top half of the Monmouthshire, built over by a railway in 1848. There used to be eleven locks up through Pontypool and then a level stretch to Pontnewynydd. I walked up into Pontypool to visit the public library, only to find it shut on early closing day. Then I went up to Pontnewynydd (about a mile beyond) to try to find the end. I found a bit of probable towpath beside the railway and some possible cottages. I then asked a man by the bus stop about a bus to the station and we got chatting, and I mentioned the canal.

He seized me and we rushed back to the canal, where he showed me another stretch of towpath beside the railway (locally called Canal Bank), and then, solitary in the middle of the town, a Lock House (so called) with a huge garden. In front of it they were rebuilding the road, and we asked the foreman if he'd found any of the locks. He had, and showed us some remains, complaining bitterly that the old work had been so good that it had bust his drills. One up for Mr Dadford [the canal engineer]. My friend was now well away, and we happily rummaged in people's back gardens and rubbish heaps, but unsuccessfully, as the old line was under the railway.

None of these descriptions found its way into *South Wales*, but the visits enabled him to envisage what he was writing about. In May 1959 he would return to participate in an RCHS visit to the area.

Charles often sought local experts to guide him around. For *South Wales* he was shown significant sites on the Wye and Lugg Navigations in 1957 by I. Cohen, an early RCHS member who, since retiring to Hereford in wartime, had published papers on the Wye and the Leominster Canal, based on field visits for the Woolhope Naturalists Field Club. One of his sources was a series of railway and canal references from Hereford newspapers between 1789 and 1860; almost every chapter in *South Wales* made use of these. Such secondary sources were usefully rendered down by early RCHS members and others. One curious source discovered by Mr Cohen in 1957 was an old book in which chemists' advertisements had been pasted over pages which recorded traffics on the Wye.

Charles had found that prospectuses and the records of the railway company which acquired the Leominster Canal were its only available sources, and the fieldwork and Mr Cohen's paper proved essential. He also consulted a range of secondary sources, among which D.R. Phillips's *The History of the Vale of Neath* of 1925 was perhaps the most useful, along with general sources like *Rees Cyclopedia*.

Written composition followed a pattern outlined in his RCHS paper of 1955. Once sufficient materials had been produced, he would type these into a coherent account, leaving part of the page blank. Each piece of information would be backed by footnotes, so that he could record its source. Successive handwritten additions would then be made, until the whole would need to be retyped and final queries settled. Finally, the whole would be cut down to a reasonable length; his method made it impossible to write to length without later cutting.

He had drafted much of the book by the end of 1957, and then sought to deal with queries which his drafts raised. Final queries concerned the later history of canals; the BTC London Press Office provided details of the final traffics on the Monmouthshire and Brecon Canals, which were faithfully reproduced. Details of the final traffics on the Glamorganshire Canal came in June 1959 from Ian L. Wright, who had grown up in Cardiff. He had photographed many of the canals in South Wales, and Charles used his photograph of the Cardiff Tunnel, which was later destroyed, taken in 1944 when he was still at school. He had witnessed some of the last traffics on the canal, and, in an early example of oral history, recorded the reminiscences of many canal workers. While Charles did not set much store by oral evidence, this turned out to be the only recorded source. Ian L. Wright also helped Charles to identify tramroads leading from Taff Vale for the map on page 92, and clarified the reasons why the short Doctor's Canal had so many alternative names.

The book proved difficult to place; Phoenix House was unwilling to take on *South Wales* on its own, and the University of Wales Press only agreed to publish if no royalties were payable. The final manuscript was completed in the summer of

1959, and Charles suggested to the Press that they print 1,500 copies. It agreed only to 1,000, and the book sold out before publication in the early summer of 1960, necessitating a further printing.

Charles's study presented many new discoveries, and exposed much about the importance of tramroads to canal history, but Professor T.S. Willan's review in *History* in 1961 drew a broader conclusion: 'the belief that wicked railway companies strangled innocent canals dies hard. Mr Hadfield knows too much about both canals and railways to give any countenance to such popular legends.' His praise was tempered by only slight reservations:

> This book is based on the best available sources, both manuscript and printed; it shows a great knowledge of local topography, and here the reader is assisted by a number of useful maps. In places, perhaps, the detail seems a little excessive, especially in describing canals which were only a mile or two in length and in discussing projects which proved abortive. Even so, considering Mr Hadfield's mastery of his subject, it is better to have too much than too little. His work is a valuable contribution to the economic history of South Wales.[7]

Later books which Charles would write in the 'Canals of the British Isles' series would follow a similar pattern of research, although these could draw upon the experience accumulated through visits by boat and by trips organised by the RCHS and others.

EXPLORATIONS BY BOAT

Until Easter 1955 Charles had not spent a holiday on a boat, and had only spent occasional days and rarer nights on the water. Once his children had grown to school age, he spent a week on the kind of holiday which he had described in Chapter 4 of *Introducing Canals*. These trips enabled him to combine a family holiday with further familiarisation with waterways whose history he was researching for the *Midlands* volume.

He hired *Venturer* from the Canal Cruising Company at Stone, on the Trent & Mersey Canal, run by the Wyatt family. They arrived from Euston on 9 April 1955, and left Stone Wharf at 3.30 p.m., with a mechanic on board at first. They worked through the first six locks in Stoke, where Charles later recalled

> one bad moment when my visual memory showed me a paddle-bar not fully down on the lower gate of a lock below the one I had just left. There followed a successful struggle of conscience with laziness, and I walked back, in time to see the pound below my lock running itself dry. Hoping no lock-keeper would arrive, I hurriedly shut the paddle, ran back to the lock above, opened everything and restored the situation.[8]

They worked through the top lock at Etruria in darkness, and moored above, at the junction with the Caldon Branch. Charles later depicted the view:

one can look over the valley to works where every so often a bright glare lights the sky as furnaces are tapped; and just along the towpath, beside the canal, Josiah Wedgwood's original eighteenth-century pottery building stands [it would be demolished in 1968]; and down a side street is a pub where an old, old gentleman told me that Stoke-on-Trent was the healthiest place in England – and he ought to have known, for he had never been out of it.[9]

The next day, after a night in which 'Boat banged against fenders all night. No sleep for anyone much', they travelled through the Potteries towards Harecastle Tunnel. Alice Mary's diary was unsentimental:

Number of boats by Anderton Co. wharf, with ?gravel. Snowflake, Sunshine. Passed Etruria factory, through steel works. Rain all the time, potteries, waste land, mountains of broken china dirty white and brown, lakes and pools of slimy water, ruined factories, ranks of tiny red and black houses, no trees, gardens, fields, no people or children no animals, no life but smoking chimneys of kilns. Mountains of waste everywhere.[10]

The children and Alice Mary left Charles to take *Venturer* through the low Harecastle Tunnel alone. They turned up the Macclesfield Canal, where, at Bosley Locks, Alice Mary, steering, 'bumped every lock entrance, in spite of my struggles, some slightly, some with a wallop and following rebound'. Above, they found that the '18 mile top pound was drained by a boat which yesterday left the paddles up'.

On the 12th they moored at Marple, where they visited the Ring O'Bells pub, where they found 'No bitter, only mild. Read papers. Macc C to be closed.' It would not happen, but closure was then a possibility. The evening there was recalled somewhat lyrically: 'as darkness falls, watching the lights come out on the hills all round as the towns transform themselves to glow-worm embroidery worked on the Pennine slopes'.[11]

They next walked down the sixteen Marple Locks to view Marple Aqueduct at their foot, and later took a hired car to explore the Peak District and search for Hadfield relatives; page 137 explains the latter connections. They returned down the Macclesfield, where they saw their first moving pleasure-boat at the bottom of Bosley Locks. Turning north along the Trent & Mersey, they encountered several narrow boats carrying pottery materials and flour.

On the Shropshire Union Middlewich Branch, they followed a British Waterways pair carrying spelter from Weston Point to the Midlands. Alice Mary's earlier comments on boat children 'reared on strong contrasts and sharp effects' did not apply to the crew of this pair: 'man and wife, grandmother, 3 kids + dog, all dirty beyond all ordinary dirtiness. They put a child ashore and hurled a rusty old tricycle after her which must have been picked out of canal. She got on and struggled along the towpath.' Charles later wondered whether enthusiasts for narrow boats, like Tom Rolt, would have condemned people to this.

They moored at Nantwich Basin, and Charles and Alice Mary went for dinner in the Crown Hotel with Mr and Mrs Marsh; Christopher Marsh told them of proposals to keep open the Macclesfield Canal and the summit level of the Staffordshire & Worcestershire for water supplies, but to close the locks. They discussed a current IWA agitation to rehabilitate the Caldon Branch for a promised traffic, which Marsh regarded as blackmail. At Norbury Junction David Wyatt had to come out to repair the engine. On 22 April they left Wheaton Aston at 6 a.m., to climb the 21 Wolverhampton Locks, pass a section by Wolverhampton Power Station congested with coal boats, and along the Birmingham Canal to moor 'by the Dirt Boat' (a refuse-carrying boat) at Farmers Bridge at 7.45 p.m., 26 miles and 24 locks later. During that night they were disturbed by the sound of rats running over the deck. By 24 April they had only met two pleasure-boats since leaving the Macclesfield Canal, both on the Shropshire Union Canal; another one would be seen on the Coventry Canal near Huddlesford.

They visited the Swan at Fradley Junction, then perhaps between two worlds: 'public bar, loud radio music, serious darts practice by team, big fire, dominoes, cards, quantities of local people, all very village kind'. Charles was ambivalent, as a modern pub would attract some boaters. Above Wood End they met the *Angela*, Wyatt's converted half narrow boat, and they returned to Stone on 26 April. Every pleasure-boat they saw moving during the sixteen-day trip has been mentioned above.

The following year they hired *Venturer* again, from 29 March. They again went north, but this time directly along the Trent & Mersey Canal, to moor at Wheelock. From here Christopher Marsh drove them to dine again at the Crown Hotel, where he confirmed that while the BTC had dredged the Caldon Branch to Consall, the traffic promised by the IWA had not materialised. The next day they saw some traffics on the Weaver, including ICI barges, from above Anderton Lift. Barnton Tunnel, then controlled by traffic lights, followed, and Preston Brook Tunnel, then internally lit, leading into the Bridgewater Canal.

At Runcorn, they moored near five canal boats, and walked down Runcorn Locks. These were then still in use, although in the previous year Alfred Hayman of the Bridgewater Department had told Charles that the development of Runcorn Docks would necessitate their closure; he had been very surprised when Charles expressed his approval. During an evening spent in the Duke of Bridgewater public house, they raised glasses to the Duke and to James Brindley; Charles would discover later that the latter's involvement in the Bridgewater Canal's engineering was less than he then thought. The next morning James MacColl met them and drove them across the Transporter Bridge to his Widnes constituency, and then joined the boat for a cruise to Lymm, during which they met several pleasure and working boats.

On 4 April they encountered increasing numbers of barges and narrow boats around Trafford Park, and waited behind two coal barges at Barton Swing

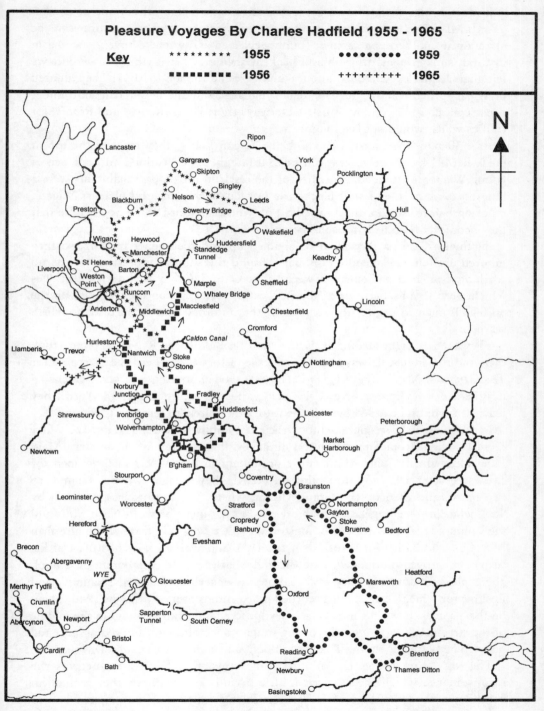

Pleasure Voyages By Charles Hadfield 1955 - 1965

Key
* * * * * * * * 1955
● ● ● ● ● ● ● ● ● 1959
■ ■ ■ ■ ■ ■ ■ ■ 1956
+ + + + + + + + 1965

Diagrammatic representations of Charles's four holiday voyages; there were day trips elsewhere. Selected places visited by Charles by road or rail are also included.

Aqueduct, while a ship drawn by several tugs passed along the Manchester Ship Canal. Mooring beyond Worsley, they walked back to view the entrances to the abandoned underground canals: 'Totally neglected and wretched overgrown basin in front, sunken boats rubbish and broken fencing . . . Everything so derelict we felt angry.' Charles would explore the underground tunnels in 1961. They moored in Wigan, where Charles met the depot manager, saw the new repair yard under construction, and two new British Waterways short boats, *Kennet* and *Ribble*, for traffics which would not last long.

At 3.30 p.m. they started to climb the Wigan Locks; they reached the top at 6.45, helped by a twelve-year-old boy, although 'At every lock an audience of young Wiganese attended. . . . Most of the rest and the oldest inhabitants were a hindrance.' Later they found Blackburn 'not half such a cheerful place as Wigan'; mooring before Nelson, they visited a pub whose landlord could not believe that they had never been to Lancashire before.

Barrowford Locks proved to be chained up and the keeper missing, so they moored and climbed Pendle Hill. They found the summit level deserted, as no working boat had passed for a week; after Gargrave they found swing bridges which were 'a nuisance', especially in the wind. At Skipton they walked up the Springs Branch to inspect the remains of the tramroad and inclined plane which served it.

They spent a night at Bingley, where Gordon Biddle, the RCHS secretary, took them out for dinner; he was later to write the history of the Leeds & Liverpool for *The Canals of North West England*. The next day, in pouring rain, they watched a barge go down Bingley Five Rise Locks, and on the final day, 14 April, they reached Leeds and handed over the boat for other hirers to return it to Stone.

In 1959, again in spring, they took their last family boat holiday, in *Maid Mary Jennifer*. Hired from Thames Ditton in Surrey, this was one of the modern Maid Line fleet, which Lionel Munk, now prominent in the IWA, had developed for canal use after 1954. With a pilot on board, they went down the Thames to Brentford, and then up the Grand Union, where Kit Gayford helped them by 'lock-wheeling' – going ahead by bicycle to set the locks between Nash Mills and the summit at Marsworth. At Braunston they met Michael Streat of the hire firm Blue Line; he had been involved in the IWA and was initially hostile, but his suspicions proved unfounded. Later he and Charles would collaborate on a book about pleasure-cruising. They saw coal on the wharves at Cropredy, Banbury and Enslow, for which Charles had recorded nineteenth-century traffics in 1940. Then, on the Thames, beyond Kings Lock, they 'proceeded to run aground in the middle of the stream, still pouring rain, owing to ignorance of the meaning of a large red buoy'. They came down the Thames in flood, and so back to Thames Ditton.

The logs from these trips record some consistent features. One was the inconvenience which they experienced, especially on *Venturer*, the mechanical breakdowns and the discomfort. Charles later recalled that 'one night I had to balance a pudding basin on my stomach to catch the drips through the cabin roof'.[12]

The second is the very limited leisure use of canals in the 1950s, and the difficulties envisaged in their adaptation for pleasure purposes. The contents of chemical toilets had to be buried, while they found no means of swilling-out at an emptying station on the Thames. Charles would later consider that pleasure-boating would only develop if the track was adapted and proper waterside facilities and attractions were provided. Finally, these were holiday trips rather than historical explorations; for the 'canal man' there is no assiduous or desperate recording of so much which was to disappear, and few expressions of regret. This lack of sentimentality would prove helpful when he joined the British Waterways Board.

One postscript to the contact with officials made for *Introducing Canals* was that they invited Charles on occasional trips. For instance, Christopher Marsh arranged for him to join an engineers' inspection trip through Standedge Tunnel, the longest in Britain, on the closed Huddersfield Canal, in 1956. Charles felt that the journey through this low tunnel was like travelling down a drainpipe; he never supported its restoration. The journey was enlivened by the engineers chipping off loose stone to assess the tunnel's stability; some of this fell into the boat and on to its passengers.

On this trip Charles met Philip Weaver of Kenilworth, who had explored the derelict Sapperton Tunnel in the 1930s; he was interested in tunnels and in mechanical engineering. He was beginning to carry out detailed and meticulous research into the Birmingham Canal Navigations, and agreed to read a long run of *Aris's Birmingham Gazette* for Charles's research for the *Midlands* study. Charles told Philip Weaver later that he could never have carried out this study without this help.

Contact with Alfred Hayman of the Bridgewater Canal brought Charles into even smaller bore tunnels, in the underground system at Worsley, at the time of the canal's bicentenary in 1961. Much later, he recalled this trip, which included many RCHS members:

> a party of us having put on overalls were taken down the shaft of a coal mine and put into the original mine boats which were called 'starvationers'. Owing to the subsidence we had to lie on our backs for part of the trip with the tunnel roof about 6" above my nose. We were legged – the only time I have been professionally legged – and eventually emerged in another mine shaft where we returned to the surface. It gave me an opportunity actually to see the underground inclined plane which connected two underground canal levels. Danger of further subsidence then closed the canals for ever. It was a wonderful experience but I was thankful I did not suffer from claustrophobia.[13]

By this time many of Charles's visits to waterways were organised by the RCHS, or by its members. For instance, for a week in 1963 he stayed in Heywood with Alan Voce, RCHS secretary since 1960, who had been researching north-west waterways through visits and documentary work since 1958. By road they toured many waterways in northern England, including the Rochdale, Huddersfield, Ashton,

Bridgewater, Manchester, Bolton & Bury, Lancaster, and Leeds & Liverpool Canals. Charles was then in the later stages of the *Midlands* study, but a *Northern England* volume was under consideration. However, as he was by then on the British Waterways Board, he also sought to familiarise himself with waterways which he did not know well, without the formalities involved in an official visit.

THE RCHS DEVELOPS

By the end of 1955 Charles was no longer the only RCHS member interested in canal history, after members such as Tom Rolt, Hugh Compton, Howard Williams and Edward Wilson joined. Younger recruits included Maurice Berrill and Martin Palmer, whose 1958 article on the Dick Brook, based on fieldwork, was one of the earliest waterways pieces not written by Charles or Edward Wilson in the *Journal*.

While Charles Clinker was in a dominant position as President, Charles Hadfield greatly helped shape the Society's early course. Many early meetings were held at Charles's house at 28 Newton Road, while others were held at Clinker's house in Rugby. The Society settled down to a regular programme of visits and lectures, some organised by the regional groups as these were formed. Charles and Gordon Biddle organised many of the early visits, including one in London on the trip boat *Jason* on 14 April 1957; this included the Islington and Maida Vale tunnels ('not at all fearsome') and a practical demonstration of boat gauging at Paddington toll-house, then still in use. Several visits returned to places which he had explored with Clinker and Cook in the early 1950s.

The RCHS *Journal*, under Jeoffry Spence, its long-standing editor, continued until 1965 in duplicated form, after which it was printed and with much longer articles. The early instructional pieces expounding approaches and methods tended to give way to short articles reporting the results of research, including some by Charles on Midlands waterways. Without any express intention, it was the publishing of serious canal history which developed in the *Journal*, perhaps because railway history had other outlets. From early 1957 Charles proposed that the best articles be extracted and published in printed annual *Transactions*, like those of the Newcomen Society. He suggested that the RCHS separate its 'learned' and 'publicity' sides for written material, and that the *Transactions* should be sold to the general public. Views diverged over the value of this idea, but the costs involved may have deterred; although in 1962 a first volume had been assembled ready for printing, it never appeared.

At Charles's instigation, the RCHS set up a Publications Fund to back its own publications. It took until 1962 for the first in a steady stream of publications which would continue into the 1990s. By 1962, however, Charles was less enthusiastic about RCHS publications, since some members' work could now be published by his firm David & Charles and other publishers. In 1958 Charles also founded a research sub-committee, which among other matters sought to locate and record transport history materials in museums and archives, to supplement the general bibliography project already launched by the Society.

One problem encountered by the RCHS was the preservation of historic transport structures; interest in both historic railways and canals was growing, partly because so much appeared at risk of closure, and also because railway modernisation involved the destruction or alteration of many features. Industrial archaeology was steadily growing; one spur was the establishment in 1959 of a special committee of the Council for British Archaeology to study it, and to consider which structures should be scheduled for preservation. One celebrated example was the proposal to demolish the Euston Arch in the rebuilding of Euston station; the RCHS decided that it could not campaign against this, but it did monitor developments.

The RCHS did participate in the Consultative Panel on British Transport Relics; from January 1959 Charles was a member, and by May had drawn up part of a list of canal structures recommended for scheduling. He remained a member until October 1960, when Charles Klapper replaced him. Pressure to prevent the loss of archive materials, and to enlarge access to them, was more forceful.

A further issue, which would continue to be raised into the 1980s, was a proposal to widen the scope of the RCHS to include other forms of transport, especially the history of roads. This was initiated by Dr T.C. Barker, who joined the Society in 1958; a piece in the *Journal* in 1960 drew a trenchant and apt analogy:

History – any sort of history – is more than a mere collection of facts. Facts only make the bricks of the historian's craft. At present, more and more writers of transport history are taking great pains over fashioning the individual bricks – and then putting them aside on a neat pile. This is not wasted effort: those who are capable of building will come along and make use of them. But is it not a pity that more transport historians themselves do not try to build?[14]

Dr Barker's appeal lay towards the more academic pursuit of economic history; he himself had perhaps carried out some 'brick-making' in his 1948 paper on the Sankey Navigation, but would go on to engage in business history, in a major account of the St Helens glass manufacturers Pilkingtons. Charles supported his proposals to widen the scope of the Society, but the main opponent was Clinker, while others were cautious. Dr Barker was to join the Council in 1961, and his views were the subject of a paper at the Birmingham AGM, the first addressed by Charles as RCHS president.

Clinker stood down as president after seven years, partly for personal reasons, and partly because of differences between him and other members. Much of this stemmed from his founding role, and his influence, often benign but sometimes over-dominant, over younger members; in some respects, he felt that it was his Society, and he did not like opposition, over either the workings of the RCHS, or the kind of history to be encouraged. Charles secured changes to the constitution which meant that future presidents would serve for a maximum term of two years, so that he himself only served until 1963.

After that date, Charles continued to play a part within the RCHS, but one which relied upon the existence of wide nuclei of enthusiasts, building on the foundations laid by the early 1960s. The emergence of new publishing houses, including one which he founded, changed the environment within which the Society operated.

DAVID & CHARLES: EARLY DEVELOPMENTS

Charles's experience in publishing had led him, as early as February 1951, to consider plans to start a small publishing business around 1957, with a view to retiring to South Cerney about five years later. At that time he envisaged Gloucestershire books such as Humphrey Household's *The Thames & Severn Canal*, and reprints like Temple Thurston's classic semi-fictional *The Flower of Gloster*, along with canal and local booklets.

The roots of David & Charles (Publishers) partly lay in the difficulties involved in publishing books on transport history, which Charles's problems in publishing *Southern England* and *South Wales* reflected. The main publishers in the field were Ian Allan, founded in 1943, which specialised in popular railway and locomotive books such as those by Oswald S. Nock; and Oakwood Press. The latter had been founded by Roger Kidner and Michael Robbins, who had met at school and in 1932 began publishing a quarterly journal, *Locomotion*. They had begun to publish railway history monographs from 1936, on very short print runs, for an uncertain market, and revived operations after wartime service.

Other small-scale operations had been launched from time to time, but authors often had to subsidise publications, many useful manuscripts remained unpublished, and much remained unwritten. Against this, Charles perceived an increasing membership of railway and canal societies, including LANT, the RCHS and the many railway and locomotive enthusiast societies, which were not well served by trade booksellers.

There was therefore a gap in the market for a new publisher of transport books, aimed at a specialist readership. Most publishers were London-based; they took a traditional approach, and used printing firms in central London. David St John Thomas had connections with a Dawlish printer, W.J. Holman, whose charges were much lower than those of London printers, and a base in South Devon would provide the means to sell local interest publications in the West Country.

David St John Thomas (henceforth 'David') was a generation younger than Charles, born in 1929. He had been interested in railways since 1942, and had been collecting material towards a history of West Country railways since 1952, when, as a journalist, he had witnessed the last train on the Bridgwater branch of the Somerset & Dorset Railway, watched only by a few railway enthusiasts. During 1958 he was actively writing this history for Phoenix House. He was spurred by an anonymous letter which suggested that his talents could be more widely employed, and he later asserted that the new firm was 'a glorified hobby, or at most a further ingredient of my freelance practice, which already included journalism of several kinds, radio and television, authorship, and fruit farming. Why not also publishing?'[15]

David was very ambitious, but ambition in journalism at that time meant Fleet Street, not writing for the *Western Morning News*. To set up a successful publishing firm in South Devon presented a challenge which could satisfy those ambitions.

David joined the RCHS late in 1956, and in 1957 met Clinker, who mentioned that Charles Hadfield was also interested in publishing. Charles hardly knew David, but was attracted by his ideas, and by December all three had joined forces, aiming to publish railway and canal books. Clinker withdrew in March 1958; he wanted to secure the publication of railway monographs of higher standards, and he would not agree that the firm should publish books of West Country interest or about industrial archaeology. Clinker was at first the Historical Editor of the series 'A Regional History of the Railways of Great Britain', and his monograph *The Hay Railway* would be the first booklet published by David & Charles. He also read the proofs of the second edition of *British Canals*, which Phoenix House published in 1959.

While Charles's views were closer to David's, he was then too busy to proceed, but they revived discussions in February 1959, and by November they were considering titles. Charles suggested that canal pamphlets, by RCHS members, should be sought for the autumn of 1960; one possibility was David's study of the Bude Canal, upon which he was already working in 1957. In the event, the first three publications included David's *The Rural Transport Problem*, a 20,000-word pamphlet partly based on his journalistic investigations, and a reprint of an 1878 history of the Salisbury & Yeovil Railway in time for its centenary.

On Charles's insistence, a company rather than a partnership was formed; the original 'David Charles' clashed with other company names, and on 1 April 1960 David & Charles (Publishers) Ltd (henceforth D&C) was formed. Charles planned to play a larger part after retirement from the COI in 1962, but in the meantime David tackled much of the everyday work on a part-time basis from his home near Newton Abbot. The initial capital was around £500; to set up a London publishing firm at the time would have required around £30,000.

The initial plan was to sell by post to specialised booksellers and the public, rather than to mainstream booksellers, with orders being dispatched by the printers. Following Charles's suggestion, John Baker of Phoenix House agreed early in 1960 to place D&C books on their list, in order to pick up library and some general bookshop sales. John Baker had encouraged David to write his first volume for the 'Regional Railway History' series, and David would later describe Phoenix House as the precursor of the firm which D&C would later become.

The connection with John Baker and Phoenix House soon proved useful. Charles proposed to commission short biographies of engineers, such as James Brindley and William Jessop; he approached Tom Rolt, whose studies of Telford and Brunel had done much to popularise engineering biography, to consider a study of Thomas Newcomen. In July 1960, however, Tom Rolt suggested an alternative. His *Railway Adventure*, published in 1953, had related his experiences with the first two years of the Talyllyn Railway Preservation Society, and he now suggested a reprint in paperback for sale to the Society, which they could in turn sell to visitors to the line. Charles saw a wider market for this, and by September it was agreed that this should be sold simultaneously by Phoenix House; it appeared in February 1961. This proved successful for both publishers, and the basis of future publications.

One publishing opportunity arose with the bi-centenary of the Bridgewater Canal in 1961. It was too late to commission a publication, but in October 1960 Hugh Malet submitted a new book on the Bridgewater's promoter, *The Canal Duke*. Other publishers had rejected this semi-popular biography, and its production in a hardback format required the whole of the company's capital. Despite its unusual appearance, this book sold well after publication in April 1961, and its outlay was soon recovered.

One early project was on a much larger scale. Charles proposed a four-volume series to relate the general history of travel and transport between 1600 and 1960. He planned to tackle the 1750–1830 history himself, to approach T.S. Willan for the 1600–1750 volume, and suggested that David should tackle one of the remaining volumes. This would greatly enlarge the general discussions of transport history which Charles had outlined in *Southern England*, but for which he would not find space (or research time) in later volumes. David was unenthusiastic about the research involved, and this project was shelved in 1961.

Flooding in the Exe Valley in October 1960 provided an unanticipated publication. Using his journalistic flair and resources, David produced, in 48 hours, an illustrated booklet, *Devon Flood Story*, whose royalties were donated to flood relief funds. This went through five editions in a month, being rewritten as events unfolded; there was a matching flood of interest from local booksellers and bookstalls, with no great certainty as to when this, like the actual flood, would subside. Despite its success, this publication caused friction between Charles and David; David had moved so rapidly that Charles had not been informed even that the booklet was being written, let alone published, and their views diverged over the risks involved in this venture. Afterwards, Charles insisted on joint financial responsibility; as he put it in October 1960, 'I do not propose to be the sleeping and acquiescent partner in a dictatorship.'[16]

More friction resulted from Charles's own publications. After Clinker's *The Hay Railway* was published, David persuaded Charles to write two booklets of his own, about the Warwickshire Avon and the Stratford Canal, despite his reluctance to divert time from *Midlands*. However, as he was a member of LANT (then actively restoring the Avon), while the National Trust were negotiating a lease to restore the southern Stratford Canal, the booklets would cover a topical subject with the prospect of specialist sales. A third booklet, on the Stratford & Moreton Tramway, which served the canal at Stratford, was written after 1960 by John Norris, who had helped Charles's researches into the Herefordshire &

Gloucestershire Canal in 1957. He had been interested in railways since his schooldays in Worcester, and had first explored the remains of the tramway in 1945, studying records relating to it since around 1953.

Charles began work on the Avon and Stratford booklets in July 1960, and within twelve months had completed most of the research. An argument then developed over whether the three should be combined into one book, *Waterways to Stratford*, to be published by Phoenix House, or whether Holman should print three separate D&C publications. After this was resolved, Philip Weaver was hastily entreated to prepare an itinerary and photographs of the Avon, which he rushed to produce. The book was placed in what was now called 'The Canals of the British Isles' series, edited by Charles, although it did not cover the canals of a whole region like the *Southern England* and *South Wales* volumes which began it. It was an incongruous beginning for the most important group of British canal history books to be published.

One public reception of *Waterways to Stratford* is discussed at the end of this chapter. Behind the differences between David and Charles over this book lay, partly, David's feeling, voiced as early as August 1961, that these smaller publications were not as marketable as they had expected, and that the new firm should produce larger books in future. It was soon forced into this position, when Dent's, who controlled Phoenix House, ordered John Baker to cease handling D&C books. This led to further differences, after Charles proved unable to persuade Martin Dent, the chairman of Dent's, to change his mind. When David suggested that he might intervene, Charles asserted that his youth would tell against him, but David was to prove successful.

By the end of 1962 MacDonalds, introduced by Charles, had agreed to take over Phoenix House's role, while Phoenix House had agreed to transfer the railway and canal history series for which David and Charles were respectively editors. After this, D&C were primarily hardback publishers.

Charles's researches for the *Midlands* volume were continuing, albeit slowed by *Waterways to Stratford*, and two glimpses of the research process involved must suffice here. He had great difficulty finding records of the Trent & Mersey Canal and its tributaries in Newcastle. Much later he was to discover that most of the Trent & Mersey records had been systematically destroyed, but he wrote to numerous solicitors in the Stoke-on-Trent area to discover if they had any papers. In July 1960 he stayed in Stoke to carry out research, and visited the offices of the Borough Surveyor for Newcastle-under-Lyme, which had acquired and filled in most of its local canal. They provided useful plans but no documentation, and he then tried Knight & Sons, local solicitors. As he recalled later

I myself once penetrated to the muniment room of Knight & Sons. They assured me they had no canal records, but grumpily escorted me down. Facing me as I entered the door was a tin box with Newcastle-under-Lyme Junction Canal Co., painted on it. They were most annoyed, but allowed me to make extracts from the minute books.[17]

In March 1963, by which time he had joined the British Waterways Board, Charles combined an official visit to Nottingham, viewing the Grantham Canal and the eastern end of the Trent & Mersey, with an RCHS visit at the weekend. He also carried out research at Nottingham Reference Library, where he found all the materials which he had requested in advance ready, and 'the VIP treatment was laid on – the great canal author – introduced to the librarian, signed the visitor book'.[18] He was becoming well known in his field, even if it was a small one.

His letters from this period indicate that retirement was proving more busy than work. In March he was attending British Waterways Board meetings and visits, RCHS visits, research trips and field studies, planning a fortnight in the Netherlands, and finding time to talk to a Trent River Board officer about hydroelectric power; added to which there was work on Quaker committees, the South Cerney Trust – and work for D&C.

Shortly before Charles's retirement in 1962, there had been more differences with David, who was reluctant to produce detailed costings before agreeing to publish, and preferred to rely on his instincts. These had proved remarkably reliable up to this time, but Charles remained cautious.

Charles retired from COI at the end of July 1962, and moved from London to Silver Street House in South Cerney a month later. He then considered the next stage of publishing. No significant books had yet been published about industrial archaeology, although fieldwork and documentary research involving both transport and industrial remains were growing, and the subject was taken seriously by the Council for British Archaeology. In July 1961 Charles had lectured to a summer school in industrial archaeology at the University of Manchester, organised by Dr Rodney Green. Charles had then agreed to assist with a new *Handbook on Industrial Archaeology*, and had made two contacts for D&C. One was J.P.M. Pannell, engineer to Southampton Harbour Board since 1935, whose *Techniques of Industrial Archaeology*, a practical guide to techniques and approaches, would be published in June 1966.

The second contact was Dr Alan McCutcheon, whose Ph.D. study at Queens University, Belfast, included investigation into the railway and canal history of Northern Ireland. His main interest lay in industrial archaeology; his Masters thesis in 1958 analysed the history of coal-mining in East Tyrone. He agreed that, after completing his doctorate in 1962, he would write *The Canals of the North of Ireland* for the 'British Isles' series. Almost all of the canals in Northern Ireland were already disused, and there was very little enthusiast interest. As editor of the 'British Isles' series, Charles would edit this work into a similar style to his own volumes, and it would eventually be published in 1965.

Charles was to develop the idea of an industrial archaeology series during 1963, when the first significant books on the subject, *Industrial Archaeology* by Kenneth Hudson, and Dr Green's *Industrial Archaeology of County Down*, were published elsewhere. Charles secured Dr Green as General Editor for a series which began with Hudson's *Southern England* and David Smith's *The East Midlands* in 1965.

In 1962 he sought the next volume in the 'British Isles' series, *Canals of the South of Ireland*, from Vincent Delany, co-founder and leader of the Inland Waterways Association of Ireland. A law professor by profession, but with long-standing boating experience, he had researched Irish canal history for several years, and had written an article about the Shannon for the *Journal of Transport History* in 1958. He began to enlarge his earlier study, but he died in January 1964, and his widow Ruth, later to become Ireland's leading canal historian, completed the book. To conform to the general approach in the *'British Isles'* series, it proved necessary for her to add tabulated material and an additional chapter on the Grand Canal's trading years. The latter involved additional research in the Grand Canal Company's records and enabled Ruth Delany to write a full history of the Grand Canal, which D&C would publish in 1973.

Charles's researches in South Wales had enlarged his interest in tramroads, and he suggested a series on railway prehistory, building on Clinker's *The Hay Railway*. This did not emerge, but Charles did foster the preparation of Bertram Baxter's *Stone Blocks and Iron Rails* as part of the 'Industrial Archaeology' series. Bertram Baxter, one of the RCHS founders, had been interested in tramroads since the 1920s, and after retirement in 1962 had sought to write an account which would detail all known tramroads along with a general history. With Charles's encouragement, he completed this by December 1964, and the book was published shortly before Bertram Baxter died in October 1966.

Charles was to do more than edit the text during 1965; as he put it, 'The text version is virtually my work, for I completely rewrote Baxter's, and added two brand-new chapters from my own material.'[19] The text had been well researched, but the writing style had made it impossible to publish. As Charles liked Bertram Baxter and wished to see the study published, he rewrote it; a perusal of the book will indicate Charles's style in all but one chapter.

Few individual tramroad histories have been commercially published, although one published by D&C – one of the last monographs – was M.C. Ewans's *The Haytor Granite Tramway and Stover Canal*. First proposed late in 1962, this was published in 1964.

By the end of 1963 much work had been initiated, but the divergences between Charles and David had developed into crisis, as the next chapter will discuss. Charles's other retirement activities included assuming editorship of the *Wayfarer*, the national Quaker monthly magazine, although he had only joined the Society of Friends in 1957. A much more significant retirement post, which would bring lasting results, was as a member of the new British Waterways Board.

POLICY BEFORE THE BRITISH WATERWAYS BOARD

After 1954 Charles had maintained contact with some of the waterways officers whom he had met, both in the nationalised body and elsewhere, and continued to observe policy developments. He had kept in touch with Tom Rolt after he married Sonia Smith and began writing full time at Stanley Pontlarge in

Gloucestershire. Tom had had little contact with contemporary events on the canals which his books had helped to popularise. He did, however, know Brigadier Hopthrow, an early IWA member, who had been selected to join the Bowes Committee, whose remit was to consider the future of all Britain's canals. Through Hopthrow he ensured that Charles, as a civil servant with knowledge of his subject, was able to give evidence to the Committee in 1957.

Charles doubted, partly in light of the very limited pleasure-boating observed on his trips, that it would be financially possible to retain many canals for pleasure-boating; his work on freight-carrying also made him doubt that the smaller waterways, relying on narrow boats, had much transport future. As a civil servant, he was aware of the constraints imposed by the need to keep within financial estimates which were rarely generous or based on far-sighted policy, and the strong influence of the Treasury.

He was therefore pessimistic that waterways which were still navigable could be retained in the long term, let alone waterways which were no longer navigable. In his evidence to the Committee, he confirmed many of his suggestions in *Introducing Canals*, but proposed that some means should be found to restore the Kennet & Avon and southern Stratford Canals, which had become unnavigable since 1948. While the former was a celebrated cause over which the IWA had raised much publicity, the latter was yet to achieve the prominence brought about after it was leased to the National Trust and restored by voluntary labour. He was taken aback to be asked some critical questions about water supply, highly pertinent to both canals; only later did his studies of Jessop reveal the crucial importance of water supplies in waterways engineering.

In July 1958 the Bowes Committee recommended that a national network of traffic waterways should be put into good order and maintained for at least twenty-five years, so that traffic could develop. The government did not accept this recommendation, but accepted that the remaining waterways, most of which remained more or less navigable, should be subject to 'redevelopment'. This meant, in some cases, retention for amenity use, sometimes including navigation, and, in other cases, closure and partial or total elimination.

The government then set up the Inland Waterways Redevelopment Advisory Committee (IWRAC), which studied various canals to consider 'redevelopment' schemes for their future. Members included Lionel Munk, rising in prominence in the IWA, and Tom Rolt, chosen perhaps because of his interest in industrial archaeology rather than his authorship of *Narrow Boat*. Others included John Smith of the National Trust, who was pressing for unwanted waterways to be transferred to the Trust, and Admiral Sir Frederick Parham, newly retired. Although a number of canals were to be closed under Acts of 1961 and 1962, Admiral Parham proved to support the retention of most canals which had some demonstrable future; those who favoured more radical closures were disappointed.

While there had been reorganisations of the constituent parts of the nationalised British Transport Commission, it was decided in 1960 to split the BTC into separate organisations, one of them to be termed (after some discussion) the British Waterways Board (henceforth BWB); in reality, the new British Transport Docks Board was to control the more significant freight waterways of the Humber, Ouse and lower Trent.

This presented one advantage for the canals in that they would be controlled by a separate and dedicated organisation, but major disadvantages in that the subsidy for waterways masked by the BTC's labyrinthine accounts was now exposed. The Transport Act 1962 rested upon an assumption that each mode of transport could be made to pay its way, even if this meant, in the case of British Railways, major cutbacks. For the waterways, the Act provided that BWB must break even after five years, during which its legal duty to maintain waterways in navigable order would be suspended while policies to secure viability were determined.

Early in 1961, contemplating early retirement, Charles made enquiries as to whether he might join the new BWB. David Serpell (later associated with the 1982 committee which considered major rail closures) called him to an interview, in which he gently reminded Charles that candidates usually waited to be approached; Charles's reply was that he feared he might be overlooked. He heard no more until November 1962, when he was suddenly summoned to an interview in London. Before then, as Ministry of Transport files show, there were complex deliberations, as candidate after candidate was considered.

In June 1961 Admiral Parham was suggested as chairman, while others like Tom Rolt and Brigadier Hopthrow, as well as Charles, were considered. Those associated with waterways enthusiasts tended to be regarded as fanatics, whereas the required capacities were described in January 1962 as 'political wisdom, sound financial sense and a mailed fist under a very large covering of velvet'.[20] By August 1962 it was settled that the full-time deputy chairman would be Sir John Hawton, whose career with the Ministry of Health, where he had been closely involved with the formation of the National Health Service, had lasted from 1927 to early retirement in 1960. Charles was originally considered, along with Peter Scott and the chairman of the National Parks Commission, as the required 'amenity man'. In September 1962, after another candidate declined, Serpell suggested that Charles be interviewed, as 'a well-known writer on canals but not a fanatic'. He felt that Charles 'was not a world-beater', but he commended his 'level-headed approach to the canals' problems and his genuine interest', noted that his appointment might be 'taken by the IWA as a sort of back-handed slap at them', and observed that, oddly, Charles's views were 'so much in harmony with those on which the new Transport Act has been based'.[21]

It was not until late in November that Charles suddenly received a telephone call from the Ministry, asking:

Could I come up late that afternoon to see the Minister, Ernest Marples? Pausing only to order a taxi to the station and put on my best suit, I caught the next train. That evening I had nearly an hour with him and his Permanent Secretary, whom I happened to know. Mr Marples was, I think, puzzled to find that, though an amateur, I was not a crank. He began to sound me out. As the wine (he had his own vineyard) sank in the bottle, we both relaxed. I told him that I thought waterways had not only a promising future for pleasure cruising, but that some, enlarged to Continental standards, could contribute to transport. He was interested, and told me to come and see him personally whenever I wished. . . . Next day the Ministry rang; I had been appointed a part-time member of the British Waterways Board.[22]

Final appointments were made in a tearing hurry. After Ernest Marples deemed the Labour peer Lord Shackleton politically unacceptable, Frank Arney, former general manager of the Port of Bristol, was appointed part-time chairman. To represent amenity interests, Pauline Dower, deputy chairman [sic] of the National Parks Commission was appointed, along with a retired trade unionist, James Matthews. The latter appointment ominously revealed some of the government's expectations: he would be valuable 'in relation to redundancy problems which may arise with the redevelopment and disposal of inland waterways no longer required for transport'.

They were a strange combination, but one guided partly by a perceived need to keep out IWA supporters; it is unlikely that Charles would have been acceptable had he remained a member, although, since further divisions in 1958, the IWA had become a more hysterical body from which Charles might well have resigned. The deep disdain with which Ministry officials regarded the IWA leadership is illustrated by a letter which followed an IWA memorandum circulated to MPs in November 1961 about the Transport Bill; the IWA was described as 'well known to the Ministry as a body devoted to promoting, behind an allegation of general concern for the waterways, the interests of pleasure boaters (commercial waterway carriers are represented by a different body). . . . In prosecuting these interests the Association has shown tremendous energy and an unhesitating readiness to falsify facts provably known to it.'[23]

Aickman's private correspondence over the appointment of BWB members shows that David Serpell had accurately predicted Aickman's reaction to Charles's appointment. In December 1962 Aickman wrote that 'you will not be surprised to learn that I regard the appointment of Hadfield as both the most personally insulting yet, and also the most damaging to the waterways'.[24] The upheavals in the IWA had led to the formation of local societies, such as the Staffordshire & Worcestershire Canal Society, founded in 1959, which were to play a significant part in the survival of their local canals. The influence of the IWA, much of it negative, upon policy in the 1960s remains difficult to assess.

Two further events in 1962 need to be covered. In May, just before retirement from the COI, Charles was sent to Belgrade, where he saw the Danube, and on his return took a trip downstream on the Rhine from Köln (Cologne) to Düsseldorf. He encountered a level of traffic which he had never seen before, including various passenger- and pleasure-boats, 1000-ton self-propelled barges, tugs towing up to seven barges, tankers from Hamburg and Switzerland, a Finnish coaster, and a

French pusher tug. The smallest barges seen were about 150 tons; even these could only have traded over a very small number of BWB navigations, where a waterway of 80-tons capacity was considered large, and the majority carried boats of 20–25 tons.

Quite separately from D&C, Blackwells had asked Charles to write a short book for younger people, *Canals of the World*. In this, he described waterways like the Suez and Panama, which he would never see, and waterways in North America and continental Europe. He took almost all of this from books and from press cuttings, bar his description of the Rhine traffic. This was the first manifestation of his interest in overseas waterways, from which he began to propound ideas for British waterway development.

Another event, which amused rather than affronted Charles, was a review of *Waterways to Stratford* published in the IWA *Bulletin* in November 1962, just before his appointment to BWB. The review complained that Charles had covered the Stratford restoration in four paragraphs, implying that it was a local scheme, rather than the trailblazer which the IWA leadership felt it to be. It was suggested that this was the 'official attitude',

> because if a wider view were to prevail, the entire national policy for the waterways would collapse. It is for reasons such as the above that we do not like Mr Hadfield's books (even though the present one is unfortunately being recommended to all members of the National Trust). We shall not trouble people with their other defects such as the dead quality of the writing, or the confusing scheme of arrangement. . . .[25]

Charles had been somewhat disingenuous in not even mentioning the IWA, especially as David Hutchings, who was managing and leading the restoration, was a leading IWA member. It is not known whether this attack reached the notice of those who appointed Charles, but it would certainly have improved his chances of being appointed.

By 1963 Charles had ended his career in the civil service, but his second career as a writer and publisher was well established, and he was able to encourage others to write for what seemed to be an expanding market. He had not, however, had much opportunity to apply his developing knowledge of current inland waterways in Britain. His new position on the British Waterways Board would provide him with an opportunity to influence their future.

CHAPTER FOUR

DEVELOPING PAST AND FUTURE: 1963–8

In later years, Charles would stress that he was as much interested in the future of waterways as he was in their past; this interest became a practical one with his work for BWB. The work of the new Board, and Charles's contribution, will be considered here mainly through two parallel themes: amenity and freight development. While he was concerned with the future, Charles continued to write and to influence the publishing of transport history, although not in the manner which he had envisaged on his retirement from the COI. During the mid-1960s he was living at South Cerney; as Chapter 13 reveals, it was not quite a retirement to a quiet rural retreat.

BRITISH WATERWAYS BOARD AND AMENITY

Charles's first BWB meeting, delayed by the severe winter, provided a negative experience. BWB dealt with a minor element in transport, one which was seen as declining and loss-making. The previous general manager, Sir Reginald Kerr, whose independent (if capricious) approach had apparently offended too many, had not been re-appointed, and the new general manager, Arnold Allen, was not yet in post. Charles later recalled his feelings:

> Looking round the table, only Admiral Parham knew anything about canals, and his work had lain with those on the borderline of dereliction. Arney's first move had been towards economy – to ask all departmental officers for proposals for a ten per cent cut in expenditure; and I could well see the Board settling down to economy and abandonment as a policy.[1]

The new chairman's initial act was understandable, if negative. The meeting agreed to three closures authorised by the previous administration, including the St Helens Canal (Sankey Canal). At the meeting on 16 January, Charles requested that appropriate bodies be offered the opportunity to photograph waterways structures of historic interest if they were to be demolished; while modernisation could remove some structures, the possibility of extensive closures was uppermost.

There were some positive sentiments. Pauline Dower suggested that there was a greater emphasis on amenity since the time of the Bowes Committee, and proposed new waterways classifications. Charles suggested that waterways not

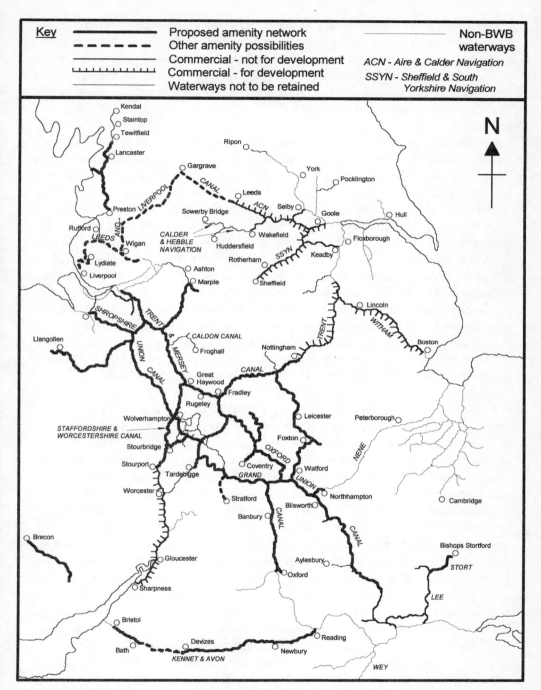

Key

— Proposed amenity network
- - - Other amenity possibilities
Commercial - not for development
⊥⊥⊥⊥⊥⊥⊥ Commercial - for development
Waterways not to be retained

Non-BWB waterways

ACN - Aire & Calder Navigation
SSYN - Sheffield & South Yorkshire Navigation

Kendal
Staintop
Tewitfield
Lancaster
Ripon
York
Pocklington
Gargrave
LIVERPOOL
CANAL
Leeds
ACN
Selby
Goole
Hull
Preston
Sowerby Bridge
Wakefield
Floxborough
Rufford
AND
Wigan
CALDER & HEBBLE NAVIGATION
Huddersfield
Keadby
LEEDS
Lydiate
Liverpool
Rotherham
SSYN
Ashton
Marple
Sheffield
Lincoln
SHROPSHIRE
TRENT
&
Llangollen
UNION
CANAL
MERSEY
CALDON CANAL
Froghall
Nottingham
TRENT
WITHAM
Boston
CANAL
Great Haywood
Fradley
Rugeley
Leicester
Peterborough
Wolverhampton
Foxton
STAFFORDSHIRE & WORCESTERSHIRE CANAL
Stourbridge
OXFORD
NENE
Stourport
Coventry
Watford
Tardebigge
GRAND
Worcester
Stratford
Blisworth
Northampton
Cambridge
Banbury
UNION
CANAL
CANAL
Brecon
Gloucester
Aylesbury
Bishops Stortford
STORT
Oxford
Sharpness
LEE
Bristol
Devizes
Reading
Bath
Newbury
KENNET & AVON
WEY

N

Charles's 1963 proposals for a BWB amenity network and selected improvements to waterways for commercial traffic. It should be stressed that some of the most important freight waterways – the lower Trent, Humber and Thames, for instance – were not owned by BWB and not then included in national waterways statistics.

we could greatly extend the cruising ground for craft of this description, we ought to get a sharp increase in pleasure craft tolls, which might be increased further if we could introduce a system of charging that gave us more for a broad than for a narrow cruiser of the same length. Moreover, if such an extension could link together important rivers, themselves the nurseries for such craft, then the prospects could be improved.[7]

That this did not prove to be the case – the dominant pleasure-craft on all BWB canals, broad or narrow, would prove to be of narrow beam – does not detract from the logic of these ideas. Charles felt that enlargement would link three cruising grounds – the Thames, the Trent, and the Nene and East Anglian waterways. The main barriers to the passage of broad craft between the Thames and the Trent were the flights of narrow locks at Foxton and Watford at either end of the Leicester line summit. His researches for *Midlands* had revealed that the widening of these locks had been authorised in 1900, when the Foxton inclined plane was opened to by-pass the locks there with a lift of barge capacity, but countered when the Watford Locks were rebuilt in 1902 at narrow gauge.

He now proposed a reversion to this scheme, although on a modern scale; this was inspired partly by another Canadian example, the two marine railways on the Trent–Severn Waterway, specifically built for pleasure-boats, which then dated back to 1920. He suggested that two of these could be built to replace the locks at Foxton and Watford. His proposed marine railway at each site, would involve 'a line of rails connecting the upper and lower pounds of the canal, along which runs a four-wheeled trolley big enough to carry a broad cruiser, and which is powered by a cable operated by a small electric motor in charge of an attendant'.[8] This would open up the route to the Trent for Thames cruisers, if the line between was dredged. He proposed a similar scheme to replace some of the narrow locks on the Northampton Arm, which linked the Grand Union with the broad Nene. In both cases he suggested that a special charge be made, but believed that the new route would bring greatly increased traffic. However, it is surprising that Charles did not note why the locks had been built narrow; this was then the prevailing size of craft, and barge traffic was discouraged as it would mean single line working through Blisworth Tunnel. BWB engineers investigated the costs, and proposed instead a tractor and ramp at each site; the estimated costs at Foxton and Watford were unexpectedly low, but costs for the Northampton Arm were prohibitive.

Relations between the IWA and BWB had begun acrimoniously, partly owing to Aickman's deep suspicion, but his involvement was reducing during 1963. A dinner party for the new Board was arranged by Lionel Munk and other IWA members on 14 March 1963, but Aickman refused to attend, on the grounds that 'people like Marples, Hay and Hadfield are absolutely hopeless, because they are not men of honour'.[9] He threatened to resign at the AGM if members did not endorse his views. Lionel Munk, who saw some merit in cooperation with the BWB, urged caution; after Aickman met Sir John Hawton on 2 May and found him surprisingly sympathetic, he felt that 'any new hope lies with Hawton personally'.[10] For once, he was probably right.

Charles's experience of the IWA was revived at a weekend course on Inland Waterways (his last) which he ran at Dillington Hall, Ilminster, in March 1963. The other speakers included Aickman, who left before Charles arrived. Charles dealt with the aftermath of his talk on the future of inland waterways, and heard that by David Hutchings, in which an interesting illustrated lecture on the Stratford Canal was punctuated by sneers about BWB, described as 'Marples and his cronies'. Charles, who spoke on 'The History of British Inland Waterways' and 'Inland Waterways Overseas' described his reception:

> I have not for many years met a predominantly IWA audience. They are deep in fantasy. Aickman has filled them so full of wild ideas, mutually contradictory in many cases, that they have no real interest in what really happens, or ability to form a judgement on it.

Nobody, for instance, demurred at Hutchings's assertion that between London and Birmingham the narrow boat was 'in fact the fastest means of transit' (some years after the main section of the M1 motorway had opened). The level of hostility, which only lessened when Charles discussed overseas waterways, about which the audience knew little, approached the sinister: 'A curious experience of mass hypnotism – one of my friends who had been at Aickman's sessions referred to them as "like a Hitler Youth rally".[11] Afterwards, Charles spoke to David Hutchings, objecting to the 'cronies' accusation; he stressed that was not a 'stooge' to be pushed around by a Minister. He suggested that past enmities should be forgotten and they should 'attempt to work together in future'. David Hutchings confirmed that it was hoped that the BWB would foster the restoration and development of the waterways.

On 12 November 1963, with Pauline Dower, Charles visited the Stratford restoration, which had now reached the most difficult section, on the approaches to Stratford, where an army unit was dredging the canal using a dragline from the bank. It was presumably on this occasion that Charles witnessed the dredging out of the puddled clay lining the bed of the canal, which was deposited on the towpath; as he put it much later, 'I looked at the puddled clay and at David, and said nothing, while David looked at the puddled clay and at me, and said nothing.' The Stratford restoration, mainly by volunteers, was a major achievement, but at the cost of major future maintenance problems. Even David Hutchings would stress afterwards that the use of volunteer labour was not always reliable and that military and prison labour was essential.

The Stratford Canal was reopened formally on 11 July 1964 at the IWA National Rally. Charles was surprised that the Board, as freeholders of the waterway, and whose water supply made it possible for the canal to be navigated at all, only received invitations to the ceremony a few days before.

The question over the Stratford was whether the Trust would let the lease run out in 1965, or opt to acquire the freehold. Charles's view, and that of Admiral Parham, was that the BWB should take back the canal; in February 1965 they stated their opposition to enclaves in what should be a united network. In March 1964 the Trust's attempt to gain a five-year renewal of the lease was rejected as BWB could not guarantee what policy would guide it by 1970, and it is perhaps not surprising that the Trust, influenced by the uncertainty involved, opted to take the freehold in 1965. However, it rejected an option to renew to the end of 1967, when the general policy would be clear.

During 1963 it was mooted that the National Trust might take over all waterways which BWB did not want, but this was not the approach favoured by the Board, which was that initiated on the Stourbridge Canal. This linked the Birmingham canals to the Staffordshire & Worcestershire; it had been of limited commercial use since 1950, and it mainly attracted pleasure-boating only as a through route. It was unnavigable in the early 1960s, and the BTC had engaged in acrimonious actions over attempts by David Hutchings and others in the IWA Midlands Branch to dredge a section of the Stourbridge Branch before the Rally at Stourbridge in 1962. Decisions over the BTC's proposals to weir the Wordsley Locks and retain this section for water supply, and to fill in the Branch, with local authority support, had been deferred by IWRAC to the new BWB.

A gap had opened up between the IWA and the Staffordshire & Worcestershire Canal Society (henceforth SWCS); the latter had been formed in 1959 in the face of divisions in the IWA Midlands Branch and the perceived threat to the S&W, upon which there was no regular traffic. The SWCS was less inclined to see BWB as an enemy and more inclined to make a case for the revival of the Stourbridge. Support for the BWB was boosted when Sir John Hawton overrode a local BWB refusal of access to the SWCS for a trip through the disued Dudley Tunnel in June 1963. When the SWCS complained about the condition of the Stourbridge in July, Hawton replied that policy was still being examined but

> In the meantime I can at least assure you that it will not be the Board's policy to try to enforce any closure by a process of deliberate neglect and damage; indeed I am a little surprised that you should think that this might be their approach.[12]

The SWCS soon requested a meeting with the BWB, and in September 1963 Hawton asked Charles if he and Admiral Parham could visit the Stourbridge; Charles agreed, as he had never seen it before. On 16 October they walked up the Wordsley Locks and the Stourbridge Branch, and the next day, with the Area Engineer, went to see parts of the connecting Dudley Canal. In the evening between, they talked to the then SWCS chairman and secretary. Charles later recalled how

> we asked our engineers, who said it would cost some fantastic sum. They weren't against it but they were perfectionists, they felt it had to be done properly. So the Admiral and I went down and walked every inch of the Wordsley Locks, making notes of the exact state of each lock. Then we met

the representative of the Society and eventually asked, 'How many boats do you think will use the locks each year?' They took a deep breath and, I give them every credit, they told the truth and said about 200. That, in fact, was exactly the Admiral's guess and we took to them at once.[13]

Charles suggested that within five years the route might not be marginal, but he recommended the elimination of Park Head Locks and the Stourbridge Branch. He felt that a third of the gates on the sixteen locks, rather than the half the Area Engineer stated, would need replacement.

Early in 1964 it was agreed that the SWCS could carry out some clearance work on the Stourton Locks from 6 June 1964 – the first case of voluntary cooperation between volunteers and any public waterways owner. Charles was invited to the SWCS Rally in May 1964, and suggested a four-year trial during which the number of voyages would be recorded.

The BWB invited the SWCS to a meeting in London on 3 June, attended by Charles and other Board members. At this, it was agreed that while the cost of restoration to impeccable condition was £30,000, the sum of £7,400 would suffice to restore it to a passable state for the time being. David Tomlinson, by then SWCS secretary, later recalled that Sir John Hawton stated that the BWB would demonstrate a better approach than the Stratford restoration. Jim Robbins, the new chairman of the SWCS, agreed that the Stourbridge Branch might be let go if the main line could be restored.

On 17 September 1964 it was announced that the canal would be jointly restored by BWB and by SWCS volunteers, to test the potential of a restored canal; volunteers were to carry out the less skilled work with BWB providing gates and technical assistance. The SWCS work was organised throughout by David Tomlinson, who wrote of the first fifteen months that

> excellent relations exist between ourselves and British Waterways local staff. It would, of course, be foolish to pretend that there were never divergences of opinion but regular meetings on the site with the Waterways' staff, and full and frank discussions have soon sorted out possible sources of friction to our mutual satisfaction. . . . Never in the past have what might be termed the criticised and the critics come together with such happy results. We hope that the friendly spirit of co-operation now existing will be one of the lasting results of the Stourbridge project.[14]

He also recorded the shortage of volunteers, which meant that by the time the canal reopened, in May 1967, general waterways policy had been determined.

The principle of cooperation with volunteers was established, and a similar approach applied to the Kennet & Avon Navigation, which Charles and Pauline Dower visited unannounced on 6 September 1963. Charles had earlier suggested a joint restoration, and that a marine railway could be built to replace the twenty-nine locks at Devizes.

He and Mrs Dower felt that the arguments for reopening lay with its position, linking the broad Thames and Bristol Avon, its scenic nature, and that it was also 'the main practical objective of most waterways enthusiasts, and therefore a decision to restore has political value'.[15] Charles favoured beginning at the Reading end and working as far as possible towards Devizes. On 11 September it was noted that the BWB had no resources to fund restoration on its own, while to pipe parts and keep the rest in water would still require forty-seven maintenance staff with little return. Joint restoration with the aid of voluntary labour was therefore approved. Much rested on the ability of the Kennet & Avon Canal Trust (as the K&ACA, of which Charles was a member, had become in 1962) to raise funds and organise work. It was then anticipated that Stage 1 restoration, from Reading to Devizes, would take at least five years. During the restoration period much higher tolls were to apply, part being donated to the Trust.

Following the Interim Report, a meeting with the Kennet & Avon Canal Trust on 8 April 1964 agreed to the restoration of Sulhamstead Lock, a derelict turf-sided lock on the Kennet section, for which the Trust was already raising funds. After lengthy fund-raising, restoration of the lock, by military and prison labour as well as volunteers, began early in 1965; in September 1964 the report of a joint working party into the restoration of the whole navigation had been accepted. Reopening of the whole line, however, would not come until 1990.

A further restoration proposal was that of the Caldon Branch, part of which had become unnavigable in 1962; Charles would originally have omitted it from the amenity network. Plans to transfer it to the National Trust had failed, and a Caldon Canal Committee was formed to press for restoration. On 11 September Charles and Pauline Dower walked the derelict length from Froghall to Cheddleton, before meeting local representatives: 'we had had a hell of a day fighting our way in pouring rain along the Caldon's overgrown towpath from Froghall to Cheddleton, but had come back convinced that the canal could be restored – and so we recommended'.[16] Charles proposed initial restoration to Cheddleton, but the canal's future would have to await the results of general legislation.

On the previous day, 10 September, Charles had met representatives of the Peak Forest Canal Society (henceforth PFCS), with less happy results. The Ashton Canal and Marple Locks, on the lower Peak Forest Canal, had become unnavigable by 1963, after maintenance was reduced. Charles saw no future for these waterways, although they linked the attractive canal above Marple to the independent Rochdale and Bridgewater Canals in Manchester. The PFCS, formed mainly by local interests in Marple, sought an agreement like that for the Stourbridge, but this was refused, as was support for the aims of the 1966 IWA National Rally at Marple. While the BTC had restored the Marple Aqueduct below the locks, restoration of the locks was seen as a prelude to restoration of the Ashton Canal, which was opposed. The closure of the Ashton Canal was to have been included in a 1966/7 British Waterways Bill, but it was decided to postpone any private Bill until general legislation was completed.

Charles saw the Ashton as a low priority, but he did favour the retention of the isolated Lancaster Canal. The upper section of this, above Tewitfield Locks, had been unnavigable since 1949, and a leaking section north of Stainton had been closed. While BWB's predecessor had favoured closure of the section north of Tewitfield, IWRAC had suggested its retention for small pleasure-boats. The M6 motorway extension from Carnforth to Carlisle was to cross the unnavigable length at several points, and in 1963 the Ministry of Transport sought BWB's views on the kind of crossings required.

The Board agreed that the crossings north of Stainton could be at ground level, but insisted that the crossing at Kellet Lane, on the navigable section, be of full dimensions. Between Stainton and Tewitfield the options centred around the costs of culverted crossings, full-sized bridges, or what were termed 'aquatic creeps', which would allow through most pleasure-boats. Although the BWB approved the construction of 'creeps' in June 1964, Charles opposed this and sought details of relative costs. It became apparent that the creeps would produce a saving in construction cost, but the real problem was the cost of restoring the canal between any new crossings. Against Charles's wishes, the provision of culverts was agreed on 14 October 1964, although the Board was keen to publicise that this did not set any precedent and 'had been motivated by means of national economy'.[17]

One factor was the lack of local support for the canal's retention; a rather vociferous Association had been formed, but only late in 1963, when the M6 plans had been published. Much the same applied to the Shrewsbury and Newport branches of the Shropshire Union Canal, where a restoration society was formed shortly before long-standing agreements to drain and fill in most of the canal were implemented. Charles's visit to these canals with the RCHS in 1964 would prove a valedictory one.

These steps towards restoration were tentative, in the face of the requirement for the BWB to review policy and promote general legislation to enshrine a more positive future for the amenity waterways. The Interim Report published in January 1964 was very much based on Charles's original paper, identifying waterways which should be retained for general amenity, for water supply, for transport and for cruising, and waterways which would provide links to form a cruising network. Hawton's main concern was to establish all the facts, so that when challenged by the Ministry of Transport and the Treasury, they would be able to counter any arguments. In February 1964 a special engineering survey was ordered, to be collated until 1966 by Christopher Marsh. The critical elements in the investigations were financial – comparing the costs of maintenance for commercial traffic, for pleasure traffic, or for water channelling, against the potential revenues from these activities, and the annualised cost of elimination works. For the large number of waterways upon which carrying was now insignificant, the last three categories were critical.

The results were published in a second document, *The Facts about the Waterways*, in December 1965. This identified a group of 'commercial' activities, upon which a reasonable return on capital could be expected. The 'non-commercial' activities were mainly the operation of waterways with limited or no traffics. The report established that the difference in running costs between waterways maintained for pleasure and commercial use was, in most cases, limited. However, in all but two cases economies could be achieved by the conversion of waterways to unnavigable water channels. It was argued that the minimum irreducible annual loss was about £600,000, with an additional annual cost of around £350,000 to retain a network for pleasure-cruising. The Report explicitly sought to establish 'facts' for others to decide, but the position was clear: without a capital reconstruction the commercial part could not break even, and, if 'the nation' wanted a pleasure-cruising network, this could be secured for an annual subsidy of £350,000. The financial matters were considered by the Honourable Alexander Hood, who had joined the Board later in 1963, with much experience in the City but little in waterways. He helped to argue the financial case for a completely different nominal capital upon which interest should be paid, and provided invaluable assistance to counter some of the Treasury criticisms of the BWB's case for subsidy.

After the Report was published, the Board was asked to consider which waterways should be included in the amenity network. In 1965 it was agreed to exclude from the proposed network a number of waterways: part of the Calder & Hebble Navigation, much of the Birmingham Canal Navigation, most of the Erewash Canal and the Shropshire Union north of Chester; later, the Rufford Branch of the Leeds & Liverpool Canal was added.

There was, however, a consensus that the Kennet & Avon (after restoration, the additional maintenance expense would not be major), and the Caldon, could be added, along with the Brecknock & Abergavenny, for which the new National Park authorities had agreed to meet some costs of restoration and subsequent maintenance.

The detailed survey had, however, revealed that much of the deficit was attributable to two large waterways with no significant traffic revenues. The Leeds & Liverpool Canal incurred especially large deficits and featured very little pleasure use. Annual savings of about £45,000 could be achieved if much of its main line was converted to a water channel, while the Grand Union main line accounted for about £65,000 and the Leicester section £24,000; the total came to almost half the estimated additional cost of retention of the canal for pleasure-cruising. Alexander Hood, while admitting that he did not know these waterways, stressed the financial benefits of their closure.

Exclusion of the section between Liverpool and Lydiate or Scarisbrick, and the Rufford Branch, was agreed, but BWB members differed about the rest. For instance, Arnold Allen (by now a Board member as well as general manager) agreed that the Leeds & Liverpool was not very heavily used, but stressed that there was an attractive section between Bingley and the summit, and structures of industrial archaeological interest.

Charles produced a carefully reasoned paper which envisaged the likely political implications of the proposed network. He realised that there would be repercussions, but

I don't think, however, that the resulting row will be unmanageable, nor will lead to the National Trust or any other body taking over any of the lengths (with the <u>possible</u> exception of the Aylesbury Arm and the Calder & Hebble), nor will re-open the demand for a separate pleasure waterways trust.[18]

He opposed the latter, while the *Facts* report made it clear that a separate organisation would lead to diminutions in staff quality and the duplication of work. The idea of a National Waterways Trust to own and run 1,000 miles of amenity canal had been developed by the IWA during 1965; one advantage was that it could accept legacies and subscriptions, although Sir John Hawton felt that there was limited scope for this.

Charles was concerned that cuts to the remaining proposed network

will bring a different kind of opposition into being – that of the man [sic] who sees the difference between pruning away what is of no real use and pruning away what is useful, and could in the future be more so, to save what appears to him comparatively small amounts of money. Therefore any abandonment in this category will lead to proposals either to take the canal in question out of our hands, or to take all pleasure canals, on the grounds that we do not really believe in the future of pleasure cruising.

He anticipated that if 'we are driven back', then the main candidates for closure should be the Leeds & Liverpool Canal, and most of the Worcester & Birmingham Canal. He felt that pressure for development would be least in the north of England, so that, about the first priority for closure from Wigan to Gargrave, 'there would be a manageable protest', and that 'A definite restoration plan for the Caldon Branch and part at any rate of the Kennet & Avon would help to sugar the pill.'

He saw a danger that a proposal to abandon the Leeds & Liverpool, probably too large for the National Trust to acquire, could revive the demand to set up a separate Trust. He anticipated that the National Trust might take over the heavily locked Tardebigge–Worcester section of the Worcester & Birmingham. The Leicester line was seen as 'a problem. . . . All the same, I feel that the Leicester line is capable of development.' He repeated his view that widening, including boat inclines, would bring greater traffic; the detractions included the lock flights – 'many people are frightened of staircase locks'.

Arnold Allen, in a thoughtful paper, expressed doubt: 'The finances of expansion of the Leicester Section do worry me.' He saw annual costs of the ramp and tractor as about £8,000, and those of locks rebuilt to broad dimensions as £15,000. Closing the locks to existing users would prove unpopular, and it would need 1,000 boat movements to pay for the costs even of the cheaper solution; he doubted that a widened and developed line would attract such numbers. However, he noted that the line 'will be almost the "Ark of the Covenant" as far as the I.W.A. are concerned (even, I think to the more moderate elements therein)'.[19]

A final and unexpected problem was the threat to the Trent & Mersey Canal at Rugeley, brought about through mining subsidence. BWB had to pay part of the cost of dealing with subsidence, and the development of a pit at Rugeley since 1960 had already brought a collapse at Armitage Tunnel which had to be closed and propped during the first half of 1965. The high costs involved prompted proposals for the exclusion of the Fradley–Great Haywood section of the Trent & Mersey Canal, and possibly the canal north to Etruria and the section of the Staffordshire & Worcestershire Canal south to Gailey. Charles favoured the retention of the latter, but conceded that the Rugeley section might have to close, although it was heavily used and 'Its removal will cause a loud protest.' He suggested that the subsidence question

> should be used as a lever on the local authorities, the subscribing public and the Ministries to raise the necessary money to cope with it. If we can't raise it, then the worst of the blame will be removed from us.
> But lets be driven into the position, not choose it.

As a result of these deliberations, a revised list was sent to the Ministry of Transport. In July 1966 the White Paper on Transport Policy which emerged accepted the factual analysis, the division into commercial and amenity waterways, both under BWB management, the need for a capital reconstruction, and a defined pleasure-cruising network. However, it proposed that the network should be reviewed every five years, and that there should be powers for waterways to be closed to pleasure-boating in exceptional circumstances. The latter provisions created major protest by the IWA, now led by Lionel Munk, who had announced the ending of its policy of cooperation earlier in 1966. Following a Commons debate in November, Barbara Castle, now Minister of Transport, sent a circular to interested organisations to seek their opinions before a decision was reached.

Charles's appointment, which had with all others been extended at the end of 1965, was unexpectedly terminated on 13 December 1966; the others were not. In October 1966 the Board had decided to retain its own pleasure-boat hire operation, but to equip it with modern boats. Charles suggested that, given the plethora of boat types – some better than others – then available, BWB should take a lead 'in producing a prototype of a well designed and cheap craft as a standard', to encourage better boat-building standards and more confidence by purchasers. He continued to be interested in pleasure-boating, and summarised his views in *Modern Transport* in March 1967.

He was deeply critical of the review proposals in the 1966 White Paper:

> What businessman is going to invest money in a canalside business if the canal's existence is to be formally reviewed every few years, and can be ended at any intermediate time? The right way is to leave a business-like Board to develop the system, in constant touch with the Departments concerned. . . . Should exceptional action be needed, it should be by a procedure that allows for public representations, and offers compensation for those dispossessed.[20]

He noted that pleasure-cruising revenue had risen by around 8 per cent every year under BWB, despite difficulties in encouraging investment. He suggested that this could rise much further, if BWB were allowed to invest directly through joint ventures in boat-hiring and other canalside facilities, bringing hire firms and new traffic to canals like the Leicester section and the Leeds & Liverpool. BWB could also assist investment in the building of suitable pleasure-craft, by taking an equity share in boat-building operations.

He felt that a new generation of boaters would need more modern facilities, since

> The present generation of owners love the canals for their antiquity, their history, their quaintness, their romantic background; but newer recruits look on them as places where they can seek refreshment and amusement, aquatic roads which should be provided with similar amenities.[21]

He endorsed the restoration, by partnership, of the Kennet & Avon, and the Caldon, and commented favourably on the Stourbridge, which would reopen in May; however, he sounded a note of caution:

> this enterprise has emphasised, what the restoration of the southern portion of the Stratford Canal had previously showed, that canal restoration engenders tremendous verbal enthusiasm, but only a small body of dedicated voluntary workers – those who come week after week, winter and summer, and not only on a few fine summer days. All praise to the devoted ones, but the Stratford restoration was very largely done with prison labour and the help of the Forces.[22]

He continued to endorse widening at the locks at Foxton and Watford, and warned that increased numbers of boats would bring additional revenues but also use much more water, so that back-pumping at locks would need to be installed; this would prove prophetic, especially for the Kennet & Avon.

Developments after he left must be briefly covered. Civil servants at the Ministry of Transport, and above all at the Treasury, viewed the statistics in *Facts* with considerable scepticism. By varying the rates of interest on capital expenditure, by hinting at savings on new highways and urban redevelopment if pleasure navigation was not needed, they were able to challenge the Board's case, and suggest that much greater savings were possible through a range of major closures.

These closures were suggested to Barbara Castle, and it was her decision to reject them, despite financial stringency, and to proceed with a White Paper in September 1967 which announced a 'new charter' for the waterways, removing the reviews and special powers to which the IWA, Charles and BWB had objected. While there was extreme pressure on public expenditure, in the year when devaluation was put into effect, she did not need much persuading:

I had always been fascinated with inland waterways. . . . I believed that messing about in boats was a leisure activity which should be increasingly available to everyone. I was therefore horrified to discover that one of the Treasury's money-saving exercises in 1967 involved closing down miles of inland waterways which were no longer commercially viable. I was alerted to the danger by a vocal band of canal enthusiasts led by a certain Mr Monk [sic], whose main political weapon was verbal vitriol to be thrown in the faces of all politicians. I did not need any kind of threat to launch me into the attack because my heart was in their cause. Getting money out of the Treasury at that moment of economic crisis was like the proverbial getting of blood out of a stone, but when I moved in on Jack Diamond, who as the Chief Secretary to the Treasury was responsible for cutting public expenditure . . . I got him to agree to give me enough subsidy to keep open 1400 miles of non-commercially viable canals for pleasure-cruising.[23]

The Transport Act 1968 which followed amended the BWB's functions and duties to include the provision of amenity, guaranteed an amenity network, termed 'cruiseways', and left a group of waterways, known as 'remainder waterways', whose fate was to be decided case by case. Most of the Kennet & Avon and the Caldon went into the latter category, but restoration proceeded, while the Leeds & Liverpool and Worcester & Birmingham, which Charles had expected to sacrifice, were included in the 'cruiseways'.

This was a major advance on the network in Charles's original paper, which he had felt they would be lucky to secure. Other factors had reinforced support for the ideas behind his initiative. The rising popularity of pleasure-boating, the forceful but less hysterical IWA campaign, the cooperation with local canal societies, changes in local authority attitudes, and a Minister much more reluctant to close and dispose, were all significant. Sir John Hawton and Arnold Allen, neither of whom had any canal background, but had the ability and knowledge to influence civil servants, were also crucial. Had they been as sceptical as the civil servants that they had once been, Charles's initial ideas would not have been so carefully received and put into effect. Arnold Allen has stressed to me the importance of the 'incomers' in BWB, who did not share the defeatism and pessimism (not the zeal for destruction that the IWA leadership seemed to imagine) of their predecessors, who had lived and worked with decline.

BRITISH WATERWAYS BOARD AND MODERN FREIGHT

The growing deficits on British Waterways canals were partly caused by declining traffics, which yielded high toll revenues. The collapse in traffics accounted for the mounting deficits on the Leeds & Liverpool Canal main line, while in contrast, on the same canal's Leigh Branch, the heavy coal traffic to Wigan power station generated high toll revenues which made this length profitable.

There were many accusations, but limited evidence, that the nationalised owners gave little support to traffic and were indeed keen to drive it down. Much of this centred around narrow boat carrying, whose future had prompted the formation of the IWA. Under different track control, such as the IWA's oft-proposed National Waterways Conservancy, it was suggested that narrow boat carrying could be greatly expanded. The Interim Report expressed considerable doubt: 'The idea of "breaking even" financially, on a transport basis only, on these canals must surely be an illusion. As we shall explain, we have already come to the conclusion that our own narrow boat fleets cannot continue to trade successfully, whether or not a toll is charged.'[24] The BWB had inherited two narrow boat fleets, which it found running at a loss, with declining traffics, decaying boats and difficulties in recruiting crews. Charles fully supported the decision to end this form of carrying, which he felt had never been properly viable since the 1890s. He went further in advocating that all such carrying should be removed, presumably by discouragement; one motive was his conviction that carrying and pleasure-boating on narrow waterways could clash.

The BWB fleet on the Grand Union Canal was run down rapidly, while that in the north-west, which dominated traffic on the Shropshire Union route, lasted into 1964. Willow Wren, a firm founded in 1952 with enthusiast backing, took over the contracts and some of the craft, on a partly cooperative basis. Its manager, Leslie Morton, who had run the Grand Union Canal Carrying Company fleet in the 1930s, expressed confidence in 1963:

I predict without hesitation that within five years there will be vastly increased amount of traffic on the waterways with narrow boats, and that within this time it will be an economic proposition to build new craft.[25]

This followed a licensing arrangement for craft on specified routes, which BWB approved to the end of 1968. By that time Willow Wren had gone into liquidation and the boats were repossessed.

Charles's interest lay in the larger waterways, about 400 miles linked to ports and estuaries, which carried about 90 per cent of the total traffic on the BWB waterways. Closure or conversion for pleasure-cruising or water channelling were not generally options for these waterways, and they were considered to be part of the 'commercial' sector, which could be reasonably expected to pay interest on a level of capital reduced from that set by the 1962 Act.

Charles was concerned to support the retention of existing traffic and routes, but also to develop new tracks, craft, and handling methods. He had been collecting information on modern Continental waterways for some time; his first act on the BWB was to ask whether hydroelectric power could be generated from new or existing waterways, as power generation was an integral part of Continental waterways modernisation. The reply was that the fall at locks on the Trent and Severn (the main candidates) made this unviable in Britain; although Charles recommended further investigations, none was carried out.

Charles's paper of February 1963 suggested that the major waterways should be examined 'by an officer of the Board, in consultation with shipping, importing, exporting and other commercial interests, to propose a new classification, and to suggest development for each waterway, long and short term'.[26] He proposed that this officer should be assisted by a Continental waterways engineer, who could advise upon reconstruction, and he suggested that the first stage of policy which would follow should include interim measures such as the dredging of the Trent and Aire & Calder Navigations, to increase carrying capacity.

The second stage would involve decisions about which waterways could be reconstructed to take sea-going craft trading to the Continent; a capacity of 2,000 tons, for which waterways around Ghent were being rebuilt, might be appropriate. He suggested four routes for enlargement: the Aire & Calder to Leeds; the Sheffield & South Yorkshire Navigation from the Humber to Sheffield; the Trent to Nottingham and possibly, via the Soar, on to Leicester; and the Witham to Lincoln. The last appeared eccentric, as it carried no traffic, but a proposed traffic route through flat country close to Continental Europe indicated sound trade and engineering thinking. Finally, given that 1,350-ton craft were felt to have a long-term economic future, he suggested investigations into enlargements to accommodate barges of this kind, already operating on the Continental waterways, which would generate quite new forms of traffic.

Charles advocated that a date should be set after which all carrying, by BWB craft or others, on non-transport waterways should cease, as 'To my mind such traffic has fallen to a quite uneconomic figure for the Board, both as toll-takers and as carriers, and cannot, whatever is done, be revised.'[27] He recommended a reorganisation to operate this and the new proposed amenity network. The response of the Board was somewhat muted, but it agreed to close most of its own narrow boat fleet, despite the adverse publicity. It was decided to investigate the potential for improvement of the Sheffield & South Yorkshire Navigation (henceforth SSYN) route, but not the others.

The SSYN was soon faced with an unexpected challenge. The section at Keadby is crossed by a low railway swing bridge; British Railways sought to close this length and fix the bridge. BR argued that the main canal traffic on this section, coal carried from Denaby Colliery to Lysaghts at Flixborough, could be diverted to rail, which already carried part of it. The BWB's response was to refuse, but it became clear that the new BR was keen to get as much traffic as possible, and for specialised traffics like that in coal was able to modernise and gain traffics from water.

In January 1964 Charles addressed this problem in another paper to the Board. He suggested that competition from modernised roads and railways, and from the development of pipelines, made it likely that traffics on all but a few BWB waterways would disappear. He suggested a survey of practices in other countries, where toll charging for profit was rare, enlargement a continuous process, and the development of specialised craft for specific traffics commonplace. From this it should be possible to identify lines where improvements could produce traffics in the long run. After that there could be a survey of the need for new canals.

Charles advocated that the survey should be 'really radical in character. That is, it must suggest for waterways solutions as new or newer than the liner or "merry-go-round" train is for British Railways or the motorways for British roads. If the solutions put forward are in our view too radical we can moderate them, but if they are not radical enough they will be of little use.'[28] He stressed that very strong evidence would be needed if authority for the considerable capital expenditure involved was to be obtained.

Charles had perhaps overstated his case, and other BWB members tended to stress the constraints set by the 1962 Act over their activities. However, the Economist Intelligence Unit was commissioned to survey traffic potential on the SSYN; it reported in 1965, casting doubt about the future of coal traffics and the confidence of potential customers. Nevertheless, BWB began its own discussions over new traffics with carriers and potential customers. A dynamic head, Harry Grafton, was appointed to a new Commercial Department; he confirmed the planned enlargement of the Aire & Calder Navigation to secure contracts for oil and coal traffic, the latter to the new Ferrybridge C Power Station.

During 1964 Charles visited Germany to see modern waterways for himself, aided by his membership of the BWB. He visited the port of Duisberg, where the need to deepen within existing water levels had been overcome by the deliberate use of controlled mining subsidence; he also viewed the ship lift at Henrichenburg. In the following year he was invited to attend the PIANC (Permanent International Association of Navigation Congresses) four-yearly conference in Stockholm. He played no formal part, but was struck by the interest in waterways shown by governments and operators in other countries, which had sent large expert delegations, while Britain had sent him and Christopher Marsh, who was about to retire.

At the conference, Charles met Braxton Carr of Washington, president of the American inland waterways carriers. Early in 1966, having read about a newly patented barge-carrying vessel in the United States, he contacted Carr, who sent him further details. Charles saw the possibilities of modernisation which could use existing Continental craft upon British inland waterways, and put a further paper to the Board.

The *Facts* report, recommending a limited mileage of commercial waterways, had been submitted to the Minister at the end of 1965, and in May 1966 Charles suggested that BWB should start research into new developments, so that if new legislation provided it with powers, they would be in a position to start work. He stressed that further research was essential, and that outside experts might be required. When he presented a paper to this effect in June 1966, he illustrated it with maps showing the extensive waterways network of Central and Western Europe. He suggested that 250-ton barges from the Humber and Trent should be able to cross the North Sea to penetrate inland to points as far as Basle, but because they could not cross the open sea, they must be carried on a ship. There were two possibilities: special push-tug craft that could be lifted on to a ship's deck, or a submersible dry-dock whereby more conventional barges could be floated into and out of a ship. He favoured the latter, the original LASH (Lighter Aboard Ship) concept, since it could use existing Continental barges. He suggested a liner service between Hull and Rotterdam or Antwerp, where the barges would be discharged and sent upstream. From Hull, they could proceed up the Trent, the Aire & Calder or, if it were enlarged, the SSYN.

New barges would be needed to cope with the increased traffic which would develop, and he suggested the formation of a joint company with existing carriers and shipping interests. He anticipated that Continental interests might develop this service themselves, but although the BWB's response was again that this development lay outside its powers, there would be new developments in the 1970s.

Charles's proposals, bold as they were, contrasted with the IWA's proposals, published at the end of July 1965 in a booklet, *New Waterways*. Based on the ideas of J.F. Pownall's Grand Contour Canal, this proposed a large network of ship canals, for both transport and water transfer purposes, but with no discussion of traffic demand or potential. The Ministry sought comments, but this was rapidly dismissed.

One scheme which BWB did approve in the summer of 1966 was the enlargement of the lower part of the SSYN to Rotherham, to the same dimensions as the enlarged Aire & Calder Navigation. However, this would be rejected by the Ministry late in 1967.

Charles's involvement with freight development was not altogether productive, but it did sharpen his interest in overseas canals and in modern freight development after the end of his term with the Board. He had begun to disseminate ideas which others would take up later.

Probably prompted by his experience with the production of informative magazines during his time at COI, Charles was keen to foster publicity through appropriate publications. Early in 1963 he had arranged with the editor of the weekly *Modern Transport*, Charles Klapper (who was to succeed him as RCHS president), that it would publish a page featuring BWB and transport developments. This offer was not taken up, and Charles sought the launch of a specialist magazine which would have a wider popular appeal than the BWB house magazine *Waterways* or the members-only IWA *Bulletin*. He felt that no publication regularly put before the public the major part that waterborne transport could play, and that many enthusiast publications were ill-informed. For the latter, he drew invidious contrasts with the well-informed publications of railway societies, which he attributed to the provision of accurate information.

He suggested that an independent publisher should be found, and provided with practical and financial support. In October 1964 BWB found that those publishers which it approached were doubtful. The market for canal publications was growing with the increase in pleasure-boating, but it would be 1972 before the first general canal magazine, *Waterways World*, would be founded. By that time most traditional traffics had finished, but there were modern commercial traffics to report.

Charles alongside Hay Inclined Plane, on the Shropshire (Coalport) Canal, visually restored as part of the Ironbridge Gorge Museum. When he visited in the 1950s, the plane was overgrown and the canal at its foot filled in.

The party to launch the book boarding John James's *Jason* at Little Venice in Paddington, not far from Charles's then home, 1955. Charles has his back to the camera; to his left, by the boat, is Lionel Munk, then founder of the hire fleet Maid Line, later leader of the Inland Waterways Association.

Moored at the top of Marple Locks, at the junction of the Peak Forest and Macclesfield Canals. Later Charles would not support the retention of these locks. The other moored craft is a maintenance boat.

At Fazeley Junction, with Molly and Alec on the roof, on 24 April 1955.

Short boat *Leo* leaving Widnes on 17 September 1956, on the Sankey Navigation Canal. Charles is in the centre.

A visit to Bull's Bridge depot on the Grand Union Canal, 1958. (Alan Voce)

One of the Llangynidr Locks on the
Brecknock & Abergavenny Canal, with
Alice Mary standing on the tail bridge,
August 1954.

Charles pointing out features on the Llansamlet (Smith's) Canal on a RCHS visit on
16 May 1959. The dry canal bed is next to the bridge. (Ian L. Wright)

Watching Admiral Sir Frederick Parham, by then Vice-Chairman of British Waterways Board, at the opening ceremony for the mechanised locks at Muirtown, on the Caledonian Canal, 19 September 1963.

The Rideau Canal in Ottawa, whose preservation by the Canadian government for amenity purposes appears to have interested Charles. Charles would visit these locks in 1978.

Charles's proposals for pleasure boat development included the construction of marine railways to replace flights of locks at Foxton, Watford, Rothersthorpe and Devizes. This example, the Big Chute marine railway on the Trent–Severn Waterway in Canada, was built in the 1920s.

The replacement for the Marine Railway, under construction in 1978.

At the Tipton portal of Dudley Tunnel on 30 May 1965, shortly after Charles had written its history in *West Midlands*; Charles is in the centre, and his son Alec on the right.

Outside The Navigation at Sowerby Bridge, near the Rochdale Canal, on a trip to northern waterways with Alan Voce, 1963. (Alan Voce)

Charles and his daughter Molly steering British Waterways' hire vessel *Water Viper* on the Middlewich Branch of the Shropshire Union Canal near Clive Green.

Steering up Hurleston Locks on the Llangollen line of the Shropshire Union Canal, past *Peggy*, of the Deans hire fleet near Chester.

Charles opening Wrenbury Church Lift Bridge on the Llangollen line.

The Ludwigs Canal at Kelheim, June 1973.

The economiser lock at Uelzen, on the Elbe Lateral Canal, October 1975.

1,000-tonne vessels on the Elbe–Lubeck Canal.

The lift at Luneberg, on the Elbe Lateral Canal, from the top.

With David St John Thomas on Dartmoor, around 1960.

David St John Thomas and Charles at the 25th celebration of David & Charles, 1985. (Michael Martin)

On the Windermere steamer at Lakeside Pier, on a David & Charles weekend, 17 May 1981.

On the 'L', the Chicago Elevated railway, at Austin. Charles was interested in all forms of transport.

A lock chamber on the Chesapeake & Ohio Canal, with a Baltimore & Ohio Railroad crossing beyond.

On the Ellesmere Canal, looking south along the trough of Pontcysyllte Aqueduct in 1965, from *Water Viper*.

The Caledonian Canal, 1984.

On board *Sabrina*, on the Droitwich Canal, being interviewed by a television crew, on 20 May 1984. (John Horsley Denton)

One of Charles's last public engagements was in Stratford-upon-Avon in July 1989, when the freehold of the Stratford Canal was returned to British Waterways Board. Left to right: Mrs Donnelly of the Shakespeare Birthplace Trust, Dr Guy Johnson of the Stratford-upon-Avon Canal Society, Andrew Grime of BWB, Dr Levi Fox of SBT, David Hutchings, Charles.

Charles at his desk in his study, 1982. (B.R. Berkeley)

With Christine Richardson, one of a younger generation of canal historians, in his garden, on 13 September 1995. Alice Mary's study is behind them. (Christine Richardson)

Charles in his study at 21 Randolph Road; note the spines of 'The Canals of the British Isles' series on the middle shelf.

After he left the Board, Charles pressed his views further in an article in *Modern Transport* in May 1967. He reiterated much that he had already discussed in Board papers, but stressed the contrast between the approaches of the British government, which had just declined to support the SSYN improvement, and those overseas, where new freight railways were rarely built but new canals were under construction and nationally planned. He stressed the lack of expertise, not in BWB, but at Ministry level, where it was assumed that there was no future for waterways except in respect of existing traffics on existing waterways. His emphasis was on investigation based on accurate information, without which the question was not 'What should British Waterways policy be?', the title of his article, but 'Should we not undertake studies that will lead to our having a policy?'[29] He concluded:

We should consider setting up a single national authority; treating waterway costs analogously to road costs; encouraging county and city participation in development; improving the navigations that lead to Hull; and investigating how feasible it is to transport barges to and from the Continent. These things and others considered and judged, we would then know much that now is only guesswork. Are we really so sure that we can do without waterway development?[30]

No such studies would be carried out, but he would return to these themes in the 1970s.

DAVID & CHARLES: AN END AND NEW BEGINNINGS

Charles had expected David & Charles to develop a reasonable list of monographs, and, in time, to provide a steady income. Not long after he retired in July 1962, it became clear that differences with David would be serious. As David had put it in March 1962, 'What has happened I don't know, except that we don't speak the same language.'[31] One clear problem was the difficulty of running a growing firm from two addresses, with directors who had other interests and commitments, in some ways exacerbated when Charles joined the BWB. As D&C expanded, David tended to be burdened with too much routine production work, and was unable to devote enough time either to the future policy of the business or handling the paperwork which Charles regarded as essential. Charles was used to working within strict financial constraints at COI, and tended towards caution; whereas David preferred to rely on his instincts, and not to prepare estimates.

One point of contention concerned David's agreement to publish *Midland Compounds* by O.S. Nock, a prolific railway writer who produced expert monographs on locomotives. Nock later explained that he was approached unexpectedly by David, who sought a series of monographs 'to be full length books, page size 9in by 7in, 160 pages, art paper throughout, copiously illustrated, with at least one colour plate, and the intention was to provide an in-depth study of a particular locomotive class, or groups of associated classes'.[32] *Midland Compounds* would thus be the first in a series, of which O.S. Nock was to write eleven in all. Charles was angry not to be consulted, doubted that this book would pay, and sought to make David bear personally any losses involved.

Matters came to a head at the company's annual meeting early in May 1964. Charles insisted that David explain why he had not produced estimates and other paperwork; David, who felt that his workload precluded this, and believed that his efforts were not appreciated, stated that he felt like giving up the firm. They decided to appoint a manager to relieve David of some of the work, and agreed to set out new procedures, while David agreed to produce the required paperwork. However, Charles soon decided that it was wrong to enforce his ideas of business on David, and therefore offered to sell all his shares to David and to retire in April 1965.

David's response was to suggest that Charles remain a director but with a smaller shareholding, to concentrate on specialised areas like waterways history. Differences developed over the valuation of the shares, and Charles sensed that the new arrangement would not be successful; although the manager started work in August, David seemed more distant than before.

After a further meeting, David stated that he was not prepared to continue with the present arrangements, and that either he or Charles must buy out the other's interests, or the company must be sold or liquidated. They agreed that Charles would resign and sell his shares, but that he might edit books on a fee basis after the sale. Charles later expressed regret:

No one would think you had 'plotted for my removal', but it is pretty obvious that if you had really wanted to provide me with the very elementary information about estimates etc which I regarded as necessary to efficient management, you could have done so. And once [the manager] was appointed, there would have been even less difficulty.[33]

Charles's main concern was that D&C might be sold to a rival which would be influenced by the IWA; he wanted to be able to take his own books away if this happened. He was reluctant to part: 'I think that together we could have made a better firm of D&C than either of us could do separately.'[34] Charles did not, in the event, set up his own publishing operation. After the formal break in November 1964, David was to expand D&C rapidly, moving to new offices at the Newton Abbot railway station in January 1965. By April 1965 he had taken over Raleigh Press, and was expanding the range of publications.

Charles would become an editor of canal books for D&C, but the firm had fostered many developments which could continue. He had proposed series of individual railway histories and of canal histories. The earliest of the latter covered a series of waterways. Paul Vine's *London's Lost Route to the Sea* covered the Wey and Arun Navigations, the Wey & Arun Junction Canal and the

Portsmouth & Arundel Canal, completing investigations which he had begun in 1942, and seriously pursued since 1951. Completed in 1963, it had been turned down by ten publishers, all of whom felt that it would only have local appeal. While D&C might be able to attract a wider canal audience, it was agreed only to publish this book at Paul Vine's expense, with editing by Charles. Charles suggested cuts and the renaming of certain chapters, and the final short chapter was heavily rewritten before it was published in March 1965. The book did sell well, with a second edition in 1966, but his next proposal, for a history of the Basingstoke Canal, was at first declined.

Charles was not involved in the first of what was to become the 'Inland Waterways Histories' series, Baron Duckham's *The Yorkshire Ouse*, published in 1967. However, in 1964 he had encouraged Kenneth Clew, who had known the waterway since 1950, to produce *The Kennet & Avon Canal*, originally as a free-standing historical study; this was published in 1968. These would prove to be the first of many waterways titles, matched by a number of individual railway histories.

Charles was also involved in two initiatives which became major D&C series. One was the 'Industrial Archaeology' series, edited by Dr Rodney Green, whose proposed general volume did not appear. By 1975, when *Industrial Archaeology of Wales* appeared, eighteen volumes had been published in this series.

A further initiative which D&C founded was a new kind of local history book, *Old Mendip*, published in 1964, which became an unexpected success. The author, Robin Atthill, covered aspects of industrial archaeology, the history of turnpike roads and the unfinished Dorset & Somerset Canal; Charles helped with the latter. Charles dismissed David's suggestion that he should himself tackle an *Old Cotswolds* volume, but a number appeared in this series, not all to the same pattern as Robin Atthill's study.

One of the loose ends in Charles's break with David was the 'Canals of the British Isles' series. Charles had already secured the two Irish volumes, when in May 1964 the *Journal of Transport History* published an article by Dr Jean Lindsay, whose background was in economic history, about the history of the Aberdeenshire Canal. Charles, very impressed, wrote to her, and in July 1964 she agreed to write *The Canals of Scotland*; researched in the vacations from her new home in North Wales, this was published in 1968.

Charles continued work on the *Midlands* volume, but he was beginning to consider a book on the canals of northern England. He had decided early on that there was no prospect of his writing a volume on the waterways of eastern England; not only did the long and complex history of the Lea make it a daunting prospect, but sources were scattered rather than collected in the BTHR archive. Martin Palmer, one of the youngest recruits to the RCHS shortly after its formation, had met Charles in 1954 and accompanied the Hadfield family on part of their 1956 canal holiday. He had researched the very early Stamford Canal in 1959, and Charles suggested that he could accumulate materials towards an *Eastern England* volume. When he decided not to continue, the task was passed to

John Boyes, another early member, who had known canals since the 1920s. By 1966 John Boyes was at work on *The Canals of Eastern England*.

The impetus for a northern volume came from Gordon Biddle, who had written articles for the RCHS *Journal* on the Bradford Canal and the Leeds & Liverpool Canal, and who suggested in September 1962 that D&C might be interested in a book on the Lancaster Canal. Charles had consulted David over this, 'one of the most interesting in the country',[35] and offered the choice of a booklet or a longer 60,000 word book.

By January 1964 Charles had discussed the prospect of working with Gordon Biddle on a joint *Northern England* volume, partly because of the need to carry out much research from sources in the region, and partly to spread the workload. Charles sought to tackle the Ashton and Huddersfield Canals, which were closely linked to waterways which he was still studying for the *Midlands* volume, and possibly the Rochdale Canal. They agreed a division of responsibilities on 12 February 1964.

Charles was completing *Canals of the Midlands* by the end of August 1965, but, he wrote, 'Frankly, I can't face diving straight into "Canals of Northern England" without a little rest from canal research.' Instead, he decided to write a book on atmospheric railways, 'a nice manageable subject without too much research attached to it'.[36] This book, the first on its subject, was published in 1967.

In December 1965 Charles sought a grant for the cost of reading newspaper files in Manchester and Leeds for *Northern England*. After the manuscript was submitted, at the last moment, David split the very large *Midlands* volume into two, West and East, for publication in 1966. Beyond some overlaps in the opening chapter and a common conclusion, the split was not noticeable.

East Midlands was favourably reviewed in the RCHS *Journal*, although the reviewer criticised the maps. Even here economic history had not been neglected entirely: 'his summary of traffic on the Erewash could well be used to illustrate the textbook accounts of the rise of Midlands industry'. The review went on to commend the help from RCHS members acknowledged by Charles, and concluded that 'this, surely, is what the Society is all about, and we should feel proud to have shared in the making of this outstandingly fine book'.[37]

It appeared that there was a market for larger books than previous ones in the 'British Isles' series, and, as *Southern England* was then out of print, David suggested that it too be split into two enlarged volumes. These were *The Canals of South West England*, upon which Charles was working in October 1966, and *The Canals of South and South East England*, which Charles decided to tackle once Kenneth Clew's *Kennet & Avon Canal* and Humphrey Household's *Thames & Severn Canal* were complete. Separate *North West* and *North East* volumes were also suggested; Gordon Biddle agreed to this in November 1966, and they then focused on the *North West* volume.

Research was interrupted by work on further books for D&C. At David's suggestion, Charles agreed to write two slighter, popular books. He began work in June 1966 on what was at first called *Motorboating on Inland Waterways*, and then renamed *Holiday Cruising on Inland Waterways*, which was to form the first in a series. This popular guide to cruising was written with Michael Streat, who owned Blue Line, a hire boat (and canal carrying) firm at Braunston. It was published in 1968, but only after Charles experienced Michael Streat's very different approach to writing; he affectionately recalled him as 'a terrible man to get started on anything. I literally had to stand over him at midnight to get him to finish *Holiday Cruising*.'[38]

The second project was to rewrite *Introducing Canals* as *Introducing Inland Waterways*; this would not be published until 1973. Further modernisation of earlier publications included a new edition of *Waterways to Stratford* in 1968, reflecting the restoration of the Stratford Canal in 1964 and proposals to rebuild the Upper Avon, and a new edition of *South Wales* in 1967.

The latter, which Charles began in the summer of 1965, incorporated revised information from various contributors. W.L. Ives of the BWB confirmed that the remaining lengths of the Swansea and Monmouthshire Canals had been closed; much had been destroyed since Charles's explorations of the 1950s. New materials on the Cinderford and Pidcock's Canals, minor canals in the Forest of Dean, originated with Harry Paar, whose work on the Severn & Wye Railway had been brought to Charles's attention through the RCHS and D&C. Updated details of tramroads were supplied by Gordon Rattenbury, an RCHS member since 1961, whose specialism was South Wales tramroads. In November 1971 Charles was to request Gordon Rattenbury to revise the next edition of *South Wales* in due course, but changes in market conditions meant that no revision would appear.

The mid-1960s was, for Charles, a period of intense activity following retirement from full-time employment. As Chapter 13 reveals, he was also increasingly involved with local activities in South Cerney. I suspect that Charles could not have carried out so much writing had he continued to be involved in the management of D&C on a daily basis. Although the break with David was a major setback in his plans, for readers of Charles's books and the growing waterways literature, it was beneficial; probably, as a result, much more writing has been left behind. Perhaps his work for the BWB would also have had a lesser impact had his responsibilities with D&C grown as the firm and its markets expanded. But Charles never set down his feelings about this, and only speculation is possible.

CHAPTER FIVE

BRITISH AND WORLD CANALS: 1969–80

The 1970s perhaps marked a series of turning points in Charles's life: the effective ending to his investigations into British canal history; a greatly diminished involvement in David & Charles; the completion of work about Jessop and Smeaton; the rise of the Inland Shipping Group; and his developing interest in overseas canals. These were closely interlinked, but proceeded at much the same time. This was a period during which he moved back to Paddington before retiring again to South Cerney. His activities made a move to London essential, but, unlike Alice Mary, he had not liked living in the countryside.

COMPLETING BRITISH HISTORY

By the end of 1966 Charles had a firm contract for *Canals of North West England*. He spent a fortnight in July 1967 in Manchester, working on records of the Mersey & Irwell Navigation and the Rochdale Canal. The Rochdale Canal Company was unwilling to allow Charles more than four days to work on its records, and he had to select rapidly and take notes from the most useful records; after this, the Company refused access to anyone, although later it deposited its records in the Greater Manchester Record Office. Charles had drafted the Rochdale history by August 1968, when he returned to carry out more research in Manchester Central Library, and to give a lecture on the canal's history.

He and Gordon Biddle drafted most of the book during 1969, after Charles had completed *South and South East England*. Gordon Biddle had to reduce the length of his drafts considerably, but Charles suggested that he could leave material for volumes on the Lancaster and Leeds & Liverpool Canals for the 'Inland Waterways Histories' series. By October it was clear that, despite strict reductions in length, the book would be longer than *Midlands*, and David St John Thomas agreed to it being published in two volumes during 1970. Charles had found his BWB membership and connections helpful: he had arranged for Gordon Biddle to see Leeds & Liverpool records from the interwar years and, from 'an unattributable source', passed him details of the last traffics on the Ulverston Canal.

The book was reviewed in *Transport History* by T.S. Willan, now Professor of Economic History at Manchester University:

This book gives the best and fullest account of the canals of the North West that has hitherto appeared, but it has all the merits and defects of the series to which it belongs. . . . All facts are not born free and equal, and some of the detail might well have been sacrificed for a discussion of where the money for canals really came from. On this point the authors are largely silent, despite the present interest in capital formation and in the sources of investment. It would be an interesting experiment to write the history of canals, not from the usual standpoint of the canal enthusiast, but from the standpoint of the canal shareholder.[1]

Less favourable than Willan's review of *South Wales* a decade earlier, this perhaps reflected the changing nature of economic history, towards a focus on finance and profitability. Charles's researches, and especially the notes which he retained, leaned perhaps further towards the details of ownership than many other canal or railway histories, although the requirements of space, and the need to appeal to a readership more interested in the history of canals on the ground rather than on paper, would preclude the commercial publication of the kind of history to which Professor Willan's review aspired.

Charles was to continue as an editor of canal books for D&C until 1971, after which he continued editing work for D&C on a different basis. He would be editor in a more literal sense of one of a series of 'Enthusiasts Handbooks' promoted by David St John Thomas. Other handbooks covered Railways and Industrial Archaeology; Charles edited two *Canal Enthusiasts Handbooks*, in 1970 and 1973. The overseas sections of these were edited by David Edwards-May, a youthful enthusiast who had originally approached Charles in 1968 with a proposal for a book on the Canal du Midi in France, which he was about to visit. As Tom Rolt was already preparing *From Sea to Sea* about this canal, the proposal was declined, but it was later suggested that he should edit the sections on overseas waterways, to reflect the growing interest of many British holiday visitors in waterways which they could now more easily reach by air. David Edwards-May was to move to France and become an important contact for Charles, whose own interest in overseas waterways was growing.

The *Midlands* volumes had sold well, and second editions were produced in 1970. Here he took the opportunity to correct errors: in *West Midlands*, Charles's account of the alteration of the Caldon Branch summit was incorrect, a mistake he attributed to his failure to inspect the visible remains on the ground. In the *East Midlands* volume, he had invented a summit level for the Oakham Canal which had to be removed, and there had been some confusion over railway schemes affecting the Chesterfield Canal. The latter section was rewritten by Peter Stevenson, an early RCHS member who had graduated from Charles Clinker's extramural classes; given his insistence on accuracy, it is amusing to note that Clinker had checked the railway references in *East Midlands*. Peter Stevenson had to remove a section on pages 197 and 198 and to rewrite a section to precisely the same length to fit.

This was a period of major expansion in transport history publishing, in which D&C played a large part. Kenneth Clew's *Kennet & Avon Canal* was submitted in 1967; Charles wrote a Foreword, and it was published in April 1968. Kenneth Clew had left out material on the Somersetshire Coal Canal, which served the Kennet & Avon, and, at Charles's suggestion, began work on a history of this canal, published in 1970. His next project, on the Dorset & Somerset Canal, carried out between 1969 and 1971, covered a canal which had never been completed or used; the study developed work carried out by Robin Atthill for *Old Mendip*. He signed contracts for books on the Exeter Canal and the Wilts & Berks Canal, but while the former was announced, problems had arisen with D&C, and it was to be published by Phillimore & Co. Humphrey Household's *Thames & Severn Canal*, which greatly shortened his thesis completed in 1950, was finally published in 1969.

David St John Thomas had long been interested in the Bude Canal, and Charles in the Grand Western Canal. Histories of both were produced by Helen Harris; that on the Bude, published in 1972, in collaboration with Monica Ellis. David provided a Foreword to *The Bude Canal*, in which he recalled a quarter-century of interest and exploration, and regretted the lack of time, much of it owing to D&C work, which had prevented him from producing the definitive account. Charles, naturally, provided a Foreword in 1973 to *The Grand Western Canal*, in which he amusedly commented: 'After reading Helen Harris's book, I feel myself a part of history.'[2]

Alan Faulkner, who had been interested in waterways and especially narrow boats since the 1950s, planned a series on the Grand Union Canal constituents, beginning with *The Grand Junction Canal*, published in 1972. He intended to follow this by volumes on the Warwick Canals and the Regents Canal, and finally the Grand Union Canal into which they were all merged.

Others would cover the Leicester section of the Grand Union. There was a provisional arrangement whereby Peter Stevenson and Philip Stevens would, between them, cover the histories of the Erewash, Nutbrook, Leicester line, Leicester Navigation and Derby Canals. Philip Stevens produced *The Leicester Line* in 1972, and Peter Stevenson the small *Nutbrook Canal Derbyshire* in 1970. The Nutbrook study involved a slightly different approach, in that it included elements of local history. When Peter Stevenson submitted his manuscript, it was over length; Charles counselled that it was better for an author, rather than an editor, to cut a book, and so he removed a whole chapter about the maintenance of the canal. It was planned then that he and Philip Stevens would work jointly on other volumes, one researching local sources, the other national sources. It was not to be; although Philip Stevens completed his manuscript on the Leicester Navigation, it would not be published until 1992 by Alan Sutton Publishing Ltd. Peter Stevenson researched one chapter of his study of the Derby Canal, and by then it was clear that further histories would not be published.

David & Charles ran into crisis, especially after the Middle East war in the autumn of 1973. The firm had expanded rapidly; by its 21st anniversary in 1981, it had published over 3,000 hardback titles. There was a financial expansion, in which Hambro's Bank became involved in 1970, while the firm expanded by taking over Readers' Union in 1971. It had carried out adventurous reprints of historical works, like *De Salis*, *Phillips* and *Priestley*, using Charles's own pre-war copies, some of which were destroyed in the process; some of the later reprints had not sold well. During 1974 and 1975 the firm had to cut back in many areas. David explained later that besides raging inflation, 'markets collapsed – especially badly for some of our categories'.[3] Canal history was among these. By 1977 it seemed that the firm had survived despite continual rumours that the receivers were poised to take over. New management was introduced in the autumn of 1978, and the firm had survived by 1981.

Not only was D&C affected by a general crisis in publishing, but it became clear that the market for histories of smaller waterways was too limited to make these viable. After the firm diversified into new areas it was unable to support the kind of publishing which it had been formed to promote. One canal writer summed up the changes from an author's viewpoint:

> With the cut-backs seemed to come the end of the old and friendly D&C. For instance, the proud boast that books had never been remaindered was quickly dropped and authors were asked to agree to a cut-back on the royalties. . . . Many of the older D&C staff who knew the transport world had by now retired, been made redundant or had sought pastures new. In their place came newcomers who knew very little – one even started to rewrite my . . . history until he was told I would speak to D&C's Chairman, David St John Thomas! Fortunately Charles Hadfield was still the canals editor and a never-ending source of help. We had a happy co-operation . . . he would readily answer any query and I cannot recall any occasion when he suggested changes to a manuscript.[4]

The crisis affected the future course of books in the 'Inland Waterways Histories' series. As early as 1971 Charles had agreed with David that in future only studies of major canals should be published in this series, like Hugh Compton's *The Oxford Canal*. One history of a then very obscure waterway, *The Ballinamore and Ballyconnell Canal*, was to sell very few copies. Other proposals were cancelled; one for the Trent, as late as 1976, was dismissed without hesitation. The last to be commissioned, in 1974, was *The Trent & Mersey Canal*, by the author of *The Canals of Scotland*, Jean Lindsay; this was published in 1979. By then, only four volumes in the series were advertised, two of them new editions of early books: *The Kennet & Avon Canal* and *London's Lost Route to the Sea*. No more would appear, although some projected books would be published elsewhere. Some authors diversified, like Alan Faulkner, who produced numerous studies of canal carriers, mainly by narrow boat, over the following decades. Others produced more and more detailed studies of waterways in their area: for instance, Paul Vine's long series of photographic books covering waterways in south-east England for Middleton Press.

In April 1976 Charles admitted that 'D&C seem to have come to a dead stop on canal books'.[5] Other victims of the crisis included two important projects: a canal encyclopedia and a canal atlas. The canal encyclopedia was a project first mooted in 1964, which Edward Paget-Tomlinson, a long-standing enthusiast from the museum world, had agreed to prepare in 1968. It proved to be a massive task, and after much effort reducing his original manuscript from 600,000 to 300,000 words to completion in 1973, he had taken it down to Newton Abbot himself in two suitcases. After considerable delays it emerged that D&C was no longer in a position to publish it, and Waine Research published the book in 1978.

In the 1960s Charles had proposed a detailed historical canal atlas, as part of a planned D&C series of specialised atlases. In May 1972 he passed the project over to Richard Dean, who had drawn many maps in the later 'British Isles' volumes for him. Although the latter carried out some research and prepared sample maps, by 1973 it was impossible to publish this project. Dean's work would only bear fruit from 1989, when the first of his series of detailed canal maps published by M. & M. Baldwin appeared.

The 'British Isles' series did continue, albeit to a delayed conclusion. It had been intended that Gordon Biddle should write most of the *North East* volume, but his other commitments made him unable to assist, and he passed his notes on the Sheffield Canal and other investigations to Charles. Charles began work in May 1970 on what was now renamed *Canals of Yorkshire and the North East*. One glimpse of the work involved is provided by Charles's visit to York at the end of November 1970. He first visited offices of the Market Weighton Drainage Board at Beverley, where

> I had a partner's room, where I beavered away, sustained by cups of coffee in paper mugs brought by anxious ladies who thought the work was too much for me! Unfortunately 50 years of minute books are missing – however, there's a nice lot of very miscellaneous information there, though I fancy we shall have to return to Beverley.[6]

That evening he visited Maurice Barbey, a fellow Newcomen Society and RCHS member, who, to Charles's relief, had found somebody to read files of one of the York newspapers. He then visited the historical records office in York, to work on the Linton Lock papers.

Charles largely completed his researches for *Yorkshire* in 1970, wrote most of it during 1971, and it was published in two volumes during 1972. A review in the new magazine *Waterways World* suggested a different kind of audience from that addressed by the first volumes in the series:

> Whilst the history of the early days of these northern rivers and canals is full of interest and detail, it is the last part of the book which will be of greatest interest to most of its readers since it covers the period with which we are most familiar . . . a comprehensive record of the subject is now easily within reach of the waterway historian, the canal enthusiast and the inland navigator.[7]

Charles had anticipated that the final volume, *The Canals of Eastern England*, would be delivered by June 1972, and could thus be published early in 1973. He arranged a party to celebrate this in May 1973, which took place on the BWB's *Lady Rose of Regents*; guests included Dr Jean Lindsay and Tom Rolt, who was now ill. D&C's plans for a celebratory dinner to supplement this party had fallen through.

The celebration was premature, as *The Canals of Eastern England* had been delayed, and one of the series' authors had not yet been appointed. The crisis, and John Boyes's illness, made it necessary to assign part of the task to Ronald Russell, who had carried out some researches in this area for his *Lost Canals of England and Wales* of 1971, and who had also investigated the Nene for an abortive volume in the 'Inland Waterways Histories' series. He covered the central section, around the Great Ouse, Nene and Welland, and John Boyes completed the remainder. *Eastern England* was an unusual work in that there are very few artificial navigation canals in the area, but many navigable drains and river navigations.

At the end of 1971 Charles set out his proposed future writing programme to David St John Thomas. He planned to rewrite *Introducing Canals* in consultation with the IWA; the original 1955 edition had been out of print since 1965. He expected to have to rewrite this after two years if the BWB had by then been abolished. This was one of a number of popular books which he would write in the 1970s. He had already agreed to rewrite a definitive edition of *British Canals*, but the most important plan was for an entirely new book, *Canals of the World*.

The final completion of 'The Canals of the British Isles', the decline of D&C's canal publishing, and Charles's decision to relinquish his place on the IWA Council (dealt with below), seem to have culminated in Charles's decision to bring to an end researches and interests which he had been conducting on and off for fifty years. As early as March 1976 he resigned from a number of canal societies, stating that he intended to concentrate on his membership of the RCHS and the Inland Shipping Group (discussed later in this chapter). In January 1977 he wrote that 'I think *Waterways Sights to See* is my last book about British Canals – I can't really see myself writing another',[8] and he dismissed a suggestion that he should publish an unexpurgated account of the IWA's history.

In June 1977 he confirmed that 'Except for a rather nominal link with the ISG, I've shed all current responsibilities, in exchange for acquiring some historical ones.'[9] Perhaps prompted by his work on Jessop, where the lack of collected papers made further studies difficult, he decided to deposit his files for the 'British Isles' series, indexed by canal and by other categories, in a permanent form for use by students. He felt that students of economic history could usefully develop the primary material in his collection, and arranged for the British Library of Political and Economic Science, at the London School of Economics, to take the main research files; the BWB files followed. Charles pictured this process, stating that he was keeping all non-UK material, and returning to *Canals of the World* but at a snail's pace, because I'm also clearing masses of papers out of my house in the interests of my executors, poor devils. All my U.K. canal files are going to the library of the University of London, U.K. photographs to the Railway & Canal Historical Society, etc, etc, and still more is being given away or destroyed.[10]

These collections remain where he deposited them; judging from later documents which survived his death, some of those destroyed and dispersed items would probably now be of interest. Many of his collectable materials, including books, coins and canal tokens, were sold at auction, while he exchanged his UK postcard collection for one of overseas waterways, which he was to enlarge by later collecting.

One motive was to clear space for a growing collection of overseas canals materials; another was that he and Alice Mary, who had never entirely settled in London, anticipated that they might move to a smaller house in Gloucestershire now that he had reduced ties to London. He stated later that he simply lost interest in British canal history.

Despite this, Charles continued to derive pleasure from Britain's canals and contact with those who enjoyed them. In 1971 Michael Stimpson, then an RCHS member, co-founded the West London Industrial Archaeology Society (henceforth WLIAS), mainly to organise informal day and weekend visits to various places of industrial archaeological interest such as Ironbridge Gorge and Gloucester Docks. It also held speaker meetings on various subjects, but, given many members' interest in real ale, was a social organisation too.

Charles and Alice Mary were much older than the majority of WLIAS members, but seem to have regarded it as a means of keeping contact with younger people – possibly because their own children were now adults, and Alec was emigrating to Canada. Some meetings were held in their house in Little Venice, and this included slide-shows; Charles was to ignore his doctor's orders and speak to WLIAS meetings, but more on a recreational than on a formal basis. Charles was made WLIAS president in 1976, during which he visited Dudley Tunnel, and Tringford Pumping Station on the Grand Union Canal. After 1978 he became vice-president, and remained active while he lived in London. He did deliver speeches and write articles which expounded his views on history, which will be discussed in the next chapter. WLIAS members Brian and Marty Seymour later recalled that

it seems to us that, in retrospect, WLIAS was important to Charles as a means of passing his knowledge and experiences on to the next generation. I think we recognised this to some extent at the time but now we see more clearly how much we learnt from him and how his teaching affected our approach to all sorts of things.[11]

In 1989 the Seymours named their boat *Mentor* as a tribute to Charles. Their interest was not all recreational: in 1977, on a visit to Australia, Brian Seymour carried out research there into the Murray River. Charles encouraged Michael Stimpson to write a short history of Gloucester Docks, published by WLIAS in 1980, and insisted on the listing of all Public Record Office sources which underpinned it.

The contract for *Canals of the World* specified 80,000 words, to be delivered at the end of 1974. Other tasks would intervene, and it would be fifteen years before this book was finally published, but it completed investigations which Charles had been accumulating over a number of years.

Charles's interests had broadened beyond canal history by the 1970s, as his last major involvement in the RCHS demonstrates. At the AGM of June 1976 Charles proposed a resolution, seconded by Gordon Biddle, to form a working party to re-examine the Society's role in view of the relationship of railway and canal history with 'economic history, geography and industrial archaeology'.[12] Charles drew an interesting analogy with the development of transport, when he

> likened the Society to the railway and canal companies which were the purpose of study by members in that these started out with defined aims and objectives. These were achieved by constructing the railway or canal between two points and opening it for traffic thereon. Consequently, after a number of years developments took place which required a re-examination of the route to serve other places which had come into being or new traffics originating in the area served. As a result branch lines were built or new methods of transport brought into use. The position was such within the Society.[13]

Charles cited the challenge to the RCHS presented by the development of university courses, the then boom in publications and the growth of industrial archaeology. A reorganisation was agreed, and, beyond various administrative reforms, new specialist Groups, to study tramroads and, later, road history, were founded. The EGM which ratified these changes also considered a further resolution by Charles, to change the RCHS's name to the rather clumsy title of the Railway, Canal and Transport Historical Society. Partly because of the title, the vote produced a dead heat; the alternative name of Transport History Society, was not pursued, and interest waned. Charles had, however, been a founder member of a small Transport History Group, outside the RCHS, which sought to unify the study of transport history.

LOCATING JESSOP AND SMEATON

After his contributions to the 'British Isles' series were completed, Charles decided to lay aside the *Canals of the World* project for the time being, and to pursue a detailed biography of William Jessop. This would fulfil a long-standing interest.

His interest in Jessop had been fired by Professor Simmons's essay in *Parish and Empire* of 1952, where he had described Jessop as a considerable figure of the Industrial Revolution – or he would be if he had had justice done to him. But as it is, only one account of him has hitherto been written, a brief memoir by a fellow-engineer, Samuel Hughes, which appeared in 1844.[14]

Charles had expected to commission somebody else to write a biography of Jessop, and he suggested this shortly after D&C was formed. Through Tom Rolt he had met Professor Alec Skempton of Imperial College, who had told him in February 1961 that the history of engineering was then expanding rapidly. In 1965, completing *Canals of the Midlands*, Charles had discovered that Jessop was more involved in the East Midlands waterways, and the Ellesmere Canal, than had been previously recorded; predicting an increased interest in Jessop, he tried to interest Paul Vine in producing a life of Jessop.

Charles next returned to the subject in an article in the RCHS *Journal*, entitled 'Telford, Jessop and Pontcysyllte', published in October 1969. Here he voiced suspicions about Telford's role in the engineering of the iron-troughed aqueduct at Pontcysyllte on the Ellesmere Canal; Smiles and Telford himself had asserted that this was dominant. Charles drew out parts of the discussion which he had presented in *West Midlands*, set out the evidence, but raised a lot of unresolved queries: 'I've asked more questions than I've answered',[15] he concluded.

Charles carried out much research himself into Jessop in 1969 and 1970, in which Anthea Beamish became involved as his assistant, collecting research materials. This included work carried out in Ireland by Ruth Heard (formerly Ruth Delany, by now Ireland's leading canal historian), who transcribed all Jessop's reports on Irish waterways in 1971. After completing *North West*, Gordon Biddle passed to Charles his notes on Jessop's work, very limited on the canals which he had studied. He also passed him notes on the contractor John Pinkerton; presumably Charles contemplated a study of his work.

Tom Rolt had produced a number of biographies of engineers between 1957 and 1962, including a short study of Jessop in a 1962 volume, *Great Engineers*. He began a biography of Smeaton and Jessop in the late 1960s, and when Charles learned of this, he agreed to pass over his Jessop files to Tom, in return for a share of the royalties. Tom Rolt became terminally ill, making it clear that he would not be able to complete the study, which was not very advanced. In May 1974 Charles suggested to Professor Skempton, then working on a study of the Smeatonians, that Skempton could either write a biography of Jessop or participate in a joint one with Charles, who would do the research 'of a non-engineering kind'. Charles had a personal motive: 'I confess to a feeling of piety towards William Jessop as a great canal engineer and would much like to see a biography of him that puts him in his proper place in the hierarchy.'[16]

They agreed upon a joint study, and by the end of July the broad lines were settled: Charles was to do most of the writing, while Skempton would handle all work on docks and connections with Smeaton. D&C agreed to a 75,000 word biography which would, on similar lines to Tom Rolt's work, 'stick to the hardware',[17] without much coverage of Jessop's personal life.

Tom's widow, Sonia, passed his notes to Charles soon after Tom's death in May 1974. Charles's contribution was then delayed by work on a new edition of *British Canals*, and not until September could he forward his materials relating to Skempton's side of the book. By 26 September Skempton had catalogued all Jessop's reports, and planned detailed research into the Ringsend, West India and Bristol Docks, works which he considered to be 'of monumental importance by world standards'.[18]

Research proceeded steadily, interrupted by work on a new popular book, *Waterways Sights to See*; this was almost complete by August 1975. By November 1975 Charles had drafted three chapters, taking the story up to the waterways around the Trent. He was part-way through a chapter on Telford and Jessop, and the Ellesmere and Caledonian Canals: 'I'm getting a lot of fun out of drafting this one, trying to assess what Telford really did as opposed to what he said he did. Later on, I shall want to talk it over with you.'[19]

On 23 November Skempton informed him that Jessop had been involved in the Isle of Dogs Canal; he had not realised this when writing *East Midlands*. By January 1976, through A.D. (Sandy) Cameron, author of *The Caledonian Canal*, he had recruited a researcher, Ailsa Maxwell, from Edinburgh University, to investigate Scottish sources on the Caledonian Canal; by 11 March he had drafted much of this section. By August, with his draft of the Irish chapter complete, he sought Skempton's section on Ringsend Docks, to complete this, so that Ruth Heard could examine the whole chapter. His attention was then diverted by editing work on *Eastern England*, received at the end of August 1976.

Charles's researches in 1976 included visits to new and familiar archives. In April he was back again at the ICE library, where he was 'sweating through' a three-volume list of Telford's drawings; in June, into Boulton & Watt papers in Birmingham; and during September, into the BTHR archive, for the last time, as this was due to move to the new Public Record Office building in Kew in January 1977. His final research, into the Thames, was at Berkshire Record Office. He then approached D&C to lengthen the work to 90,000 words, as their discoveries had exceeded the anticipated scope of Jessop's work, including that on drainage. After he drafted the chapter on the Grand Junction and Rochdale Canals, he took three weeks in November to finally edit *Eastern England* 'which has descended on my desk'.[20]

Another of Professor Skempton's discoveries was that Jessop had proposed a canal along the line later taken by the Surrey Iron Railway. Both carried out research into tramroads during 1976, although Charles opposed a separate chapter on iron railways. He did amend the chapter dealing with Telford and Jessop at Skempton's request, but continued to express suspicions about Telford's autobiography, leaving this for a further study.

Early in April 1977, having completed the final draft, Charles and Alice Mary visited Jessop's home and other locations in Newark, and subsequently redrafted the first pages of the final chapter. During this period Charles was also rewriting *Introducing Inland Waterways* to fit D&C's 'Leisure and Travel' series.

Published in 1978 as *Inland Waterways* in a cheap midway edition, it would prove to be Charles's last book about British canals.

One diversion during 1977 was an investigation into the story, expounded by the early railway writer Clement Stretton, that Jessop had been involved in a plan for a Liverpool & Manchester Tramroad long before the railway scheme between these cities. Charles devoted much time to this, and the greatest direct expenses incurred in any of his researches, before exhaustive searches concluded that it was a legend.

By May 1978 the final title was agreed, after some discussion with D&C, as *William Jessop, Engineer*, perhaps reflecting the title of Professor Simmons's original essay, and the book was published in 1979. In their introduction, they stressed that if an engineer's work is to be properly assessed, collected papers are essential, and as early as March 1976 Charles had suggested that they should deposit copies of all their papers to form a Jessop collection at the ICE; they met to fulfil this in January 1979.

Charles wrote later:

Skempton and I were rather pleased with *William Jessop, Engineer*, because of the complete lack of research material. It was a matter of finding each separate fact separately, and I've never done such a jigsaw puzzle job in my whole life.[21]

G.M. Binnie reviewed the book favourably for the Newcomen *Bulletin*: 'The story that the authors have unravelled is the most exciting one during a great period in the development of British and Irish waterways and docks that has come to light for many years and it will enable Jessop to take his rightful place.'[22] This praise realised an ambition for Charles, who had written that 'I feel a little mission-like about Jessop.'[23]

Jessop had been John Smeaton's pupil, and Skempton had handled the part pertaining to Jessop's relationship to Smeaton. During 1977 Skempton gained ICE support for the publication of a volume of essays on Smeaton's work, and in February 1978 Charles began a chapter on 'Rivers and Canals'. His researches had already covered much of Smeaton's canal work, but he sought to enlarge his knowledge of schemes over which Smeaton gave advice or which did not proceed.

His attention was diverted by the Jessop book and by his long trip to North America, but he did begin initial enquiries through Philip Weaver, to detail the way in which the Birmingham Canal summit level had been lowered with Smeaton's advice. One discovery was that Smeaton, checking Brindley's proposed Trent & Mersey line in 1760, had suggested a higher summit and a cutting in place of the Harecastle Tunnel which was in fact later built. He completed most of the research in the early winter, including a visit on 30 October to the Royal Society library to see Smeaton drawings. Skempton provided him with details of the Forth & Clyde involvement. He submitted a draft on 28 December, and, after some minor alterations in 1979, the whole book was published early in 1981.

During the period of the Jessop researches, Charles was living in London; he and Professor Skempton became friends, and they met on numerous occasions. He had also been great friends with Tom Rolt; the Rolts and the Hadfields had visited one another frequently while they both lived in Gloucestershire. After Tom died in May 1974, Charles paid tribute to him: 'Some men are remembered for what they did; some for what they were. Tom Rolt will be remembered for what he did and for what he wrote, but most of all, I think, for what he was. There was greatness in him.'[24] Charles became one of Tom's literary executors, and, with Skempton and others, joined the Rolt Memorial sub-committee of the Newcomen Society. This decided to promote an updated version of Tom's 1963 study of Thomas Newcomen, which was published in 1977. Charles's assistance to Sonia helped to keep as many of Tom's books as possible in print, and thus preserve memories of Tom himself as well as his work.

THE IWA AND THE INLAND SHIPPING GROUP

Between 1966, when Charles left the British Waterways Board, and 1971, when he rejoined the IWA, the position of commercial carrying on Britain's canals and rivers had continued to decline. Most remaining traffics by narrow boat had ended, bar a few specialised movements, by 1970. Maintenance practices on the 'cruiseways', with longer winter stoppages and reduced draught, would have made it very difficult for commercial traffic to continue, even if there had been a demand for it.

Traffics on the 'Commercial' waterways also declined where they relied upon traditional craft and handling methods. In 1969, for instance, Regents Canal Dock was closed, and the BWB Severn fleet, carrying general merchandise from Avonmouth and Sharpness, was dismantled. On the other hand, the BWB's remaining general merchandise fleet, in the north-east, was modernised from 1970 by the introduction of push-towing units; this reflected a trend which had begun on the Continent in the late 1950s.

Traffic on BWB waterways declined between 1966 and 1971 from 7.62 million tons to 5.38 million tons in 1971; the larger fall in million ton–miles from 111.06 to 60.96 indicates the shorter average distance of haul. Traffics disappeared altogether on some commercial sections, notably the upper sections of the Lee, Weaver and Severn. This was also a period of major changes in port location and handling, with trends towards the concentration upon deepwater ports handling unitised cargoes, and away from lighterage.

Since leaving the BWB in 1966 Charles had devoted most of his time to history, but his knowledge of large North American and Continental waterways had grown, and he had joined the Chartered Institute of Transport. He had kept contact with BWB officers, such as Harry Grafton, who were positively interested in the development of carrying. For some time he sought to form a group to press for waterways development, although many IWA members retained a strong belief in narrow boat carrying, or in the ideas associated with J.F. Pownall's Grand Contour scheme and *New Waterways*.

The IWA had, however, changed after Aickman's effective departure in 1966, and the securing of 'Cruiseways' assured by the Transport Act 1968. Robert Shopland of Bristol, whose interest had been fostered in the 1950s by Severn barges, had become IWA general secretary in October 1968. He was one of a small number of IWA members seriously interested in large-scale carrying, and from May 1969 introduced a new 'Commercial Carrying News' column in the IWA *Bulletin*, which increasingly included coverage of larger waterways.

After September 1970 Lionel Munk, the IWA chairman, had secured as his successor John Humphries, a City solicitor who had been a boating enthusiast since the 1950s; he saw him as a suitable leader for the IWA in the new atmosphere, which required persuasion rather than confrontation. John Humphries knew nothing of the divisions in the IWA two decades before, and he invited the main founders to celebrate its 25th anniversary at the Waldorf Hotel on 15 January 1971. The Hadfields and the Rolts all attended, and John Humphries was astonished to discover that his guests had been expelled twenty years before. All applied to rejoin.

Charles's unexpected return to the IWA enabled it to help him form a group to press for large waterway development. A pivotal role was played by Harry Grafton, head of the BWB's Commercial Department since its formation in March 1964, who sought mutual assistance on the strict understanding that it must be behind the scenes. A small Commercial Carrying Group was thus formed, holding its first meeting at the IWA headquarters on 2 June 1971. Charles chaired the Group, while Robert Shopland was its secretary. Others included Christopher Marsh, formerly special engineering adviser to the BWB, who had been manager of the Weaver Navigation while it was improved to take coastal ships; and Charles Klapper, who had been editor of *Modern Transport* until this folded in 1968. Charles insisted that the purpose of the Group was only 'to promote commercial development on a large scale, with particular reference to sea links. Therefore it is not concerned with commercial carrying on cruiseways. That's someone else's job.'[25] Reflecting this, early in 1972 the Group was renamed the Inland Shipping Group (henceforth ISG), at Robert Shopland's suggestion.

The Group remained small, but aimed to influence government and others who might invest in waterways development. It supported initiatives that BWB was already considering, including port transshipment terminals on the lower Grand Union Canal (for London) and Winsford (for Liverpool), the introduction of BACAT (Barge Aboard CATamaran) to the Humber ports, and a further scheme to enlarge the SSYN to Rotherham.

The ISG soon identified the need to study overseas practices, to disseminate information in the transport industry through publications and conferences, to influence government, and to press for large-scale inland waterways development in any way possible. At its first meeting Charles listed a large number of subjects for research, whose results would be steadily published through a series of simple duplicated *Fact Sheets*, some of them written by Charles himself. For instance, he studied the operations of US waterways, and drafted a new IWA policy on commercial carrying.

In March 1972 Charles published his initial thoughts in the IWA *Bulletin*, in a rapidly written but succinct article, expressing themes which the ISG would follow in the years ahead. He suggested that waterways development should be financed in the same way as roads, as in Continental countries, rather than on the basis of loans, upon which the planned SSYN enlargement was to be financed. He noted the development of the barge-carrying ship since 1966, so that worldwide there were 2,300 LASH lighters out of a planned total of 5,500, along with other systems such as BACAT and SEABEE. While the smaller BACAT system could work on the Trent, Aire & Calder and an enlarged SSYN in the interim, he advocated the enlargement of significant waterways to LASH standards, so that they could also be used by sea-going barges, which would require no transshipment and could trade directly with Continental waterways. To achieve this, what was required, among other things, was 'a well-informed, energetic and technically qualified inland waterway division in the DoE, similar to the motorway division and to those in other countries . . . , able to initiate and plan national waterway development'.[26]

Charles was surprised at the positive reception of this article, whose principles were generally accepted. His *Modern Transport* piece of 1967, from which he developed many points, had not excited much response, but the *Bulletin* article produced positive interest. Some IWA members were opposed to the modernisation of waterways because of the possible destruction of historic structures, although only in rare cases would a new waterway take up and destroy the line of an old one. Concern over the loss of historic structures was to lead the Greater London Council to drop support for the modernisation of the lower Grand Union Canal, one line whose enlargement would have involved destruction; Charles, for instance, advocated the replacement of the flight of locks at Hanwell by a water slope.

During 1972 Charles drew up proposals for the future of commercial waterways in the face of government plans to transfer the BWB waterways to the new Regional Water Authorities. A document, *Towards a Future for Inland Shipping*, was published on 31 October 1972.

Charles always felt that anyone's first duty is to train his or her successor, and he soon found his in Frederic (Fred) Doerflinger. An American who had lived in England since 1942, his background was in journalism and public relations. A passive IWA member since 1947, his experience of waterways had lain in pleasure-boating, much of it on Continental waterways. He had contacted Charles in the late 1960s, while he was writing *Slow Boat Through Pennine Waters*, published in 1971. Charles had helped with queries about W.H. Bartholomew of the Aire & Calder Navigation and had read the manuscript. The Doerflingers stayed with the Hadfields shortly before they left South Cerney, and Fred agreed to join the ISG. From his first meeting in March 1972 he provided widespread publicity; this was fortunate, because Charles would prove unable to do so after March 1973. Between 1973 and 1981 the ISG met at Charles's new home at 21 Randolph Road; it proved to be a congenial environment, but Charles was slowly reducing his involvement.

One proposal during 1973 was to study the possibility of a new 1,350-tonne waterway from the Wash via the Nene and then a new canal to a new terminal at Tyseley in Birmingham. In August a sub-committee was formed to produce what was described as 'A National Commercial Waterways Projection'. The result was published in March 1974 as *Barges or Juggernauts?*, partly written by Charles and Fred Doerflinger. It suggested a separation between the use of lorries for distribution, seen as essential, and their use as long-distance heavy transport – the unnecessary 'juggernauts' of the title. It proposed detailed studies which should be carried out, financed by government.

The report criticised the position of waterways in relation to the promotion of other modes of transport, and recommended a national marketing organisation, to match British Rail's organisation, which would cover all Britain's waterways, not just the less significant ones owned by the BWB. In relation to this, it proposed a proper basis for national statistics of inland waterway transport; the British Government's reliance upon statistics of BWB waterways alone prevented proper international comparisons.

It proposed investigations into a new waterway between the Wash and the Severn, via the Midlands. Some 170 miles long, rising through lifts to a summit of about 325 feet, this would link road and rail transshipment points on both sides of the Midlands to inland ports in the Netherlands, Belgium and Germany. It suggested feasibility studies into this route which should be followed by studies of a link with the Mersey and with the Trent, and possibly a trans-Pennine route to extend the Aire & Calder line westwards. It was noted that, while on the Continent and in North America the generation of hydroelectric power was a major source of revenue and finance, the new proposed waterways would draw revenue from water transfer, between impounding reservoirs in the Wash and the Severn above the planned barrage. Water would be pumped back from lower to upper levels using surplus electricity at offpeak rates.

Barges or Juggernauts? was well received, with publicity extending to television. By July it was generating over a hundred letters per week, and had to be reprinted. The oil crisis of 1973 had focused attention on the need for energy conservation, while the growth of road freight traffic was almost as controversial then as it would be later. One strength was that it made representations about the need for further study of track, craft and handling improvements, but did not concentrate on specific measures whose practical application might be immediately dismissed.

Information-gathering was seen as essential, and Christopher Marsh had already collected preliminary details of Continental waterways operations. Charles approached David Edwards-May, who had been overseas editor of the *Canal Enthusiasts Handbook*, to produce a detailed study of practice in four countries in Continental Europe. This was published in 1975, in time for the Freightwaves '75 conference.

The limitations of a small group of enthusiasts, only some of whom had professional experience, led Charles and Fred Doerflinger to begin discussions about the possibility of a major waterways conference, modelled on those in the

USA, which would lead to the formation of a trade association. This association would remove some of the work from the ISG, carry out work of wider scope, and develop its own policies alongside those of the ISG. They had met Sir Frank Price, the BWB chairman, in December 1973, and found that he generally supported waterways development, despite BWB's major financial constraints. He approved the idea of a National Waterways Transport Association (henceforth NWTA), and from early 1975 Charles chaired a Steering Committee to form NWTA. It came together at the end of an international conference in London, Freightwaves '75, on 13 June 1975. The BWB would play a considerable part in the development of the NWTA, although ISG members like Mark Baldwin would be on its executive committee.

Against these positive organisational developments, there were setbacks, notably the withdrawal of BACAT in September 1974, only months after its introduction, following industrial action by dockworkers at Hull. Charles wrote to the *Financial Times* to oppose the view that ports which discharged to inland waterways craft, rather than to land, would threaten port employment; he cited ports like Rotterdam, Antwerp and Hamburg where trade did not suffer from being served by major inland waterways. BACAT nevertheless remained withdrawn, and industrial action inhibited BWB craft carrying to and from Hull. Containerisation, whose applications accelerated in the 1970s, was to limit the applications of barge-carrying vessels as well as to decimate port employment and overside loading alike.

Some successes followed the ISG's work, although Charles's role in the Group until 1981 was mainly to offer hospitality and encouragement at meetings rather than to take much action. In 1978 the government agreed to compile waterways statistics on a proper basis, approved the Sheffield & South Yorkshire enlargement (albeit on the basis of loans), and, in the Transport Act 1978, made it a duty of the Secretary of State to promote a national policy for the use of inland waterways for commercial transport. Compliance with this duty proved to be more in spirit than in deed.

The ISG's role changed after the formation of the NWTA; two developments involved further publications. In 1977 it assisted with the publication of *Barge Carrier Systems – Inventory and Prospects* by Dr David Hilling, who had been a member since 1974 and who was later to become chairman. Dr Hilling, an academic transport geographer with extensive experience of West Africa, was particularly interested in the application of barge-carrying vessels to developing countries.

Mark Baldwin, another academic with a civil engineering background, succeeded Fred Doerflinger as ISG chairman in 1977; his postgraduate studies in engineering at Imperial College were under Professor Skempton, Charles's co-author. Baldwin had joined the ISG in 1973 after hearing one of Charles's last public lectures in London, and completed his doctorate on the development of inland waterway transport in Britain in 1978. In January 1979 it was decided to replace *Barges or Juggernauts?* by a more closely reasoned and factual analysis of the case for inland waterways development. Dr Baldwin took on this task, using his doctoral thesis, which included the first attempt to estimate the true level of British inland waterways traffic; the ISG's last major publication for some years, *British Freight Waterways Today and Tomorrow*, was published in October 1980. Much had taken place in the nine years since Charles so tentatively founded the ISG.

Charles had rejoined the IWA mainly to further the development of inland shipping. He was less interested in other issues of importance to many IWA members, including campaigns which followed the Transport Act 1968: to retain and restore many of the 'Remainder' waterways which were not part of the 'Cruiseway' network, and for which BWB received no subsidy, or for the restoration of the legal public right of navigation. He was surprised in 1972 when John Humphries nominated him for the IWA Council, mainly on the grounds of the developing interest in inland shipping. He agreed, 'secretly thinking that I was unlikely to be elected, given the iconoclastic reputation I thought I had. However, I suppose there were more people who knew my name from books, for I was elected easily.'[27] This was at the end of 1972, when John Heap had become IWA leader.

One activity which proved short-lived was a series of visits to IWA branches. On 2 March 1973 Charles addressed a branch meeting in Manchester on the 'Commercial Development of Waterways'; much to his distress, he found himself unable to continue half-way through. He was clearly over-working at the time, researching *Canals of the World*, editing books for David & Charles, and doing extensive work for the IWA and ISG. He and Alice Mary could occupy only part of their new home at 21 Randolph Road, with many of his materials out of reach, while builders carried out alterations which were not to be complete until May. His doctor ordered him to give up either speaking engagements or writing; he chose the former, and rarely spoke at public meetings after 1973.

He supported the need to reorganise the IWA, under a new constitution from July 1974. This provided for the replacement of branches by regions, with a somewhat more federal structure. He suggested that posts of vice-chairmen be created to reduce some of the chairman's workload, and was pleasantly surprised to find himself elected one of the former. He was very amused to observe that this gave him the unusual record of having been expelled between two periods as vice-chairman. He favoured the creation of small groups to handle details, leaving the Council to develop broad policies, in the same manner that the ISG operated as a committee with autonomy within defined parameters. The new Restoration Committee, for instance, monitored the details of restoration proposals and progress.

Charles remained doubtful about some of the plans for canal restoration which emerged in the more secure environment encouraged by the 1968 Act, the growth of pleasure-boating and the organised voluntary movement. The Ashton Canal was one example; the Thames & Severn drew more doubts. One of the more complex was the Yorkshire Derwent, which would later become an expensive *cause célèbre* for the IWA. In a rare instance where he sought to direct my study, Charles urged me, as he had others without success, to investigate this. Like the loss of Jessop's papers, he was puzzled by the way in which this had been recorded and presented. He did not survive to read the results of my investigations.

The Yorkshire Derwent Navigation had been the subject of restoration attempts since 1949. In 1970 the Yorkshire Derwent Trust Ltd (YDT), with IWA support, was incorporated, and obtained an agreement with Yorkshire River Authority to reinstate navigation by restoring and rebuilding locks. Work was carried out from 1971, and relations were harmonious until February 1974. After the formation of the Yorkshire Water Authority (YWA), which took over the River Authority's functions, YWA agreed to foster restoration on the basis that this would be carried out with voluntary assistance and that the YWA would then become the navigation authority. It seems that the original trustees, who had favoured working with YWA, were removed by the autumn of 1974, when Robert Aickman was nominated as a trustee to YDT.

Problems with the Derwent continued. During 1975 the YWA promoted a Bill to assume greater powers and to become the navigation authority; a rival Bill was drafted by the YDT, which would have made *it* the navigation authority. The IWA National Festival was held at York in August 1975, and there were plans to use this as an opportunity to attack the YWA and to campaign for the Derwent restoration. Acting on Charles's advice, a meeting proposing cooperation between the IWA and the YWA was planned, which would draw a distinction between restoration by volunteers, which he supported, and maintenance and operation by volunteers, which he opposed as impractical.

It seems that an informal meeting was held at the York festival. A leaflet was issued there attacking the YWA, although this was deemed actionable and was withdrawn; despite the YWA's considerable involvement in Yorkshire rivers, it was denied a stand at the festival. At the meeting, the attacks by the YDT on the YWA had met their target; John Heap, the IWA chairman, was accused of conspiring with the YDT against the YWA, and walked out of the meeting.

Charles recalled attending an IWA AGM, probably that in September 1975, at which Aickman, in a crowded room, addressed the meeting and declared that if the Yorkshire Derwent campaign was lost, the whole IWA cause was lost. He was appalled at the manner in which Aickman, a 'spellbinder' in his words, had taken over and dominated the meeting. Charles persuaded John Taunton, the new IWA general secretary, to stage the next AGM in a quite different meeting place, and later recalled with amusement the way in which a very large hall, with IWA officers on the platform, was found, in which Aickman's proved only a voice in the crowd.

Charles was involved in a meeting between the IWA and the YWA on 23 September 1975, at which the YWA chairman stated that the YWA would assist with restoration on a step-by-step basis, but only if the IWA was to set up a 'responsible body', not the YDT, with which the YWA refused to work. The YDT was accused of adopting a personally abusive and litigious approach.

Divisions within the IWA prevented the emergence of such a body, and further restoration work was inhibited. By 1980 a 'conservation' group opposed to boating activities on the Derwent had emerged, and the YDT diverted attention into attempts to take legal action to enforce a public right of navigation which was held to exist on the river. Many years, and substantial expenditure by the IWA later, the House of Lords deemed that no such right existed; the river remains largely unrestored. Charles later viewed this campaign as a significant source of financial problems for the IWA in the 1990s.

Charles resigned from the IWA Council on 25 September 1976 and was made Honorary Consultant, which meant, as he put it, that his advice could be sought but not heeded. He was consulted over a campaign in 1980 to revive and enforce the public right of navigation. Charles counselled strongly against this somewhat abstract right. He felt that Parliament would not, realistically, accept a right which could be used to impose open-ended inviolable obligations upon waterways owners, state or private, to maintain their waterways in good order, whatever the cost.

EXPLORING WORLD CANALS

Charles had written about overseas waterways in his short book, *Canals of the World*, published in 1964. A trip to Duisberg, on behalf of the BWB, had followed, with visits back to the Rhine, Netherlands, Norway and Sweden in 1965 and 1966. The last of these, to Bergen in 1966, was probably their last family holiday, as Alec was then twenty, John eighteen and Molly sixteen; most future holidays were taken with Alice Mary alone, often to overseas destinations where they could explore waterways. One such trip, to France in 1968, included a visit to the inclined plane under construction at Arzviller-Saint-Louis, where, in broken French and sign language, Charles gained permission to explore.

On David St John Thomas's suggestion, Charles had written *The Canal Age*, a more popular history aimed at readers who 'wonder how the waterways came to be, and what the canal age was like'. He went on to add 'short chapters on the great ship canals, and on the age on the Continent and in North America, so that readers may see a little of the wider background against which the affairs of Britain were set'.[28] He covered the Suez, Panama and North American Canals from secondary sources, but based his account of the Trollhätte Canal in Sweden on his cruise in 1965 on *Wilhelm Tham*. A later description, in a general history of British transport, dismissed this book, as one which 'glances at some foreign canals but does not noticeably enlarge our knowledge of British ones, nor set them at all securely in their historical context'.[29]

While he was busy with *Northern England* and minor publications, Charles continued to accumulate materials towards another possible publication. One catalyst was a long trip which he took in August 1969; this coincided with the end of his period as editor of *Quaker Monthly*, and his sixtieth birthday, after which he would receive his civil service pension.

In 1962 Charles had seen the Danube at Belgrade, and later read about the scheme to deepen the river through the Carpathian Gorge by constructing locks at the Iron Gates, which would provide hydroelectric power and improved navigation. In August 1969 he returned with Alice Mary to travel down the Danube on the *Theodor Korner* from Austria to Romania through the Carpathian Gorge leading to the Iron Gates.

Their journey began at Passau, on the German/Austrian border, on 23 August, and took them through Vienna, into Czechoslovakia to Bratislava, then through Hungary to Budapest, and through Yugoslavia (Serbia) to Belgrade. Downstream from Belgrade, the Danube formed the Yugoslavian/Romanian border, where on 27 August they reached the Gorge before the Iron Gates.

At the head of the Gorge, they met three tug trains, and manoeuvred through the first section before picking up a pilot. Alice Mary's notebook (using JS for Yugoslavia and Rum for Romania) pictures part of the next section:

Fast, rippling, breaking into foam current in channel. Hills on both sides thick woods, deciduous. Round 45° to the right. Hills strike down and seem to cross to stop a passage. Buoys take you round the elbow, while current rushes on. Wooded crags and mountains on either side and high peaks ahead. Spires of bare rock, pointed, run down the hills, from sky to water. Steam tug appears with barge train. Now we strike across to JS bank. Two rocks stick up in mid-stream. Steam tug filling the hills with smoke from two tall funnels. . . .[30]

They moved through the Gorge to a break where a village and road were being rebuilt at a higher level, as the water level of the Danube was to be raised once the Iron Gates Locks were completed. Beyond, they entered the most restricted section, before the town of Orsova:

Hills going bald as we approach the grey cleft. Very narrow again . . . JS road building active, tunnel through cliff point. We enter narrow neck with rock island in middle. We blow and slow. Whole Danube squeezed into this narrow neck. . . .

A tug appears, we stop, above the rock. All now blocked by huge rock elbow on left. Signal station this side. We wait. Rumanian flags pass us and we glide forward. Now we are in the cleft, bare rock, or bushes, on R. side and thin woods on JS. Cliffs close in, again, grey, and signal flag shows at cabin on right hand side. Little passage opens. . . . We go through and swing round and immediately another neck and signal cabin and grey cliff facing us. In flat scoop beside, another new village building above low one. We pass in, and another signal is ahead. . . .

Ledges at 6 ft above water by Roman engineers for their bridge. Hadrian's campaign into Dacia. Through the channel, sudden widening. Tug pulling a barge . . . Long sandy level, Dubova. Women washing, long frocks, heads tied up. Now the grey rocks give way to smooth hills, and pasture and trees. Over the low bend (with watch tower Rum.) a red-roofed town shows Orsova and

Tekyja. Long gentle valley on left to Orsova all to be flooded. Another collection of barges waiting for tow. Hills have fallen back to make wide circle, with low land as the next turn. We moored to land our pilot, and saw the half-demolished village houses, and the new houses and a new chapel . . .

Small docks at Orsova, all to submerge. Turkish island cleared of Turks, middle of stream. New road carried all round the bend, bridges, across narrow valleys and dips, walled embankments, tunnels, all on Rum. side. Hills falling back, river widening again as we see the lock works far ahead. Channel now marked by stone dike. Railway 2–10–0, one with steam up, on long stone dike up to lock works.

The railway carried steam locomotives which were used to pull vessels upstream against the flow; the new locks would remove the need for this. *Theodor Korner* moored in the first Iron Gates Lock for lunch; the Romanian lock was half-built, the Yugoslavian not started. They turned at Turnu-Severin, and were back in Vienna on 31 August. The Iron Gates Locks, upon which work had begun in 1964, would be completed in 1972, with a total lift of 34.5 metres (116 feet).

Later visits included one by road in 1972 to the deep locks, the world's steepest single rise at 34.5 metres (116 feet), on the Douro in Portugal, then under construction to make this river navigable for the first time. By this time, Charles had begun writing *Canals of the World*; they would visit many more overseas waterways until 1983.

Charles's researches into William Jessop around 1970, and overseas canals in 1971, both employed Anthea Webb (formerly Beamish) as a research assistant to trace books. Charles had previously employed researchers to search primary sources, but it was clear from the outset that any world study would rely on secondary sources; barriers of language, time and travel placed any primary sources beyond reach.

Research began with the exploration of existing sources, like Vernon-Harcourt's volumes, and articles like those by Robert Legget in the Newcomen Society *Transactions*. Anthea Webb traced more obscure sources and listed suitable extracts for Charles, before he returned to London. Charles joined the American Canals Society after this was founded in 1972; one of its aims was to trace the many small canals in North America which had been rapidly superseded by the railroads. A canal literature was beginning to develop there: for instance, Dr Legget had published *Rideau Waterway* in 1955, and William Shank had published a long booklet on *The Amazing Pennsylvania Canals* in 1956. Both they and William Trout and Captain Tom Hahn of the American Canals Society would help Charles considerably over the next decade; Charles must have known Bill Trout for some time, as he had tried, unsuccessfully, to persuade him to write a book about the canals of the United States in 1969.

Robert Legget would go on to write *The Canals of Canada* for D&C in 1976; after retirement from a Canadian Government post in building research, he was to write numerous studies of Canadian waterways, and even a book on the *Railways of Canada*, which D&C published. Curiously, just as the principal historian of English and Welsh canals originated in South Africa, this Canadian equivalent of Charles had been born in Liverpool, England, in 1904, and had attended university there before emigrating to Canada in 1929. He and Charles became great friends, mostly through correspondence; Robert Legget had greater energy than Charles in retirement and told Charles that he had laid out sufficient research to occupy him until he was over one hundred years old, although he was to die just before his ninetieth birthday, still writing.

The earliest drafts for the new book covered early Chinese waterways, where Charles followed the writings of Dr Joseph Needham. Charles had decided to draft the book in two sections, one dealing with the 'Old World' (very broadly, the European countries and their non-American colonies), another dealing with the 'New World' (North America) and a 'coda' dealing with developments in Latin America. It was not a perfect division between quite separate lines of development, but a closer chronological link would have been confusing. By 1974 he had drafted the five New World chapters, although more was to be added as research in North America, and his growing contacts with it, gathered pace. While he was diverted by the study of Jessop, he continued to receive research materials, and, perhaps more importantly, to visit as many waterways as possible.

After Ron and Joan Oakley began to organise Continental visits for IWA members in 1973, the Hadfields began to join them. Charles's first, in October 1975, was very much influenced by the ISG; it was planned by Charles and Fred Doerflinger, assisted by David Edwards-May. Based in Hamburg, which they approached and left by ship on the Elbe, the main attraction outside Hamburg was the Elbe Lateral Canal, a new canal being constructed to take 1,350-tonne craft. This achieved a rise of 61 metres (200 feet) in 115 kilometres (71 miles) by only two structures. Charles saw the first, the vertical lift with, at 38 metres (125 feet), the greatest rise in the world, on 10 October:

> Luneberg lift springs out of the hillside that carries the upper pound, an enormous version of Anderton, its twin caissons working independently, balanced by 240 counterweights suspended in the four towers that surround each of them. Lifting time, including entrance and exit, is 15 minutes, giving a capacity of 10 million tons a year. We were lucky enough to see the caissons being tested while we listened to explanations from the chief engineer of the Hamburg waterways region.

On the next day, the group saw the Uelzen Lock, with the highest rise of any canal lock, which Charles described as

> quite outstanding, not least because, in order to get its great vertical rise, half the lock chamber rises above ground. Here the site engineer, who had awaited us on a Sunday afternoon, gave a quite fascinating talk on the lock, the technical problems it had presented, and the lessons that had been learned.

Then he took us into the underground sluice chamber that controlled the outflow from the three side-ponds that together save 60% of the water used, into the pumphouse that returns the other 40% to the summit level, and into the control cabin above the vertically-rising lower gate.

This interest in a waterway of the future was matched by a concession to history, alongside a visit to the 1000-ton Elbe–Lubeck Canal: 'Just round the corner was the tiny circular lock, dating from 1724, of its predecessor, the Stecknitz Canal, built in the fourteenth century to carry Luneberg salt to Lubeck, the first European watershed canal, and the first canal in Europe to have pound locks.'

On the last night, a panel including IWA Council members Stanley Clover and Charles, engaged in a question and answer session in which they 'spent nearly as much time answering each other's questions and disagreeing with the answers as they did dealing with the public right of navigation, BWB charges and finances, regional water authorities, BACAT, et al'.[31] Charles would attend a series of these brief trips, until his last one to Switzerland and Italy in the autumn of 1982.

A further trip in 1978 was a three-month tour of the United States and Canada, involving 5,000 miles of waterway travel. Out of this, Alice Mary and he wrote what he described beforehand as 'a travel book at which we propose to try our hand'.[32] *Afloat in America*, which was published in 1979 by David & Charles, but financed by the Hadfields, described their holiday, including long rail journeys, explorations of various towns and personalities, and contained their observations on various matters. Both kept daily notebooks, and compared accounts; Charles wrote almost all of the text, which Alice Mary reviewed. The result, informative in its way, was rather flat; perhaps too few readers could identify with an elderly travelling couple, because sales proved surprisingly poor.

Charles was not then sure if he would complete what he now called *World Canals*: 'Whether I ever in fact write the book on *World Canals* that I have in mind, I don't know, but if I do I've again got a lot of background for it.'[33]

He was to complete this major piece of work during the next decade, after he had returned to live in South Cerney. In effect, Charles had retired from active involvement with British canals. It was not, however, to prove a happy or fulfilling retirement.

THE ENDS OF HISTORY:
1981–96

Parts of Charles's last years tended to be dominated, not by research into or activism over inland waterways, but by the need to deal with the decline first of Alice Mary and then his own physical deterioration. They moved to a much smaller modern house than they had lived in previously, but did not return to the life which they had enjoyed when they lived in South Cerney in the 1960s. The same Charles who had previously mapped out parts of his life now began to anticipate his death, although it came much later than he expected. As with others who live to a great age, he attempted to settle aspects of his past life which were now history. The most important practical matter to settle was his book on *World Canals*.

COMPLETING *WORLD CANALS*

Charles returned to *Canals of the World* after the publication of the Jessop biography and *Afloat in America*. *Afloat* did not prove successful; there were many returns, and in 1985 Charles arranged for the remaining stock (and that of *Jessop*) to be handled by Mark Baldwin, who was setting up a new bookselling and publishing business.

Charles had continued to amass research materials while he worked on other projects. For instance, Robert W. Passfield of Canada first wrote to Charles in October 1978, seeking details about the Forth & Clyde Canal, upon which the lock designs for the Shubenacadie Canal appeared to be based. Charles could not help, as his researches into Scottish canals had been limited, but in January 1979 Passfield sent him his article in which it was established that the Shubenacadie Canal engineer, Francis Hall, had been involved with the Edinburgh & Glasgow Union Canal, and that Scottish masons had worked on the original locks.

In September 1981 Charles was contacted by Stanley Holland, a retired lecturer and waterways enthusiast from Birmingham, who was contemplating further research. Charles wrote to tell him that

at present almost no books on canal history are being published. What was at one time a brisk market is now moribund as my own sales show. Whether it will revive is anybody's guess but if you write a book a substantial grant towards publication would be necessary in the present state of the market.[1]

He went on to explain that *World Canals* was now in very rough draft, but he was working on the final drafts of the North American chapters. Stanley Holland agreed to search through back issues of journals such as *Engineering* and *The Engineer* for materials on what Charles termed Old World waterways, using mainly Birmingham University Library's collection. He submitted a stream of photocopies, so that Charles could start work as soon as his drafts of the New World chapters were complete. Later, in 1983, he made enquiries on Charles's behalf into the current position of waterways in the Indian sub-continent, and the Nile. These enquiries were completed by the end of 1983, but they continued to discuss their collections of waterways stamps and coins, and Stanley Holland acquired part of Charles's collection at auction in 1988. Later, he wrote *Canal Coins*, published in 1992, with a Foreword by Charles.

Two examples, from Canada and the Netherlands, must suffice to portray the range of researches carried out by Charles in the second phase of what was now called *World Canals*.

Before moving into their new house in South Cerney, the Hadfields went to Canada again, for six weeks, partly to visit Alec in New Brunswick. Further enquiries to Parks Canada had provided details of the Shubenacadie and other Nova Scotian waterways. Charles has left several accounts of this trip, which convey some of his enthusiasm. They landed in Halifax, Nova Scotia, to explore canals in the area:

I had briefed myself pretty thoroughly before going to explore the canals of Nova Scotia and I laid on a taxi in order to drive us all over it. Asking particularly for a driver who knew where the locks were, we got two charming students from university who were full of enthusiasm, but totally deficient in knowledge, so I took them round. They were quite stunned when I produced quite a detailed map of the whole canal and proceeded to track down one lock site after another as well as that of the upper inclined plane.

We managed to find every lock except two and the site of the remaining inclined plane. One lock turned up in the garden of a rather surprised elderly gentleman who didn't even know it was there . . . we had hardly climbed out of the car, and before I had time to walk to the lockhouse, [this] enraged citizen erupted, shouting at us with a rifle. I tried to keep calmer than I felt, and with Alice Mary as support I explained that we were English visitors interested in canal history. Slowly he calmed down and ceased to wave his rifle quite so threateningly . . . the landowner didn't like visitors, seemingly, but our combined charm, Englishness and knowledge of his own canal enabled him to lay down his rifle and join us in mutual autographing of each other's newspapers. At the end of the day Alice Mary and I were going strong and the two girls were flat out.[2]

After visiting Alec, they went on to Montreal and Toronto, and then:

A flight to Sault Ste Marie to see our old canal friends Robert and Mary Legget, and book in to the Holiday Inn [with] a view of the great quadruplicated locks which with short canals join Lakes Huron and Superior. We enjoyed ourselves, for the site is unique, the only set of four side-by-side ship locks in the world. Robert and I explored them in detail, and all of us took a boat trip through one of the four American locks and back through a fifth Canadian one. Time to leave, we climbed into the Leggets' car for the long drive to the Welland Canal, with an overnight stay on the way. Along the north side of Lake Huron, then turning south we took the ferry across the entrance to Georgian Bay and so on south, by-passing Toronto to Burlington and then east to Thorold to stay at every canal enthusiast's dream of a hotel, the Lock Seven Motel.

It is built on the edge of the embankment to one of the great Welland ship canal locks. As we climbed into bed, we heard the first freighter approach, and I (not I fear Alice Mary, who took it for granted) shot out again to watch the lights of a seagoing ship pass maybe 500 feet from our window. Back to bed and sleep, until through my dreams I heard another one coming. Out again! After the third, even I remained in bed. We stayed several days at the motel, Robert and Mary taking us to explore remains of older Welland Canals back to the first, first opened in 1833. Then to Toronto and England.[3]

After his return, Charles tried to find out more about the Welland Canal, such as the number of locks along it; enquiries with the curator of the Historical Museum in Ontario proved unsuccessful, and it was only in October 1982 that the position was clarified by Dr Roger Squires, an American Canals Society member from Beckenham (Kent).

Charles's account of early waterways in the Netherlands, which he sub-titled 'The astonishing Dutch trekvaarten', relied on an unusual book by Jan de Vries, *Barges and Capitalism*, which broke new ground. This proved to be in English, not Dutch, and written by a respected economic historian from the United States. Charles had quoted an account by the poet Robert Southey of a Dutch passenger boat in *The Canal Age*, but de Vries's study, completed in 1977, revealed that there was a detailed network of waterways, known as *trekvaarten*, built from the 1630s onwards for scheduled passenger carrying; this provided, for an expanding economy, what Charles described as 'Europe's first mass transportation system'.[4] Curiously, this study, which included a detailed analysis of the economic significance of the *trekvaarten* and the organisation of services, had begun with a chance enquiry in an archive in Haarlem.

Charles had followed his trip to Canada by an IWA visit to Belgium, marred by poor weather, and in June 1982 he went on a private trip with the IWA organisers, Ron and Joan Oakley, to visit North Germany and North Holland. During the latter visit, he saw a *trekvaart* in the town of Sneek. By that time, however, Alice Mary had been struck down by the first stage of dementia, with her faculties progressively diminishing. Apart from the emotional consequences, in practical terms this forced Charles to leave the writing of *World Canals* after November 1981 to help complete what would prove to be Alice Mary's last book, on Charles Williams. He had completed this by April 1982.

Charles completed the draft of the Old World chapters by September 1983, and sent it to David Edwards-May for comment and checking; by then his final draft of the New World chapters was complete. While Robert Legget checked the Canadian content of the latter, it was difficult to find other experts who could cover the whole of a country's canal history. He finally completed work on the book on 9 December 1985, and it was published on 27 February 1986.

This should have been a triumphant conclusion to a major long-term project, but by now Charles's personal life was in severe difficulties, with Alice Mary undergoing a steady decline. The day after publication he had to cancel a proposed IWA trip to the Rhine–Main–Danube Canal (then slowly nearing completion), as he no longer felt confident enough to travel far from home, unless it was to destinations which were safely under his control. All holidays with Alice Mary now had to be to such places.

The reception of the book, the first of its kind, disappointed Charles. His somewhat defensive preface claimed only to provide the reader with 'an impression of the pattern that waterway transport has imposed upon time and space',[5] and he stressed that it was not a comprehensive survey. Perhaps he failed to lay sufficient emphasis upon the sub-title, 'Inland Navigation Past and Present', despite the problems which he experienced in persuading D&C to secure it. Unlike the British histories, he covered the postwar period fully.

Six months later he complained that it

appears to have sunk more or less without trace. Apart from 3000 sold to Facts on File in the USA it had sold just over 1000 in the UK up to the end of April. Only one person has written to me about anything I have actually said in the book, and his query came from the first twenty pages. . . . It is very puzzling therefore to know what is happening, if anything. Are people reading it? Have they put it on their shelves, or are they using it as door stops?[6]

He soon expressed further evidence of his disillusion:

I've learned a lot from the reaction to *World Canals*, notably that virtually no reviewer or correspondent of mine is interested in present-day commercial waterways at home or abroad. I reckoned the four 'Since 1945' chapters, two Old World and two New, were informative – but only one reviewer even mentioned them – they all went for the history.[7]

This was not quite true. John Boyes, who was not only co-author of *Eastern England*, but also editor of the Newcomen Society's *Bulletin*, and a regular participant in the IWA overseas visits, reviewed the book in *IWA Waterways*, stressing that Charles rightly draws attention to the new canal age which is with us now and to the work at present in progress. Reconstruction and new construction, virtually unknown to our parochial British outlook, is burgeoning in many parts of the world, involving distances of hundreds and even thousands of miles and engineering work on a scale which dwarfs anything which has gone before.[8]

John Boyes went on to perceive a challenge which has yet to be taken up:

one is still left with the feeling that almost every page embodies the seeds of further research, the accomplishment of which in terms of time and energy is far beyond the capabilities of any one person, even a man of the stature of Charles Hadfield. This is an outstanding, and a pioneer, book. Get it, read it and ponder on its implications.[9]

A much more light-hearted review was provided in *American Canals* by Bill Trout, who asserted that 'our water planet is a canal world, especially designed for us. God must be a canal buff too! We Americans can learn a lot from this book about canals in our own hemisphere; 141 pages of this hard-bound, 432-page work are given over to the New World.'[10]

Charles had no intention of continuing work on *World Canals*, and cancelled subscriptions to American societies, ceased to collect press cuttings, and sold his overseas collections of postcards and other memorabilia. In 1985 he deposited the remainder of his collection, mainly photographs and files, in the recently opened Tom Rolt Centre at the Boat Museum in Ellesmere Port. The book was out of print by 1991.

There was a curious postscript to *World Canals*, in that Charles was approached in 1990 with a proposal to produce extended versions of the Old World chapters, which David Edwards-May would update and translate into both French and German. Interest had been spurred by the anticipated opening of the Rhine–Main–Danube Canal in September 1992, within an apparently newly re-united Europe. It is not clear what became of this project.

HONOURS AND UNFINISHED BUSINESS

Very much had gone wrong since Charles wrote in February 1980 that the seventies were proving to be the best years of his life. There had been honours like that of delivering the annual RCHS lecture, renamed the Clinker Memorial Lecture since Charles Clinker's death in 1981. On 2 November 1985 he delivered this lecture in York on 'The World's Eternal Tortoise: A Thousand Years of Inland Waterways Transport – and Now?', to an appreciative audience.

His move to South Cerney, and his withdrawal from active involvement with British canal history and current events, made him despondent about the move from a London which he greatly missed, along with regular contact with the IWA, ISG, WLIAS and Professor Skempton. Correspondence did not quite replace the personal contact and involvement provided in Little Venice, and Charles's account in Chapter 13 reveals a growing loneliness.

Advisory work for D&C had steadily diminished, reflecting both the collapse in the market and company policy. In 1980 he noted that D&C seemed to be 'gingerly returning to the canal market',[11] but at the end of the same year David told Charles that it was unlikely that either the 'British Isles' or David's 'Regional Railway Histories' series would ever all be brought back into print. Charles took part in D&C's 21st anniversary celebrations, which included a 'Victorian weekend' in the Lake District on 15–17 May 1981. This incorporated a trip on the preserved steam Lakeside & Haverthwaite Railway, linking to a tour up Lake Windermere to the recently opened Windermere Steamboat Museum; a surviving photograph of Charles at this event suggests slight bemusement.

A different publisher, Phillimore & Co., was to publish a book of essays, *Canals – A New Look*, dedicated to Charles. The idea for this came from Mark Baldwin, who drew in Anthony Burton as co-editor; both contributed essays. The long lead time, after it was announced in April 1981, allowed the contributions to be successfully edited and published on 3 August 1984, just before Charles's 75th birthday. It comprised seven essays on themes of interest to him, and a short biography and bibliography of Charles himself. This was followed by two events, the first in Gloucester, where the authors formally presented the new book to Charles. Later in that month there was a joint BWB/D&C celebration, involving lunch and a cruise in London on the Board's *Lady Rose of Regents*. A further honour was that he was made a vice-president of the IWA in October 1982, ironically succeeding Aickman, who had died in February 1981.

In time for Charles's 75th birthday, there were moves to put some of the 'British Isles' series back into print. A new impression of *East Midlands* had been published in 1981, but new editions of two more volumes, *South West* and *West Midlands*, the latter the most popular book in the series, were to be published in 1985. In both cases the book was revised by combining some of the preliminary pages and writing a longer, updating preface. That for *South West* commented mainly on changes on the ground; that for *West Midlands* attempted to provide what other regional volumes had not: notes on the period since 1948. In this, he reflected upon his 1955 trip, summarised the development of the amenity network in the 1960s, noted completed restorations and proposed restorations, and the growth of museums. In both volumes he recalled explorations made to research the books, which were perhaps themselves starting to fall into history, and in *West Midlands* he concluded the new preface on an odd note, scarcely related to its content:

We who love waterways have a world of interest and enjoyment open to us in what our predecessors did. In turn we have to ensure that we do better than they, so that our children will in their time come to study our achievements – and find them both good and enjoyable.[12]

These were Charles's last published words on general canal history. He had been reflecting upon the uses and meaning of history, a theme taken up below.

Charles also needed to update *British Canals*; he had briefly revised this in 1979 for its sixth edition, but for a more radical revision, he employed Mark Baldwin during 1983 to collect and sort material, as Charles felt his own interest had waned. The new edition was published in 1984.

Charles attempted to secure a future for the 'British Isles' series; by 1986 there seemed to be no prospect of publishing new editions of the volumes on Scotland, Ireland and Eastern England which others had written, while no second editions of the four northern volumes appeared. There was a proposal that Mark Baldwin should become general editor of the series, and commission revised editions, but meetings with David St John Thomas in 1984 proved inconclusive. Charles felt that whereas railways which had closed had no further history, many canals which had declined or closed did, given the number of proposed restoration schemes and the interest which these attracted. However, these would mostly need radical revision to bring them up to date; only the *South West* volume did not feature much restoration, and minor updating did suffice. In 1988 he tentatively suggested to David that the *South and South East* volume, where almost every canal featured restoration, could be revised and published in paperback in two volumes. David responded that there was now no market for large expensive books on canals, railways or industrial archaeology, and that only smaller local studies of canals would be viable. In that sense, the wheel had come full circle, back to the aims and approach of the original D&C.

By 1986 D&C was considering reprinting some of the 'Inland Waterways Histories' series, but the last to appear was a third edition of Kenneth Clew's *Kennet & Avon Canal* in 1985. Surprisingly, this included the Foreword written by Charles in 1967, unaltered. Charles continued advising, upon a declining number of book proposals, until D&C was sold to Readers Digest late in 1990. Readers Digest had very nearly acquired the company in 1984, but this move was defeated by D&C shareholders; its main interest seems to have lain in the book clubs and Readers Union.

Amendments in the new edition of *British Canals* concentrated on alterations and extensions to the final chapter. The subjects of these amendments provide a convenient point to consider Charles's concerns in the 1980s. These were restorations, freight development and the viewing of history.

While waterways secured by the Transport Act 1968 had been retained or restored, a burgeoning movement had provided varied schemes for the restoration of waterways which had previously been thought beyond recovery. Charles's views on waterways restoration were influenced by the example of the United States, where waterways which had soon become disused after the railroads opened (not, as often in Britain, long after), featured only fragmentary remains. There was little prospect of restoring these for pleasure-boats, but scope for retaining structures and routes for roadborne visitors. The Chesapeake & Ohio Canal had closed after severe damage by floods in 1924, but the towpath had been retained, the remains of locks and other structures maintained, and a short section restored for use by a trip boat, as part of a National Historical Park.

Charles commended the approach taken by the IWA West Country Branch, where the restoration of short isolated canals was impracticable; they had adopted a similar approach to that in the United States, producing leaflets which highlighted the remains of local waterways. In 1986 the West Country Branch invited Charles to celebrate the 40th anniversary of the IWA, and presented him with a decorated cake honouring the writing which had enlarged their interest in, and enthusiasm for, their local waterways.

Charles felt that this approach should apply to waterways in his locality, like the Wilts & Berks Canal, whose line through Swindon and Melksham had totally disappeared; on page 323 of *British Canals* he commended what appeared to be the approach of the Wilts & Berks Canal Amenity Group. He would be disappointed to find that the Group set full navigable restoration as a long-term goal, and in April 1984 he declined membership for this reason. He was very sceptical about the purpose of the 'Big Dig' to clear parts of the same canal in 1992. Although he did become a member, he twice declined to be president of the Trust which aimed to restore the whole of the Thames & Severn Canal for pleasure-boating.

He continued to support some restorations, including the Kennet & Avon, upon which through navigation was restored in 1990; to the end, he urged the replacement of the Devizes Locks by a marine railway. He particularly supported the restoration of the Rochdale Canal, steadily proceeding since 1974; his visit to it in 1991, with Fred Doerflinger, was one of his last. He also supported the restoration of the Sleaford Navigation in Lincolnshire, partly because it involved a realistic programme, capable of gradual achievement in stages.

In May 1984 the RCHS AGM weekend included a trip on *Sabrina*, owned by the Droitwich Canal Trust, to reopen the top three miles of the canal, which formed an isolated summit level running through Droitwich to Ladywood. John Horseley Denton, a long-standing RCHS member, has recalled how

We began the voyage by passing under a new railway bridge on what was, in fact, a brand new section of canal and we were extensively filmed and photographed by reporters and others as we moved off. The BBC TV unit started to interview Charles on the importance of the occasion and presumably the canal's history but almost immediately we ran aground! The forty or so members aboard were conscripted into a systematic rocking of the boat which enabled the skipper to . . . get us under way again. I seem to remember Charles coolly saying that these things happened in the best circles and then they went on with the interview.[13]

Charles was, in fact, not impressed with the progress of this restoration.

Charles did attend other RCHS events, although the last one in which he spoke was at Gloucester in May 1988, where Professor Barker, then retiring president, arranged the dinner to be given in his honour; I witnessed a very amusing speech which brought to life some of the endearingly eccentric early RCHS members, but in which he expressed his views upon restoration in trenchant style.

The last RCHS AGM which Charles attended was in Oxford in 1991. There a move to rename the RCHS the 'Transport History Society' was unsuccessful, but two new specialist groups were formed, in Road History and in Air Transport. Rather surprisingly, Charles drafted two short papers for the latter, detailing his experiences with the R101 in the 1930s, and the journeys by air taken in 1951 and 1960. However, away from the RCHS, a move in 1990 to revive the small Transport History Group, of which Charles had been a founder member in the 1970s, did not meet with success; Charles himself insisted that he was now too old to assist.

One of Charles's last public appearances was on 11 July 1989; he was asked by the Shakespeare Memorial Trust to open an exhibition to celebrate twenty-five years since the southern Stratford Canal reopened. By this time, negotiations between the National Trust and BWB had resulted in the transfer of this section back to BWB. At this, he paid tribute to the Lower Avon restoration, which was the first to restore a navigation for pleasure-boating and the first to use volunteers, and to the Stratford Canal, the first canal to be restored by volunteers. Their example had led to cooperation with the BWB and then to the Transport Act 1968. In turn, this had meant 'the flowering of a *second* Canal Age so fecund indeed that old men like I am watch with amusement present-day enthusiasts trying to limit this fecundity, which inspires all manner of bankside developments, some a bit peculiar, and some slightly improbable restorations'.[14] He also spoke at a presentation to celebrate the work of Peter White, chief architect to the BWB, at Hillmorton in July 1991. Peter White's essay on conservation in *Canals – A New Look* dealt with themes in which Charles had developed an interest; his views on this are discussed below.

His amended conclusion to *British Canals* in 1984 provided the view of the future which he had declined to provide in previous editions, and one which addressed the concerns of more general transport history:

> an age-old pattern is showing through. . . . Our turnpike mania widened and improved road facilities, and the subsequent canal mania did the same for waterways. The two, along with maritime-linked rivers and canals, made the first industrial revolution. Then came railways, to sweep away much road and water transport alike. But now railways are of minor importance for most freight and passenger carrying except specialised traffics, and we find ourselves back with roads and waterways, fulfilling their old functions, but upon improved roads and improving waterways, and with very different vehicles and craft.[15]

Charles's optimism about the future of freight waterways, 'running fast to keep up with technological, traffic, vessel and political changes',[16] was partly based on the successes of the ISG, in which his involvement had diminished. The ISG's pressure and support had led to the compilation of national waterways traffic statistics on a sound basis for the first time. These confirmed the importance of waterborne freight, although not on the Industrial Revolution canals nor, increasingly, on BWB waterways. The SSYN enlargement had finally commenced in 1979, but by the time it opened in 1983, the recession had reduced the number of customers, and traffic failed to develop. Charles's main BWB contact, Harry Grafton, retired at the end of 1982, and Charles paid tribute to him privately:

> the main change in the inland waterways freight scene has been due to you, Harry, and don't you forget it. How anyone could have kept his cheerfulness and his energy as you did through all those years of many reverses and few successes is a miracle.[17]

However, the reverses continued and the successes became too few and too short-lived. Charles's last involvement with the NWTA was to attend its conference 'Water Freight 80s' on 26 October 1982. There a waterway operator from the Netherlands struck a note of caution which reflected badly on the 700-tonne SSYN enlargement; he asserted that ships below 1,000-tonne capacity could not be operated profitably, and suggested that improvements should be based on a capacity of 1,500-tonnes. General IWA support for the NWTA would be limited; late in 1985 Mark Baldwin had to persuade the IWA Council to pay the annual subscription of £95, when it had just made a grant of £6,000 towards the Yorkshire Derwent campaign. NWTA was subsumed within a much larger organisation in 1993.

Similarly, IWA support for ISG activities was waning. The ISG had proposed to follow up *British Freight Waterways Today and Tomorrow* with a practical guide, *Inland Shipping – How It's Done*. After much preparatory work, the IWA Council refused to sanction expenditure upon it. Despite pressure from Charles, the project had to be abandoned in 1984. He described his reaction: 'I took the stickiness hard – I had originally suggested the title, though done nothing on the book itself, except back it strongly, but a lot of other members had worked very hard.'[18]

The early 1980s saw the beginning of interest in more recent waterways history, going beyond the curious to the factual. One catalyst was Tom Rolt's autobiography of his canal involvement, *Landscape with Canals*, published posthumously in 1977. This evoked an era which was now firmly in the past, when pleasure-boating on canals was minimal, and when the early IWA had developed and diverged. While the latter events were now history, the book had to be shaped to avoid litigation from Aickman, whose own account, *The River Runs Uphill*, would not be published, posthumously, until 1986.

Charles had seen Aickman's manuscript when it was, surprisingly, submitted to D&C for perusal, but commented that his blood pressure would not stand another reading. There was controversy over Aickman's book, when the IWA, perhaps fearing the raking up of old disputes, refused to accept advertisements for the book. Perhaps its appearance in the IWA's 40th anniversary year might have been seen as an official endorsement of its contents. The book displays many of Aickman's prejudices but also his ability to tell a very entertaining story. In later years he became, after all, a writer of fiction.

Further interest developed with Ian Mackersey's researches, in the early 1980s, which concentrated on the history of Tom Rolt's involvement with canals; he tracked down some of the survivors from the 1940s, and studied the IWA minutes from the period. His account detailed people whose books were known, but whose personalities and personal histories were not; in some respects, this was true of Charles. Ian Mackersey's researches included interviews with Charles late in 1981; Charles helped by lending him books and documents. His study was largely complete in 1983, and parts of the book were serialised in *Waterways World* during 1984. Charles completed this serial by relating part of his own story in the same magazine.

Charles's article was one of a number of occasions in the 1980s when he sought to set the historical record straight. In 1983 he was concerned over appeals in *IWA Waterways* for voluntary labour to restore what was reputed to be a navvies' barracks on the Herefordshire & Gloucestershire Canal; he felt that this had no proven historical basis, and secured the deletion of this scheme from restoration projects featured in the magazine.

JESSOP, TELFORD AND THE END

Perhaps Charles's COI background, dealing with information, made him aware of the ease with which information can be handled, suppressed and slanted to make a case, whether in current propaganda or in the presentation of history based on selective reading and falsified records. His work on Jessop had uncovered doubts about Telford's role in the engineering of the Ellesmere Canal, and, as *World Canals* neared completion, he wrote to Professor Angus Buchanan of Bath University in October 1984 about 'an idea for a possible research project in which you might be interested for some of your students. . . . The improbability of it all so intrigues me that I would like to talk to you about it, even if it turns out to be a mare's nest.'[19]

He discussed this with Professor Buchanan in May 1985, and began work himself on a new study in September 1986. He anticipated that he might not complete it, and planned to leave Professor Buchanan the files in his Will, as 'it is on the cards that I shall not live to complete this piece of research'.[20] Charles's highly developed sense of his mortality was perhaps heightened by Alice Mary's deterioration. In an earlier Will, he had arranged to leave his *World Canals* papers to Mark Baldwin in case he did not finish that book, and over what became *Hadfield's British Canals*, he repeatedly told me between 1990 and 1993 that he would not live to read the book.

For what was then called *Telford and William Jessop's Reputation*, he re-established contact with Ailsa Maxwell and Sandy Cameron in Scotland, who had helped with *William Jessop, Engineer*; by July 1987, however, he regarded the research as hamstrung by the failure to locate Jessop's papers. Meanwhile his attention was diverted, not only by the increasing problems of looking after Alice Mary, but by a renewed interest in Africa. Up to December 1988 he spent much time on a partial autobiography, entitled *Round Africa in 80 Years*, which included his reflections on his upbringing and visits back to Africa, and observations from a long holiday to South Africa with Alice Mary in November 1986. His observations on the apartheid regime, which he thought should be left to slowly and gradually reform without outside interference, show how far his political views had moved from those of a 1960s Labour Party member; even the right-wing periodicals in which he sought a platform for his views seem to have been unimpressed.

During 1988 he and Alice Mary visited the Caledonian Canal, which he had never seen from end to end before. He had drafted a chapter on the Ellesmere Canal, with a very detailed analysis of the successive texts in Telford's original and revised accounts of Pontcysyllte. By April 1989 he had drafted his Caledonian chapter and sent it for comment to Sandy Cameron; when his response was anger at what he saw as the demolition of other writers' work, Charles rapidly climbed down: 'I have upset you, and therefore I at once apologise.'[21]

Shortly afterwards Charles wrote that what was now called *Thomas Telford's Temptation* was in abeyance, although he now had a draft manuscript 'in the Hadfieldian sense that it is a written up account of everything I know and is not of course anywhere near being a publishable book'.[22] By that time, there was interest in publishing a shorter version as an article in the *Journal of Transport History*, and Mark Baldwin expressed interest in publication.

Alice Mary finally died in August 1989. Although Charles had long anticipated it, he took the bereavement hard, and seemed, in a sense, to be waiting for his own end. Sonia Rolt, who knew them for nearly fifty years, wrote of 'Charles-and-Alice-Mary': 'It seems natural to think of them collectively because this form of unified creative and lived-out love was what both intended and gave to the world.' She went on to refer to 'the last years, when Charles really wished to be gone to Alice Mary'.[23]

Charles took a long holiday in South Africa in the winter of 1990/1, and began work on a project, not for publication, to write a biography of Alice Mary, so far as possible in her own words. It might have been therapeutic and a means of paying tribute to someone he so greatly admired, but he seems to have become disturbed by his investigations into a life which had not included him. (I must stress that he found nothing derogatory, but she had loved others before him.) By the end of 1990 he was returning to *Telford*, circulating the draft for further corrections. The book was eventually published in 1993; Charles had expected to have to cut it, but Mark Baldwin did not require this.

Charles had expected *Telford* to cause a furore, given Telford's reputation: some years earlier, he had jocularly asserted that 'If I ever get to the end of my research I look forward confidently to spending the rest of my days enjoying myself on the pension that the Institution of Civil Engineers will pay me for not publishing the book.'[24] His thesis was the somewhat pained accusation that Telford, keen on self-publicity, had been tempted deliberately to conceal evidence of Jessop's involvement in the Ellesmere and Caledonian Canals; he could find no other explanation for the way in which Jessop's role, which his chapters clearly established, had been diminished in Telford's autobiography, and the way in which the Jessop papers had disappeared.

Criticisms, often expressed in private, saw this thesis as weak and without foundation. One feature which grated with some was Charles's invocation of 'Miss Marple', Agatha Christie's fictional detective. In 1985 Charles watched a television version of one of her stories, where Miss Marple said something like 'The trouble with you, my dear, is that you believed what you were told. I gave up doing that long ago.' It seems strange that a popular fictional detective should be invoked in an era when so many historians and commentators have engaged in the analysis of inaccurate texts. Maurice Barbey of York neatly demolished Charles's use of 'Miss Marple':

> Unlike Telford and Jessop, Miss Marple is a fictional character. Both the story she is in, and her own reputation in it, are entirely dependent on a) a large number of red herrings being floated around and b) her being the only person able to smell them.[25]

Perhaps Charles's study would have fared better had he left the ambiguities to stand alone, with an open verdict. However, he had experienced for himself the way in which others took the credit for one's achievements; experience and observation of the IWA certainly provided many examples. From the same quarter, he had witnessed people hanging on to convenient myths, and Telford seemed to provide one such example. Some reviewers doubted the explanation of the 'temptation', but approved the scholarly nature of the Ellesmere and Caledonian coverage. Professor Jack Simmons, to whom Charles had dedicated the book, wrote privately and perceptively that 'your inquiry must have been one of the most frustrating possible when nearly all your evidence has to be negative not positive, from the absence of the documents that ought to have helped you to a firm conclusion'. He went on to praise Charles's scholarly prose:

> you have pursued a fascinating inquiry and shown us all the stages it went through, which makes your narrative of it all the more interesting than the plain statement of conclusions: you are actually sharing the whole process with your reader.
>   And of course it is such a bonus to that reader that he finds what you have to tell him written in the English language, the well of English undefiled.[26]

Charles would be the first to describe his own prose as dull; he once expressed doubt to me that anybody had ever read one of his 'British Isles' volumes from cover to cover. Yet his writing was always competent, careful, clear and scholarly, if unsensational. He had very early on mastered the craft of writing; cutting his concise sentences and paragraphs, as I have now attempted twice, proved very difficult.

Telford was not Charles's final publication about canals, for late in 1993 he agreed to prepare short contributions for the *Oxford Companion to Railway History*, edited by Jack Simmons and Gordon Biddle. He contributed sections on William Jessop and (after discussions) on canals until 1840, which were completed in July 1994. The whole volume was published in October 1997; it includes an entry about Charles himself by Gordon Biddle.

Charles's final years involved him in much tying up of loose ends. David St John Thomas, doubtful about other canal books, felt that *British Canals*, Charles's first major book, should be kept in print through successive editions. Charles felt unable to deal with this, but suggested to me in July 1990 that I might produce an entirely new edition, including new coverage of the twentieth century. Roger Sellman's maps were re-drawn, new photographs provided, and the coverage of Ireland and Scotland expanded; a new sub-title reflected the wider coverage. The needs of a new audience had to be addressed, one to whom narrow boat carrying no longer lay in recent memory, and for whom the near-loss of much of the system was a matter of history. Charles's only contribution to the new book was to update the preface slightly; he only read the book through after publication. The book, *Hadfield's British Canals*, was published in 1994.

Charles was also keen to see a new edition of *The Canal Age*, and attempted to persuade two parties to prepare new editions of *Yorkshire and the North East* and *South and South East England*, on similar lines to my own radical revision. In the latter case, he succeeded; Paul Vine, who had by now published extensively about this area, agreed in 1995 to work on a new edition.

Charles's last involvements with the IWA were to display, perhaps, his feeling for history, or perhaps merely his capacity to vacillate between amused inaction and outraged forceful action. They also suggest strongly that he was keen to secure an accurate record of his own life and contribution.

In May 1989 David Bolton of Stratford, who had written *Journey Without End*, an account of three years which he spent living on a boat, wrote in *Waterways World* that he was writing a book which would relate how the waterways had been saved from closure between 1945 and 1965, and how much was owed to particular individuals. Charles agreed to be interviewed by him, and when the book appeared in 1990, it proved to be entertaining and based on much research into primary sources. However, an admiring review described it as 'inevitably, something of a biography'[27] of Robert Aickman, and Charles felt that it focused too heavily on Aickman's involvement; Charles's work on the BWB, the subject of a detailed article in *Waterways World* in 1988, was not mentioned. The book's dust-jacket stated that Aickman had masterminded the waterways campaign, and its conclusion was that the real memorial to Aickman's life was the 3,000 miles of waterways saved from closure.

Charles was at first unconcerned about *Race Against Time*, but seems to have been stirred into action by the conclusions which some in waterways circles had drawn from it. Although its author had covered the involvement of other contributors to the waterways movement, and although he set out the facts about Robert Aickman, including some which did not show him in a good light, some drew the conclusion that Aickman had single-handedly saved Britain's inland waterways – and began to propagate this view.

The possibility of an official IWA history arose as its 50th anniversary approached. IWA Council members were aware of David Bolton's account of its first twenty years, and David Stevenson, then IWA chairman, approached him to write a further book to cover the next thirty years. Charles felt, although others disagreed, that this would be taken to be the second part of an official history and that both the existing and proposed volumes would appear to be endorsed by the IWA as the approved version of events. Perhaps he had in mind the controversy from 1986, over the 40th anniversary and Aickman's own book.

In 1994 Charles therefore, suddenly, threatened to resign from the IWA, and to make his reasons public, if David Bolton's proposed new book was to appear as an official account. He persuaded other prominent and long-standing members to issue the same threat. In the face of this, David Stevenson had to withdraw his invitation to David Bolton, who did not then write the book, although he produced a series of articles on the history of the IWA for *Waterways World* during the anniversary year of 1996. It was uncharacteristic of Charles, who had spent at least thirty years of his life persuading others to write, to try to discourage somebody from writing, especially when they had used primary sources. As will be noted in Chapter 7, he seems to have despaired about the presentation of waterways history in the 1990s, and perhaps made David Bolton a convenient scapegoat for his disillusionment.

Charles also advised that the IWA should change radically after its 50th anniversary had passed. It had, he suggested, become too large, and should disband in a 'blaze of glory' in 1996, reducing to a coordinating role between enthusiast societies and pressure groups like the ISG, with a small direct membership. Not surprisingly, this has not come about.

In 1989 Charles stated that he never intended to write an autobiography: 'Unlike Messrs Rolt and Aickman I have no intention of writing one!'[28] However, in 1974 he had written a private family history, *Youth Shows But Half*, the *Round Africa* project in 1988 was a partial autobiography, and between 1990 and 1992 he worked on an incomplete biography of Alice Mary. In September 1991 he commissioned Harry Arnold, the editor of *IWA Waterways*, who had considerable experience in waterways journalism and photography, to produce a biography. Charles's motives seem to have stemmed from the impending 50th anniversary of the IWA in 1996, and his indication that 'it's important to get down on paper what really happened before the fictional history writers get started'.[29]

Harry Arnold began work, but by December 1993 it was clear that he would be unable to proceed, and, given my interest in how Charles's canal work had developed, a partial biography became possible. Early in 1995 the project which led to *Canal Man and More* began. Charles spent much of his remaining time working on drafts from his autobiographical writings and dealing with my queries, although he was increasingly dogged by illness and decreasing mobility.

He was unconcerned about his eventual demise; as he had put it in September 1992: 'The sooner I can get back to Alice Mary the better!'[30] He had anticipated the need to move to a retirement home in Cirencester as early as the autumn of 1991, but he found sufficient support to prevent this. He and Alice Mary had been assisted by a series of secretaries since they first moved to South Cerney in 1962. He was, in my view, fortunate that his last secretary was Jackie Stratford, whose support extended well beyond her duties; on two occasions her intervention saved his life.

Early in July 1996 he had a stroke; he had come close to one in Canada in August 1986. He was taken to one nursing home, and then another. In my last conversation with him, he told me that I was now on my own with this account of his work, but another visitor, David Hilling of the ISG, had a different response on 25 July:

> I had about half an hour with Charles and in that time we sorted out most of the world's problems. In particular we got on to Africa where he had spent his early days and I had started out my career. . . . it was clear that for both of us, it had been the experience of travelling in Africa, often over great distances, sometimes with considerable difficulty and by different modes that had stimulated our life-long interest in transport, and especially the movement of the many goods on which all of us depend. Charles was, for all who knew him, a great source of encouragement and he was genuinely delighted to know of my own soon-to-be-published work on Transport and Developing Countries. We discussed its content and perhaps inevitably he wanted to know what I was going to do next.
>
> The ISG's *Blueprint for the Future* was also discussed and he expressed his general approval of the ideas presented but with his usual sense of realism. . . .
>
> Charles was in great form that afternoon. He was clearly over the worst of the stroke and little did I think that in just three weeks I would be in Cirencester – this time for his funeral.[31]

On the morning when he was due to return home, on 6 August 1996, he suffered a massive stroke and died immediately. A large funeral followed, at his parish church, attended by representatives of organisations which he had founded as well as family, local and personal friends.

Obituaries appeared in the four main quality daily national newspapers, in the waterways press, and in scattered places like the *Halberton Parish Council Newsletter*. In late August, at the IWA's National Festival in Dudley, celebrating its fifty years, pathways between stalls were named after the founders; thus 'Charles Hadfield Way', named after its last surviving founder, passed near to the ISG stand. Charles would have been amused at this belated acknowledgement. He would probably have been impressed by the ISG's *Blueprint*, a plan for modern freight waterway development to 2025, dedicated to him.

In the opening pages of *World Canals* Charles the historian quoted from *The Book of the Dead*: '"to sail for ever in a boat along those intricate canals where the reeds are continually bending in the heavenly wind" is one of the pleasures of Paradise. Let us hope that it still is.'[32]

There seems little to add to that.

CHAPTER SEVEN

CHARLES HADFIELD'S CONTRIBUTION

It remains to consider Charles's contribution to the fields which he helped to make: the growth of transport history and the making of historical events. His study and appreciation of transport history may be examined in terms of his views about history and its uses, and his contribution to the developing field of transport history; the final section deals with his importance to events and developments which have now passed into history.

CHARLES HADFIELD AND TRANSPORT HISTORY

Charles lived on into an era in which history, presented as 'Heritage', has come to prominence; at its worst, an ossified past provides the setting to achieve sales or is itself the subject of sale. One of the outward manifestations of the development of 'heritage' has been seen both in pressure to maintain the traditional appearance of canals, and in the development, sometimes incorporating an uneasy ambivalence, of 'heritage centres' and museums. Charles's views on the latter were expressed after a visit to the growing Boat Museum at Ellesmere Port in the 1970s. While plans were later changed, it was then proposed to convert the Island Warehouse to 'a two-storey covered area in which the past will be seen becoming the present, traditional boats being built, etc.' Charles voiced some doubts about this:

> To us, who have seen narrow boats actually working, it will be fascinating, but to our grandchildren who have never actually seen a real narrow boat earning its living, what will it really mean? Won't it be similar in kind to the excellent Roman Museum at Cirencester; a vivid reconstruction of an irretrievably dead past? Won't they perhaps be more interested in a museum of early pleasure craft, made out of one of the first pleasure cruising bases?[1]

Charles's general view of all industrial archaeology, was that 'we should work hard at recording, but go easy on preservation'. His caution derived from the long view:

> The most fascinating period to most of us is that of which we just caught glimpses when we were young and that's the period each of us is unconsciously trying to preserve. So when we are making our choices – to preserve or not to

preserve – then if to preserve, how to preserve, we must think less of what we would like to preserve than of what our children will be interested in, for they are the industrial archaeologists of the future and we are building what they will be measuring and recording and preserving. How, in the year 2078, will those of the third generation from us judge us here and now? What shall we have achieved in which they can take an interest, or will our achievement be only what we have preserved and not what we have CREATED?

This evokes his earlier views that former transport canals would need to be *developed* for pleasure use, sometimes using old structures, sometimes involving new ones, and 'it will be the latter, surely, that our children will be interested in'.

Charles was, therefore, interested in recording the past, but opposed to indiscriminate preservation. He stressed that preservation involved choices:

We all agree, of course, that we want to preserve some examples of the work of the past – let us say, a canal warehouse. At once we have choices; do we preserve it unaltered and, if so, do we leave it empty (and empty buildings quickly decay or are vandalised) or do we use it for something quite different from its original purpose – and then what are we preserving?[2]

He urged that preservation for its own sake should not get in the way of progress, with the exception of 'artifacts – boats of all kinds, steam locomotives, buses and suchlike'.

What of Charles's own views of history? He drew a sharp distinction between the industrial archaeologist, observing and recording, and the historian, recreating and interpreting. He suggested that industrial archaeologists were in danger of confusing their discoveries for history:

In our enthusiasm for what we have discovered, we often go further than we ought and appoint ourselves historians. Now history is an art and a difficult art at that. Historians have to recreate the past – let us say the canal age – so that if William Jessop or William Praed of the Grand Junction Canal could be brought back to life, either would recognise the historian's effort as a reasonably accurate picture of what was in fact going on in his own time.[3]

Charles certainly aspired to do this through his accurate factual accounts of canal history. In 1983 Jack Simmons paid tribute in seeking to dedicate to Charles, 'to whom all students of transport history are deeply indebted',[4] his book, *The Railway in Town and Country, 1830–1914*:

as a salute to your really wonderful work on canals. I have made a great deal of use of your volumes, as the footnotes will show. They have what is surely one of the greatest merits any such work can have, and one of the least common: they almost always tell one straight what one wants to know. That is for me one of *the* tests, and they pass it most handsomely. I very much admire the comprehensiveness of what you tell us, based on so much research (your secondary sources were much less useful, I think, than mine) and its excellent organisation.[5]

What about Charles's interpretation of the factual? In many of his writings, space precluded much discussion of what were previously unpresented materials from primary sources. In that sense, he was one of Professor Barker's 'brickmakers'. He suggested that interpretation provided many pitfalls: 'historians have to recreate this past in terms that we, in our very different circumstances, can understand. If they can present without distortion the past to the present, then they understand the art of history.'[6]

Here he invoked two problems: interpretation and distortion. With regard to interpretation, by the 1970s Charles's views leaned towards what Professor D.C. Coleman has described as the 'neutralists' among economic and social historians. For instance, his comments on the human costs of the industrialisation process in Britain come close to those of T.S. Ashton, and opposed to those who criticised industrialisation for its adverse effects on working people, couched in romantic terms, like Tom Rolt, or in those of 'reformist' historians like the Hammonds or E.P. Thompson. Charles felt that it was a mistake to apply today's moral ideas to the past: for those moving from the land to the cities, 'these represented a chance to get out and get on'.[7] There are quite different interpretations of the urbanisation process, historical and contemporary, and its human costs and benefits.

However, Charles usefully attacked the double standards of those who would denigrate the present, including industrial and urban development, in favour of a vision of the past. His warning about the distortion caused by attributing 'present day motives to people who in fact had quite different ones', useful in general terms, could be seen to undermine his own attempts to explain Telford's motivation towards Jessop 150 years before. The dangers of romanticising past artefacts may be compared here to what may be seen as a rose-tinted view of past social conditions. He presented a portrait of paternalistic bosses, presiding over what was 'Basically . . . a human system and its humanity redeemed many injustices. We are in no case to criticise.'[8] He might have disagreed, but it is difficult to see this (and much of the conclusions of the 'neutralists') as an *impartial* view of the past.

Charles felt that the publishing of serious canal books had come to an end by the 1980s. In 1992, he said that

canal books have changed completely. . . . people are not really interested in detailed canal history now. They're interested in what – it would be harsh to describe as fictionalised history – but certainly history with a point of view very prominent in it. In my day I tried to be as impartial as possible, having been brought up in the old tradition of the Oxford University Press of being completely impartial, and so books like mine just don't sell any longer.[9]

These comments were fired by what appeared to him to be increasing numbers of 'historical' studies which appeared not to be based on any factual research, or based on a sketchy reading of secondary sources – much like those pre-war railway articles condemned by Charles Clinker. Perhaps the differences here, however, lay less in unwillingness or incompetence in handling factual sources, than in interpretations of that evidence and the selection of supporting facts (and suppression of others) for presentation. Despite his claim to impartiality, Charles's excellence in investigating, rendering and interpreting primary sources was perhaps not matched by equal skills in considering alternative interpretations of the results of his investigations. To employ an extended version of Professor Barker's metaphor, he may have been a competent builder, but the evidence of his architectural capabilities and flair is unclear. If it is towards interpretation rather than the uncovering of factual detail that future histories must lean, Charles's work on primary sources will be more useful than the working assumptions and interpretations which he employed. This work will stand no matter what alternative approaches and conclusions are formulated.

This discussion of the parochial field of inland waterways, with history written (or attempted) by enthusiasts rather than academics or professionals, is a long way from history produced to academic standards. To the end Charles remained puzzled by the disregard of his work by some academic historians, and the lack of any honours such as the award of honorary degrees.

One instance indicates how his factually accurate histories were apparently brushed aside. At a conference in Swansea, Charles met Michael Flinn, later (from 1967) Professor of Social History at Edinburgh University, and suggested that he might usefully study the Poor Employment Act of 1817, under which the government had subsidised the construction of canals like the Gloucester & Berkeley. Although Charles had written about this in *British Canals*, he was surprised when an article by Flinn subsequently appeared in the *Economic History Review* in 1961 which did not acknowledge his work. Professor Flinn's history of the British coal industry, published posthumously in 1984, included a chapter on transport which resolutely avoided recourse to any of the 'British Isles' work. It preferred to cite Ph.D. theses from the 1950s rather than Charles's work, or failed to use his work to track down and use the primary sources upon which it was based.

Against this, it has to be said that many academic historians admired Charles's work. These included Dr Gerard Turnbull of Leeds University, then co-editor of the *Journal of Transport History*, whose 1987 review essay of *World Canals* acknowledged that 'Academic historians have been slow to absorb the implications of Hadfield's work.'[10] He attributed this to a disinterest in canal history, apparently sandwiched between an emerging academic interest in turnpike history and studies of the major significance of the railways to economic history. The 'British Isles' series volumes, he stressed,

made available a wealth of detail on numerous topics not previously accessible. He did not set out to write the economic history of canals. He invited others to do that and, in order to help them, he deposited not only his books but also his research files in the . . . London School of Economics.[11]

Charles regarded these files as a quarry for academics to use and develop, although it is not clear how many have consulted his LSE research files. His largest contribution to history lay in the opening up of a previously unknown and poorly researched field, taking advantage of the major widening of sources provided inadvertently by nationalisation. While future historians may need to return to his records to develop more detail, so much of the essential searching and sifting has been carried out that nobody will need to repeat this work. Much the same applies to his work on Jessop, where the foundations are clearly laid. However, there are far too limited signs that anything is being built on these foundations.

Dr Turnbull pointed to a second contribution made by Charles. In researching his history of the carriers Pickfords in 1965, he had early on received from Charles 'the unsolicited loan of his file notes from canal company records which contained references to Pickfords. This was a degree of generous sharing of research which I had, and have since, not experienced very often, an openness which raises certain guilt feelings when contrasted with much academic practice.'[12] One legacy of historians is the assistance and encouragement which they can provide to others. While many investigators of transport history have encouraged others' efforts, it is a field with a minority of jealous hoarders and Job's comforters. Charles would answer the most trivial queries patiently, rather than brush them away. He sought to develop his successors, and usually provided personal encouragement; as Christine Richardson, a more recent canal historian working on a study of James Brindley, has put it: 'he "collected" canal historians. Like a gentleman angler he "played" us well, landing us from the bank from where we went off to research the subject Charles had always intended.'[13]

D&C was one useful fishing ground, as was the RCHS. The former, which grew far beyond Charles's expectations (if not David's) was a catalyst which enthused a generation not only in reading transport history and industrial archaeology but also in producing, and seeing published, their own work. Its effective withdrawal was one factor, among others, which has tended to stall the growth of serious transport history and industrial archaeology.

Charles's contribution to the literature of waterways history was to enter a field which was practically barren, and to leave it fertile and cultivated, if no longer quite flowering in the same way as it was by the early 1970s. Before he began research, there were only a number of out-of-print books, and T.S. Willan's work, to inspire interest; after him, there was a whole literature and numerous practitioners in a well-tilled field. Yet it bears repeating that Charles attributed much of his own work in history and transport to a single man, Tom Rolt, and a single book: 'little of it, except maybe one or two canal histories, would have happened had not *Narrow Boat* been written. The time, the need and the man came together to produce the book.'[14] Charles was one who developed the seeds sown by Tom Rolt, and by T.S. Willan, and while his lighter works have served their ephemeral purpose, his solid historical work in the 'British Isles' series, *Jessop* and *World Canals* will stand, even if copies are available only in libraries and second-hand bookshops, and even if the fertile literature for which Charles hoped lies somewhat fallow. They are unlikely to be superseded. As this book may have demonstrated, Willan, Rolt and Hadfield did not set out to propagate a literature in some linear form of progress; much is owed to the unintended and inadvertent turn of events. Such, perhaps, is history.

Charles's motives for his work may be discerned from his own account in this book, but he did expound a sense of order:

> I have always maintained that one way to happiness in life is to be the greatest living expert in *something* – whether it is the history of a canal or a locomotive or a parish or a building . . . Because when you seek excellence like that (and having sought it, put your knowledge on paper for others to learn from) you have given yourself your place in life – alongside all the others who have also sought excellence and become the greatest living experts on their subjects.[15]

He drew personal satisfaction from his work, in Jack Simmons's words, 'remaining the standard work for much of his life: let alone the galaxy that shines around it'.[16]

CHARLES HADFIELD AND THE MAKING OF HISTORY

Unlike some historians, Charles was keenly interested in the future. One instance is his angry response in 1990 when the Chartered Institute of Transport, of which he had been an associate member since leaving the BWB, wrote to advise him that he would only now be considered an affiliate member, as it was assumed that his connection with transport lay with history. Ceasing membership, he retorted: 'I am, and always have been, a transport man, for, as you well know, transport cannot be stratified: tomorrow's is projection, today's is actuality, yesterday's is history.'[17] He detailed his involvement with transport, not its history, for forty years, which can be summarised by abbreviations: IWA, PIANC, BWB, ISG and NWTA.

His contribution to the present position of Britain's canals has partly been to assist in their popularisation; even if interest in serious history has subsided, Charles's histories helped to enlarge popular interest in canals in a way which academic work like that of T.S. Willan, on its own, did not. Perhaps more marginally, they influenced the survival of historic structures, at least through the raised historical awareness of those pressing for retention. Here his contribution was as one of a generation, mostly born in the first twenty years of the twentieth century, which has helped to raise and develop public awareness of the history of transport, engineering and industry.

To my knowledge, the detailed history of the movement towards transport history and industrial archaeology has yet to be written, while its impact on the preservation and interpretation of historic environments, and in turn on the development of 'heritage', has yet to be interpreted and assessed. If that task is ever carried out, Charles Hadfield will feature prominently among many others like Tom Rolt, Michael Rix, Professors Willan, Simmons and Skempton who, in highly diverse ways, contributed to literature and practice.

What was Charles's role in the retention of Britain's smaller waterways for amenity use? It is probable that the IWA would have been founded without him, but it is hard to speculate what would have transpired had Robert Aickman been defeated by the dissenters in 1950 and an alternative organisation formed in which Charles could have played a part. The alternative IWA would have been better informed, but probably more prone to defeat and prepared to accept priorities and compromises. Charles's exclusion meant that he only played a small part in this movement.

His part in the 1963–6 British Waterways Board is the most significant; his early proposals for an amenity network was an unequivocal catalyst for change in what could have been a very stagnant environment. It was perhaps fortunate that he was addressing an audience of incomers, who did not share the reluctant defeatism of those who had run the waterways before 1963. The contribution of Sir John Hawton, the chairman, and Arnold Allen, the general manager, between 1963 and 1968, must not be underestimated. They knew that the Treasury would argue against the costs involved in the retention of an amenity network, but also knew how to present the case in the right terms. They could have easily dismissed Charles's initial ideas as impractical and continued the course begun by the first chairman, to cut back and minimise financial losses.

Much, however, relied on the right environment: a growing holiday industry, increasing numbers of legislators who had experienced pleasure-boating, a more realistic and supportive pressure group in the IWA after 1966, and a government which regarded public expenditure restraint as a painful vice rather than a virtue. To say that any individual or group of individuals 'saved' the waterways is to fly in the face of history; *Narrow Boat* might never have been published, Robert Aickman might have found some other outlet for his energies, Charles might have become MP for Paddington North or written about quite different subjects, but there would still have been some pressure to preserve and develop inland waterways for amenity, although it might have been pursued in different ways and by quite different people. Pressure to develop amenities and conserve historic environments was developed in other fields during the same period. Unquestionably, though, Charles influenced the shape of that process; the right person in the right place at the right time, he applied the right kind of pressure at the right moment.

If others continue to be awarded the credit for Charles's achievements, this would not surprise him. In another context, he expounded his view that 'with the politician, public man, side of me, I know that the old rule applies, "One can *never* achieve anything and get the credit". That is because one needs to give someone else the credit in order to get most things done.'[18] He was writing about Fred Doerflinger of the ISG, but he could well have been writing about his own work. What of the private man, implicit in his statement? There was undoubtedly a private man behind his writing, but that remains private, and in a study of his contribution speculation about his possible aspirations and disappointments comes close to irrelevance.

What of Charles's influence over the development of modern freight waterways? His efforts in this direction went unrewarded, despite the apparent flow of events and expectations in his direction. The ideas which he put before the BWB helped to publicise, within BWB, the need to investigate the freight possibilities of barge-carrying vessels, and the viability of enlargements. It cannot be said that any flowering of modern waterways transport resulted, although modernisations slowed the pace towards probable extinction upon the BWB waterways. His efforts in founding the ISG did publicise the need for national public information about waterways, including freight waterways outside BWB control, and influenced the course of information gathering, even if little of this has yet been put to use.

The enthusiasm fostered by the ISG in the early 1970s, however, was not followed through. Against a background of economic crisis, investment generally dominated by short-termism, and, in the transport industry, the massive and unforeseen impact of containerisation, linked in Britain to road haulage, calls for national waterways freight planning, a national government policy (still awaited), and major public investment could not be expected to be well received or acted upon. In this respect Charles was unsuccessful and not influential, although his writings, especially on overseas waterways, and the ISG which he founded, are still in place should the tide turn. One influential participant summed up the position in 1984: 'Very few people know the real facts behind the battles with Governments. . . . Had we allowed the politicians to win we would have lost a lot of the system by now. The mandarins still want to kill off the freight waterways.'[19]

Signs that the tide could turn are provided by the impact of the environmental movement, ranging from anti-road protests, through concerned and transforming professionals to the kind of free-market environmentalism which has meant, in Andrew Ross's memorable phrase 'every major corporation transforming its image overnight into that of a gentle green giant'.[20] Should this move from rhetoric towards realities, modern freight waterways must play a part in a transport system which respects rather than exploits this planet's potential. Charles and others have ensured that the ideas have been committed to paper, and they may be resurrected from the history to which they are temporarily assigned. The ISG's latest publication, *Blueprint*, which sets out a plan to develop modern freight waterways till the year 2025, under preparation when Charles died, suggests one way forward.[21]

As Charles so often found, and his life and work illustrate, when the conditions are right, individuals can foster what appear to be miraculous changes in ideas and practice. When they are not, individuals appear as lone prophets, even as cranks. So far as the period of British canal history since 1945 over which Charles had some influence is concerned, when a full historical account is finally written, it will have to reflect this factor.

Single-handed saviours rarely exist outside the world of fiction. Charles often quoted Charles Williams's phrase expressing the choice between 'the King for the kingdom or the kingdom for the King'. Charles was more interested in furthering the kingdom which he made than in exalting his own leading role. Yet his own insistence on the important part played by others should not be used to deny his own significance.

PART TWO

Scenes from a Life by Charles Hadfield

EDITED BY JOSEPH BOUGHEY

CHAPTER EIGHT

TRANSVAAL BOYHOOD

I remember sitting in my brown wood high-chair, pushing large coloured beads that ran on a wire round the semicircle of the tray. At Mountain View, with its white walls, deep pillared stoep [verandah] and corrugated iron roof painted green, my memories begin. The house was on the hillside of Orange Grove, a suburb of Johannesburg – a small garden and hedge in front, a rough road to other houses, and then a sharp drop to an old quarry. From our stoep we could look down to the tramlines from the city running to Norwood, and beyond the brown veld stretching far and flat into the distance.

Early memories jumble: of running out of the house at my mother's call, to watch a crowd of strikers dynamiting a tram in the 1913 Rand riots; of my dislike for my Scottish nurse, Cooper, who had succeeded my beloved fat African Esther; of the little girl next door and I taking off all our clothes under the hedge by our front gate to settle an argument upon our respective structures; and of running into my parents' bedroom one morning only to burst into tears when I found my mother in bed with a strange man. I took a deal of persuading it was still my father even though he had shaved off his moustache.

Maybe to each memory I can attribute a subsequent conviction. Certainly I never had any race feeling – I regarded Africans as people like everyone else. That I disliked Cooper so much was perhaps my first reaction to undemocratic authority, to which I have never taken kindly; joining my girlfriend under the hedge my first essay in romantic love; losing my father in my imagination a foretaste of losing him just after my seventeenth birthday. I knew irrevocability then.

My father, Alexander Charles, was a New Zealander. An odd family, my father's. Hadfield is a widespread Derbyshire name; my own part of it came from near Edale in the Peak District. In the 1770s sons moved to Manchester and manufactured fustian (corduroy) so successfully that my great-grandfather Joseph was able to make the Grand Tour in 1779 and meet Voltaire. In November 1784, aged twenty-five, he sailed for America to collect considerable debts owing to the firm from before the Revolutionary War, and in about May 1785 visited George Washington at Mount Vernon and was taken over his plantation by the general – I suppose one of the first Englishmen to meet him after the war. Joseph endears himself to me by his determination to see whatever was to be seen, for I also am a globetrotter. Moving to Canada, he was paddled in an open bateau from Montreal up the St Lawrence, through the earliest locks, to Lake Ontario and Niagara.

There he got down under the falls. 'I had heard', he wrote, 'of this body of water being so great as by its density to become opaque. I was determined to prove it. I entered boldly . . . I did remain long enough to ascertain it, for I found the heat to be so intense my breathing became difficult, and in a violent perspiration I sought the opening and was happy to emerge freely again.' Then he went back to Montreal.

He also held definite views on women. After visiting the Ursuline convent in Quebec, where he argued celibacy with two of the novices, he wrote: 'certainly Heaven never formed woman for a life of celibacy, at least for women under thirty. At a more advanced age their life cannot be better devoted than in attending the sick and such like useful institutions.'[1] Anyway, he had a good eye for the sex, for he later married Amelia White, daughter of a Bengal Army general, whose enchanting golden hair and blue eyes under a poke bonnet are on a miniature in the Victoria & Albert Museum. Though now thirty-five, he wasted no time with eighteen-year-old Amelia; they had sixteen children. He lived to be ninety-two, she eighty-four.

The business was judiciously disposed of, and Joseph became a gentleman of leisure, living first on the Continent, later at Bonchurch in the Isle of Wight. His youngest son and tenth child, Octavius, born in 1814, was my grandfather. Clever, but suffering from asthma so badly that he had to leave both Charterhouse and Pembroke College, Oxford, he decided when twenty-one to be a missionary. Joseph who, I imagine, was an eighteenth-century rationalist, faced his youngest son with liberal distaste: 'I would prefer him to become a chimney-sweep rather than a missionary,' he said, 'but he is a sincere enthusiast, and it's useless to annoy him by making any objection to his plans.'

Octavius, aged twenty-three, sailed for Australia via Simons Bay at the Cape in a 600-ton sailing ship: it took him four-and-a-half months. At Sydney he was ordained deacon, and went on to New Zealand to join the Paihia mission at the Bay of Islands in December 1838. In 1904, having cured his asthma, translated portions of the bible into Maori, championed his protegés, as he regarded them, more than once against the Government before later becoming adviser on Maori affairs, bishop of Wellington and first primate of New Zealand, he died, aged ninety. He and his wife Catherine Williams, the daughter of archdeacon Henry Williams, another missionary, had ten children.

Devotedly religious, learned, practical, determined, constructive, obstinate, speaking his mind too often, grandfather was a remarkable man. It is odd to read his biography,[2] his letters and writings: every now and then I find a phrase I could have used myself, and then, over the page, another I could never use. Such is ancestry.

His fourth son was my father Alexander, born in 1864. After two years in Corfe's House at Christ College, New Zealand, during 1877–78, he was sent to Trent College in Derbyshire. (I have a leather-bound copy of J. MacGregor's *The Rob Roy on the Jordan*, stamped with the Trent College insignia, and awarded to him at Midsummer 1879 for mathematics.) By 1883 he was back in

New Zealand. He then read law, and on 23 December 1889 was admitted barrister and solicitor (one can be both in New Zealand). However, he seems to have left the law about 1896 and taken to working on farms. In 1899 he joined the 2nd New Zealand contingent to the Boer War as a private, and sailed in January 1900. His war medal is inscribed '373 Corpl A.C. Hadfield, NZ'land M.R.' {Mounted Rifles}. He arrived in time to fight in the battle of the Tugela River before contracting typhoid and being invalided home.

Back in New Zealand in August 1900, stiff-legged and -footed from the effects of typhoid, he took a temporary job as a committee clerk to the Legislative Council. When it ended, he tried for another, but failed. He seems not to have recovered his health, for the bishop wrote to his brother Henry on 15 August 1902: 'I am sorry Aleck has been disappointed . . . If his health was stronger I should advise him to take up law again and work in the country . . . his abilities are much greater than half the country lawyers.'

Maybe he remembered the stretching veld, the bright stars, the sound of the crickets, and the clear air of South Africa. As early as August 1902 he had return in mind, and on 12 November 1902 signed on as seaman on the *Surrey* of 3,497 tons for the voyage to Port Natal, where he was discharged on 30 December. He was back. In June 1903 he was enrolled as an attorney, and set out to learn a new kind of law, Roman-Dutch, before becoming a Transvaal Colony magistrate. There, at Barberton, a decaying small gold-mining town in the eastern Transvaal, he met his fate, and I became a possibility.

They must have made a striking couple: my father, 6 ft 3 in tall, black-haired and -moustached, blue-eyed, an outdoor man's man, a racing man, rising forty-four; and Marion Francis Fulford, vicar's daughter from Devon, now a nurse in the Barberton railway hospital, herself almost 6 ft, handsome, with masses of fine brown hair and a very fair skin, over thirty. But 'vicar's daughter' does not fully describe my mother.

The Fulfords are an old Devon family. The elder branch still live at Great Fulford, a manor house at Dunsford between Exeter and Moretonhampstead; the younger branch, mine, had moved to Crediton, later becoming serge manufacturers. My grandfather, artistic, musical, something of an original, was for much of his life an ecclesiastical architect, working for Fulford, Tait & Harvey, church architects, of Exeter. A restorer of Devon churches, once reviled, now respected, he turned parson in later life. His temperament being unsuited to Devon vicarages, he spent his holidays tricycling through France, Belgium and Austria with an easel on his back, painting good watercolours. When that palled, he took his son and three daughters to livings abroad. First to Ballarat in Australia, where he met his match in the gold-miners of that day; and later to Grenada in the West Indies.

My mother herself then took to roving before the century's turn: to Sweden in 1896 and to Smyrna in a French ship to become companion to a Frenchwoman. Not liking either Smyrna or her employer, she came back on a French ship during the Fashoda incident, over which France and Britain approached the brink of war.

Deciding then to become a nurse, she trained at Battersea General Hospital, and in 1901 went to South Africa, where her brother, formerly a merchant sailor, had gone through the Boer War and was now in the police. After a spell nursing in an African general hospital, she transferred to the railway hospitals and found herself at Barberton in 1903.

My father was appointed Assistant Resident Magistrate in the small rural town of Pietersburg in the northern Transvaal from 1 February 1906. My mother, who seems to have been based at Pretoria, was in Pietersburg between 28 October and 3 December 1906.

It must have been then or soon afterwards that they became engaged. On 30 November 1907 they sailed together for England, and were married on 29 May, in grandfather's Hennock Church, near Bovey Tracey in Devon. Then they went back to Pietersburg, having bought as a basis for housekeeping a full canteen of Prince's Plate table silver engraved with 'H' that, some eighty-nine years later, still serves me every day. There, on 5 August 1909, I was born, a month or two before my father was transferred to Johannesburg, and almost nine months before the independent dominion of the Union of South Africa was formed from the four older colonies. The local Pietersburg newspaper's contributor was obviously an Afrikaner unaccustomed to English, for he wrote: 'Congratulations to Mr and Mrs Hadfield on the birth of a fine son. Our estimable Assistant Resident Magistrate is exceedingly well pleased with joy over the happy event.'

I am, therefore, what Kipling called one of the native-born, with a colonial-born father whose own mother was herself also born in New Zealand. The British Empire came naturally to me as a fact: I never thought or felt it to imply domination, but always as being part of a family. Octavius had known the Maori as equals before God; my mother had nursed African lepers and railwaymen; my uncle commanded Afrikaner and African policemen; I had black Esther as my nurse, and our house-boys as my friends. When later I went to school, I learned alongside English, Afrikaners and Jews, being taught English Language and Literature by Mr Rocher, an Afrikaner master himself of French Huguenot descent. My next girlfriend after her of the hedge, when I was about twelve, was Lexie van Dalsen, whom I adored from afar, the pretty fair-haired daughter of the local Afrikaner bank manager.

At the end of 1911 my parents paid a visit to England, taking me with them, and returned in early 1912; one way on *Guildford Castle*, the other on *Dover Castle*. I have one memory of the visit, of winning the 'chalking the pig's eye' competition at the ship's sports. For a long time I possessed a little souvenir mug with the crest of the *Dover Castle* – my prize.

Around Johannesburg I quickly learned something of family quarrels. My mother used to tell of the threatened Israelite native rising. Asking her house-boy whether, if fighting came near, he would kill her, he replied, smiling broadly: 'No, missus. I kill next door missus; next door boy kill you.' In 1913 there were the Rand strike riots. Then in 1914 my mother and I left for a holiday at Parys on the Free State side of the Vaal River which forms the Transvaal boundary.

I was five when I looked out of the first floor lavatory window of our hotel, and saw de Wet's rebel commando unsaddling in the courtyard. The rebellion, joined by about 10,000 Afrikaners led by Generals De Wet, Beyers and Kemp, was a protest against South Africa's decision to invade German South West Africa at the beginning of the First World War. My father, acting like God to me, sent down a Johannesburg taxi to a farm across the river, where the driver enterprisingly immobilised it and hid it behind a haystack. A little Afrikaner girl in bare feet brought a note across the river to my mother; and that night we crept out on foot, crossed the dam in the dark, and reached the farm. Five golden sovereigns for their kindness, and we were on our way in the dawn, a revolver beside the driver on the front seat, my mother and I out of sight at the back. Farm gates cross African country roads every few miles, and at each we expected to find a rebel guard. But there were none to stop me as I hopped out to open the gates, and, more quickly still, hopped back. So we came to Johannesburg and my father, coming out of his club to greet us.

I was now sent to a sort of pre-preparatory school in a private house kept by someone called Blacklock. But not for long. I was taken away when my mother, who all her life seemed to enjoy danger, decided in 1915 to visit her sisters in England. So, sharing a coupé on the train, we set off for Cape Town to embark on the *Miltiades*. Of the Aberdeen Line, this was one of the last passenger steamer lines to give their ships a bowsprit and figurehead.

I loved South African trains. With single-line, 3 ft 6 in gauge track, speeds were low, and we used to take 48 hours to cover the near thousand miles from Johannesburg. While we went to supper in the dining car, the attendant converted our day compartment into two sleeping bunks, and while we breakfasted, he turned it back again. In between, one could sit on tip-up seats on the balcony ends of the coaches to watch the veld go by, the wide Karroo across which the line runs straight to the horizon. I used to lean out to watch the driver and fireman: when not working, they sat one each side on a little seat swung outside the locomotive cab, to get away from the boiler's heat. When we stopped, Africans would sell us oranges, and later we would watch ostriches racing the train. Then the Hex River pass, the edge of the plateau on which the interior of South Africa lies, down which the train snaked its way. Once past the Hex, the train ran through fruit and wine country to Cape Town, Table Mountain and the sea.

For me, all mountains are epitomised in Table Mountain, its flat top usually hidden in its cloudy cloth that, so I had read, was there because two Dutch dwarfs held an endless contest beneath its summit to decide who could puff his pipe the longest. All seas, too, and all sands are in the great white-foamed breakers of the Cape – the blue, deep blue sea.

I remember nothing of the voyage, and of this second visit to England in six years, only a few incidents. We stayed in my aunt Ada's house in Bedford Terrace, off Tavistock Hill at Plymouth, and from the window of her first-floor sitting room I could watch the flash of the Eddystone light. There was no rationing, but sugar was hard to get, and I remember returning from a grocer's, proud of a 2 lb bag of granulated that I had obtained. The highlight of our Plymouth visit was the snowman. I had seen a few flakes of snow once in Johannesburg, and tried to catch them before they melted, but here was real, deep snow. I made a full-sized snowman by my standards, and crowned him – her – with my aunt's oldest hat. There was another moment, when I looked out from the blackout curtains of our Lancaster Gate hotel room in London, to see a Zeppelin caught in centred searchlights, and heard the clatter of the anti-aircraft guns.

The submarine danger was greater when the time came to return. My mother bought me an inflatable waistcoat, and we slept in the saloon and not in our cabin. It was very rough all the way across the Bay of Biscay and further south. My mother, when able to say anything, passed on the news that we were being followed by a submarine. Peering hopefully over the stern, I failed to spot it, but we put into Dakar, where I sent my mother ashore to get me some Senegal stamps. The submarine shaken off, we left for home.

I was now sent to a girls' school, St Andrews, which took a few miserable boys in the lowest form. It was shameful to creep to school surrounded by hordes of girls, large, small, short, tall, all laughing, I felt, at me.

In March 1918 all three of us set off for New Zealand. My father must have saved his leave, and wished my mother to meet his family. It was, of course, still wartime, and we went to Australia in the Union-Castle's *Balmoral Castle*, currently an HM Australian troopship, bringing back Australians from the Gallipoli campaign. I frequently got under the barrier to fraternise with the troops, thus acquiring Anzac badges and buttons for one of my by then numerous collections, when not leaning over the bow watching the paravanes cutting through the water and, I understood, thereby pushing aside any mines we might encounter.

We called at Fremantle, Albany, Adelaide, Melbourne and Sydney, where we arrived during a race meeting week. Our hansom-cab driver, having tried several hotels, eventually offered us a bed in his own house, which we thankfully accepted: I slept on a sofa.

My mother was so bad a sailor that she was sick before she reached the boat. I remember supporting her up the gangway of the *Manuka* for the voyage to New Zealand while my father, a true New Zealander who picked quarrels with Australians on principle, fought a rearguard action up to the ship.

New Zealand did not interest me. I spent almost all the time with my aunt Nina at the small town of Marton, where I was parked while my parents went to see such interesting things as the geysers at Rotorua. Existence was, however, mitigated by my aunt's four step-daughters. They taught me to ride a girl's bicycle. At least, they put me on one and, so eager was I to learn, I started off downhill without enquiring how one stopped. At the bottom I met a main road, then occupied by a timber waggon. I festooned myself over a few planks protruding from the tailboard; the bicycle went beneath. Sorting myself out, I was delighted with my new experience, and frequently borrowed the bicycle. Much later, at Wolmaransstad, my father bought me a pony, hoping I would become a horse-lover like himself. But I disliked and feared my pony, which had no brakes. My father sold him and bought me a bicycle instead, which, by judicious use of the back-pedal brake, I could turn in its own length in the dusty road. I was suited, but my father sadly realised that I was not his kind of boy.

In July we returned, catching the troopship *Marathon* from Sydney to Durban, arriving in mid-August, and thence travelled by train to Johannesburg. We had no house, and now lived in the first-floor front rooms of Roseneath boarding house, a big detached building in Park Town which had a superb bath with a canopy, and rows and rows of knobs which, when pulled, manoeuvred water out of all kinds of improbable apertures. I was there on 11 November, when the war ended.

I was then put to the preparatory school of St John's College, and had been there most of the Lent term when I went down with typhoid, which, as was later found, I had caught from a carrier at a hotel where we had spent a few nights. Fortunately, my mother being a trained nurse, I was kept at Roseneath. I had five or six weeks in bed, and so missed the Victory processions. I was very ill for a time, but all I remember was an endless longing for golden syrup, which the doctor eventually prescribed in minute doses. Typhoid left me with what my mother alleged were weak ankles. I never noticed them myself, but later this interesting complaint was to get me off all compulsory football.

Back to St John's, and then, catastrophe; at the beginning of 1919 my father, who had spent ten happy years being a character in his Johannesburg court, was moved for the last three years of his career, nominally on promotion, to the little western Transvaal town of Wolmaransstad. This meant boarding school. I was entered for P.T.S., Park Town School, though it was no longer at Park Town, but on the top of the hill and beyond our old house at Orange Grove. I was 10½, and I had never been away from my parents.

Wolmaransstad was some eight hours by train from Johannesburg to Maquassi (now Makwassie), then nine miles by car. As one entered the long main street one came on the left to a big hard-baked open square where the Afrikaner farmers would gather for 'Nagmaal', a communal Holy Communion. On the right the Makwassie Hotel, A. Lewinsohn, proprietor. Beyond was the town hall with its little tower, also on Saturday nights the cinema, and on one Sunday morning a month, the Anglican church. Beyond, on the left, the Residency, where we lived, with a flagstaff outside our white gateposts, and, across the road and a strip of veld, the spruit or stream where whiskered barbel swam, and ox-waggons crossed at the ford. On our side of the square were shops, on the top side, facing the hotel, the post office and my father's court.

Wolmaransstad was what the locals called a dorp – a miserable little town. I loved it.

The Residency was a large bungalow: facing it, at the right-hand end of the stoep, was my room, where I slept and had my books and my collections. Round two sides of the house, fruit trees of many kinds – I remember peach, plum, quince, almond, figs, and of course vines. At the back, a baked open space for games. Beyond, the servants' quarters, the water tank that a prison gang came and hand-pumped full once a week, and Bridget's sty. Bridget was my black pig. On the fourth side was our vegetable garden, and, surrounding all our land, a double row of tall trees in which the vinks [weaver-finches] built their swaying woven nests and laid the eggs I sought amid peril of hornets for my collection. House and garden occupied me – I read, climbed trees, built huts, lived a hundred boys' lives. When these palled, I explored the town, calling at the Indian-owned stores, the library, the post office, my father's court, or rode out over the veld on my bicycle.

These were highlights: on Saturday nights I went in the taxi to fetch the film from the station, then helped unpack it and load the projector, finally seeing the film from the projection box. My parents were dim below. At the end of the performance, the piano would pound out 'God Save the King'. My parents and a few others would stand stiffly: the Afrikaner majority tramp out. We took it calmly; so did they. Views having been asserted, five minutes later my father would have been found propping the hotel bar alongside those who had tramped.

Every now and then was diamond-buying day. In those days Wolmaransstad was a centre for widespread alluvial diggings. I often used to go out with my father or one of the policemen to the diamond fields, among the shanty towns, where white or black families lived in tents, sacking huts or houses made of flattened petrol cans. Claims had been staked, and each man worked away, digging the gravel. When he had enough, it was washed, and then picked up a sieveful at a time. The sieve inverted and tipped on to a table, the heavy diamond, if there were to be one, would be at the top. Dozens of times a day the sieve was turned, and each time the digger and his helpers peered at the wet stones, longing, searching for the elusive money the dull stone represented. For in those days there was much distress on the diggings: my father and mother collected money and helped to organise relief works.

Beside Lewinsohn's hotel a row of little cubicles stretched down the street. Here the buyers sat, one to a booth, while the diggers moved down the row, seeking the best price. No cheques, of course: only banknotes. If I kept quiet I was allowed to sit in a cubicle to watch the buying and selling, the weighing of the stone on carat scales, the careful examination under the magnifying glass, the thoughtful pause, the bid. Sometimes the seller would nod; more often he would silently replace the stone in its little wash-leather bag, and go to try his luck next door. I was used to Johannesburg's gold mines, though all one saw was the dust blowing off the powdery white dumps beside each mine. But on the diggings one could see the mining; in the cubicles see the diamonds.

Once a month, Mr White the Anglican parson came – his parish as large as an English county. He would arrive on Saturday to sleep in our spare room. My mother and I would get our drawing room ready for early Communion service, and after the Saturday night film we would re-arrange the Town Hall seats and prepare an altar. Morning Prayers on Sunday was a town event. There were only half-a-dozen Anglicans: the rest of the congregation consisted of Roman Catholics, Nonconformists, Jews, a selection of members of the Dutch churches, and the Theosophist lady who ran the library. Hymn books having been distributed from the parson's box, my mother at the piano, I stood next to my father and obliged. I never could sing a note correctly, but he didn't mind, though in the home I was a sore trial to my musical mother. The service over, the parson came home to lunch, then set off to take evening service thirty, forty miles away.

All in all, Wolmaransstad suited me fine. An only child with busy parents, my father in court, in meetings, or just talking, my mother housekeeping, organising servants, chairing committees, running fund-raising functions, giving tea and dinner parties, I liked being on my own while knowing I was at home, within the framework of the family. I knew some boys, of course, but had no wish to know them better, and stoutly resisted all efforts to make me cooperate and be sensible. I am glad I did, for my life's foundations were being laid.

I hated boarding school: not school, but boarding school, being cooped up with boys and masters, Give me learning, I might have cried, but give me freedom too. My wife hated boarding school too. Both feeling that children should be brought up at home, we sent our children to day schools, private or State as came most convenient.

I had many enemies, and a few friends. Of the enemies, Fishy was the greatest. Fishy was the headmaster's wife. When I used to say, 'Can I go upstairs?' she replied: 'You can. The question is, may you?' I could have strangled her. Sweet days were worse. Sweets, a bag for each boy, were kept locked in a cupboard, being replenished once a week by two seniors. Twice a week the sweet cupboard was opened, and for half an hour we could gorge, BUT, each boy had to offer a sweet from his bag each time to Fishy, who presided, and usually she took one. Only the innocent, therefore, bought large sweets. Did she eat them all? I have a photograph of Fishy, and her substantial figure confirms that she did.

I liked learning. At first, being behind in work owing to my travelling and illness, I cheated to keep up. Detected, beaten, and talked to by an excellent master who appealed to my better nature, I found I had one, and decided to go straight. It was also less painful. Before long, I was doing well in my work. This, combined with my hopeless performances at cricket – played all the year round on a matting wicket, athletics – though I once won a pocket knife in a relay race, and Cubs, where I performed incompetently as acting leader of the Eagle patrol – did not endear me to my school fellows.

So I learned a useful lesson: not to seek popularity, because it was not for me, but to get on with my own affairs. I did, however, do some successful stamp swapping; I was a founder member of a small Meccano Club which gathered at the house of Wentzel, a day-boy friend of mine; I had another day-boy friend, Carter, with whom I stayed, and with whom, in a go-cart, I perilously used to race the trams down the long hill to Orange Grove; and I helped to produce a number or two of a mimeographed school magazine. No. 1 of *P.T.S. News*, dated 18 August 1920, carried school news; appeals, such as that 'James major and Montgomery are collecting bullets, and will be very grateful for contributions to their collection' (we used to pick up Boer War bullets that had been flattened on the rocks of the kopje [hill] on which the school stood), lost and found, Cub notices, and the beginning of an article on pigmies and baboons, clearly extracted from somewhere. My dramatic career began and ended with my performance as the knock in the porter's scene from *Macbeth*, and I was not chosen to appear at the end of the year's prizegiving, when Oppenheimer major (Harry Oppenheimer the industrialist), recited 'La Conscience'.

The teaching was good. The only gap, a natural one, was that I learned South African as well as British history, so that later in England I had to do some fast work to catch up, though that grounding in South African history still serves me usefully. Outside school hours I read every book in the school library, learned to smoke the cane from the inside of cricket pads, acquired some railway enthusiasm from a boy who was expert in English pre-Grouping railways and the intricacies of Walschaerts locomotive valve gear, and became an expert at marbles. It was the only game I was good at. For the rest, I counted the days, even the hours, to the holidays. The blessed sound of 'Lord, dismiss us with thy blessing', the horse-cab to Park station, the finding of my sleeping bunk after having implored the guard to wake me half an hour before Maquassi; being woken, and dressing in my bunk; climbing down from the train, for there was no platform; being welcomed by Mr Kemp the taxi-man, and then driving through the night, now and then catching a spring-hare in the headlights. And so to the Residency, where my parents and Roger, my Old English Sheepdog, would be waiting up. A hot drink and a sandwich, and into bed. I was home, in my bed, among my few books – *Alice through the Looking Glass, Freckles, Stamp Collecting*, and an old bound volume of *The Scout*.

I spent three years at P.T.S. and Wolmaransstad. Then, a few months before my father's retirement, my mother and I sailed for England on the *Balmoral Castle*, to get me started on an English education. I was 13½. There must, I am sure, have been long discussions between my parents. My mother, strong Englishwoman, looked to 'home' as the natural place for retirement and education, and by 'home' she meant Devonshire. No other county would have occurred to her. But my father had not been to England since 1912. Part New Zealander, part South African, he was quite unsuited to English village life. Yet, a few months later, he followed. I was thankful he did, but I am sure that he must have looked back from his liner's deck to Table Mountain falling astern with even more regret than I. To me, all I loved in nature was receding: the wide vistas of the veld; the daily blue of the cloud-puffed sky; the brightness of the Milky Way and the friendly Southern Cross; the dorp street, the bungalow houses with their red and green tin roofs; the mangoes, pineapples and Cape gooseberries; the mealie (maize) porridge I preferred to oatmeal; the mixture of races; the familiar trains and trams; the mine dumps of Johannesburg and . . . Table Mountain itself, sinking into the sea.

It has taken me a lifetime to understand how fortunate I was to have been born and brought up a Colonial. I had no class-consciousness, for I had never experienced it nor even heard of it. Thus I have always been able to work with those of any class. Nor were traditional ways of doing things important. How could they be, when Johannesburg in my day was not yet fifty years old? Long afterwards, when I took early retirement from the Central Office of Information, a colleague in his farewell speech referred to my 'radical mind and fresh approach'. I knew, though he did not, its origin.

I owe also to my youth two of my life's absorbing interests: politics and transport. Was there ever a South African not interested in politics? From schooldays to old age I have loved the rough and tumble, the manoeuvring and the outwitting, but above all my efforts to get the answers right. As for transport, I had travelled over 50,000 miles before I was fourteen, or passenger aircraft were known; mainly by rail and ship. In doing so I discovered other transport modes: ox and donkey waggon teams for goods, horse four-wheeled cabs for hire, or, once, a hansom, and private Cape carts, governess carts and the like, till all were slowly replaced by early motor cars (I learned to drive on a Model 'T' Ford). Bicycles and rickshaws, trams double or single-deck, even once a small knife-board horse tram that, joy of joys, came off the rails and had to be lifted back. In Johannesburg, too, electric single-decker trolley-buses (we called them trackless trams) were appearing.

My visits to Britain and two other of the then three dominions besides South Africa, and my interest in transport, helped me unconsciously to absorb a feeling for the world as a whole. On Johannesburg station I watched trains setting off for Rhodesia and the Belgian Congo; I collected steamer names and lines, and became familiar with those of France, Germany or Japan, and motorcar makes, notably from the United States. Above all, I collected stamps. Others were more surprised than I when one of my later books was titled *World Canals*. It seemed natural enough to me.

England came as a shock, to my parents more than to me.

CHAPTER NINE

FROM DEVON INTO PUBLISHING

The England of reality and not of memory was a shock to my mother, who had wanted to return; to my father only a fulfilment of forebodings. Gas-lighting in our Plymouth flat began it. In South Africa I didn't remember a time when we didn't have electricity. Now my mother had to come into a dark wintry room, grope by the door for the matches, then make her way to the gas mantles and on to the gas fire. We probably had a gas cooker, but when we moved to Halberton in Devon so that I could attend Blundells at Tiverton as a day-boy, we had a paraffin stove, though by then electric light. In between, in farm lodgings waiting for our bungalow to be built, my poor father had to struggle to light a single-burner paraffin pressure-cooker which first demanded methylated spirits to start it and then frantic pumping to give it enthusiasm. In South Africa he had had an electric saucepan on the breakfast table, so that he could cook his own boiled egg just as he liked it.

Mother was not a grumbler, and neither was Dad, but they must indeed have missed our servants, who had also been our friends. At Halberton we did have a young girl, as broad as she was long, to do a few hours a week, all we could afford.

Once I had got through a first year of being covered from head to foot in chilblains, by day I found in England a myriad things to interest me. From those early days derived my life-long love of Devon, and especially Dartmoor; my renewed enjoyment of trains, for at Plymouth I could watch the Great Western expresses approaching Plymouth Millbay in one direction and, mysterious delight – London & South Western expresses approaching Plymouth Friary in the opposite; my first published and paid for writing – 'Diamond mining in the Transvaal' in the *Meccano Magazine* for December 1925 (I think I was paid five shillings); and especially my interest in canals.

South Africa has no canals or, for practical purposes, navigable rivers. Maybe it was that, and its name, that so intrigued me about the Grand Western Canal, which began at Tiverton. One evening while my father was still alive his solicitor came to dinner, to discuss with him whether I could become an articled clerk in his firm. Over the meal I mentioned the canal, and was told of a box full of records in his office which I could borrow if I took care of them. From that chance remark derived a life-long interest.

We had by now built a bungalow, Combecot, at Halberton, 4 miles from Tiverton and 3 from Blundells, to which I cycled every day.

England frustrated and bored my father. A man's man, a racing and horsy man, a lawyer accustomed to an un-English legal system, he had nothing in common with Halberton. Having tried unsuccessfully to get a job that at his age he could understand, 'he lik'd it not, and died'. That was in 1926, soon after my seventeenth birthday. He was only sixty-one. With him died his pension, leaving my mother with the sale value of our house and a very small private income which she soon supplemented, pathetically, by making and selling needlework and raffia purses and pincushions for presents.

To tide her over the first winter she was lent Rock Cottage, outside the village in an old quarry beside the canal. It had no amenities, but it was free. In the following spring [1927] she moved to a flat with her sister in Plymouth, having arranged to board me until I left school with a clergy widow who lived with her sister-in-law and her daughter Violet. Still at school, I became unofficially engaged to Violet when I reached eighteen.

An adolescent outburst of first love it undoubtedly was, but later, when during university days I found myself in the company of clever and attractive girls, my engagement was an insurance policy. Without it, I should probably have proposed to one of at least six. Happily I emerged to marry Violet in London in 1932. Since then I have lived all my life either married or pledged to one of two women, and have never been able to envisage any other kind of existence, nor sparing the time to be unfaithful.

At Blundells the teaching was first-class. I was tried in maths and classical forms, but found sadly wanting. I owe to my classics master my first introduction to the excitement of politics, for he interrupted his class after a boy brought him a message, to say that the Tiverton seat at the December 1923 general election had been retained by the Liberals by three votes after many recounts. I came to rest in the sixth with history, English and, rare subject in those days, economics, taught by a perceptive master named Westall. He had noticed me because, during the General Strike of 1926, I had written an essay to support the coal-miners' case, probably the only one in my class to do so.

While in the sixth, my bachelor uncle Frank in New Zealand offered to pay my expenses at Oxford were I bright enough to win a scholarship. In those days before student grants, I won a Devon County scholarship in History and English, and settled down to work for an open, having been given the run of the school library. I read and read and read. Spenser and Shakespeare and the Elizabethans; Milton, Congreve and Wycherley; then a curious gap until Wordsworth, and then everything I could lay my hands on up to the twentieth century. More, I galloped through many of Everyman's and the Home University Library (what riches were spread there!). Economics – I read Adam Smith, Ricardo, Engels and Marx; history and politics – Machiavelli by way of Macaulay and Bagehot to Trevelyan – and a little science. After two failures I won an open exhibition in English to St Edmund Hall.

One day in early October 1928, I arrived at the gate. Third oldest of Oxford foundations, then the only remaining Hall (formerly the house of a master who gathered his pupils round him, rather than an endowed college) the Hall had rather over a hundred men. Some forty had rooms round its diminutive quad, while the rest lodged out, coming in to learn, eat in its tiny hall, and, if they wished, worship in its equally tiny chapel.

As an exhibitioner, I was given rooms in Hall for my first year, at the top of No. 1 staircase, overlooking Queen's Lane. It was a bit of luck because first year men with Hall rooms were few and sought after, their rooms a base wherein to leave gowns, books and games clothing. I grew from boy to man in 24 hours. I had my own sitting room with a coal-fire and a scout to bring the coal, to which I could ask people, and to which tea could also be brought – piles of hot anchovy or honey toast, and a large earthenware teapot. I had a little bedroom with no heating, and a tin jug in a tin basin. Once I found the ice on the jug too thick to break; but never mind, I had my own rooms.

I also had a scholar's gown, and in Hall academic distinction: even a £40 p.a. exhibition meant that. To one who had had no standing whatever at school, never a prefect nor even allotted a fag on the grounds, I understood, that I lacked leadership qualities, that also gave confidence. To be called 'Mr Hadfield' by scout and don alike instead of 'Hadfield'; there was equality in it.

Standing in the quad waiting for dinner that evening, I made my first friends. Faced with large men anxious to size me up for rugby, soccer, hockey or rowing, I opted for rowing, because I knew I would be hopeless at the first three. After dinner, itself impressive as dons swept in and out, long gowns swirling, a group adjourned to my room and stayed there until they had to go. That night I went happily to bed. If I had known the *Prelude* then I might have said: 'Bliss was it in that dawn to be alive, but to be young was very heaven.' I was up for four years, and loved every minute of the first three: the fourth was a mistake.

In those days the first two terms were occupied with an exam, Pass Mod(eration)s, preliminary to working for a degree. Pass Mods over, I mustered courage to ask the Hall principal whether he would allow me, an exhibitioner in English, to read economics instead, in the comparatively new School of PPE (Philosophy, Politics and Economics). It was a good deal to ask, but he agreed. Fortunately, four terms later I was awarded a University Scholarship in Economics, so showing him that my request had not been frivolous.

My bent was, indeed, towards economic history and organisation: I was poor on theory and hopeless at philosophy. The third of my subjects, politics, including theory and modern political and constitutional history, I enjoyed as much as the economics. The result of such uneven abilities was eventually a good second, when I should have scraped a first. That I did not was probably the result of a disastrous *viva voce* on economic theory.

While I was up, Teddy Hall had a renaissance in sport, which in rowing brought our one boat from the third division to the first in eights. I made no contribution. Later I was co-founder of the Hall's Diogenes Club, limited to those who did not have college colours in any sport. Its more positive aspect was to debate philosophical (in its wider sense) questions in punts on the Cherwell in the summer, and over tea and toast in front of study fires in winter.

I was a member of several Hall clubs – I remember The Makers, which demanded an original literary work each term; the Essay Society, at which we read each other's daring views on sex and politics; the John Oldham, a play-reading group, and the Debating Society, at which the officers had to smoke churchwarden pipes throughout the debates. They were happy times, discussing, arguing, far into the night as the port fell in the decanter and the coal in the scuttle. There, too, one's wits were well sharpened against the best brains of one's contemporaries, and often the dons as well.

Outside college, I joined the Oxford Union, but as a club and for its library: I never spoke in debates, though I often went, especially when visiting politicians were speaking. I shall always be glad I heard Lloyd George, although the fire was dim. Willie Graham, then president of the Board of Trade in the 1929–31 Labour Government, impressed me by speaking without notes, yet commanding his detailed economic argument; and Oswald Mosley, still a radical Labour Minister, but shortly to form his New Party. I have always loved politics, what F.S. Oliver, in his biography of Sir Robert Walpole, called 'The endless adventure of governing men', implying their good government, that what is done will work, will succeed and survived to be further improved. But, though in 1945 I was to seek the Labour nomination for the Parliamentary seat of North Paddington, I am glad I failed. I am by temperament and ability an administrator, not a politician.

My university political career had variety. When I went up, at the tail end of Baldwin's government of 1924–9, I was inclined to support Labour. However, I decided the best way to broaden my mind was to attend Conservative, Liberal and Labour meetings. Then I went to a lecture by G.D.H. Cole and realised for the first time that the Great Slump was beginning.

During the 1930 summer vacation John Farrant, a Blundellian at Trinity, and I set out on bicycles for a fortnight's tour of South Wales. At Cheltenham I discovered the delights of fish and chip shops; at Kempsey, how good bacon and eggs could taste in 3s 6d bed and breakfast lodgings; at Cardiff that the best way to find a good cheap meal was to ask a lorry driver. At Pontyates, a Welsh-speaking village, a meeting convened by the station-master decided who should put us up, and so we saw a collier who did indeed have his hipbath before the kitchen fire. But at Merthyr Tydfil I saw unemployed miners sitting on their haunches in rows along the street, backs to walls; and at Llanelli the trams bucked along subsiding tracks in potholed streets. I saw for myself a little of what slump meant and returned to Oxford determined to learn how unemployment could be avoided. In those days it never occurred to people like myself to 'protest'; if it had, we would have dismissed it. What was important was to learn how to do better and then to do it.

It seemed, however, that the Labour Government did not themselves know. It was then that Oswald Mosley, frustrated by what he considered their nervous inaction, formed the New Party. I joined it, but when the administration collapsed, MacDonald formed a National Government and went to the country in August 1931. I could do nothing, for the New Party's few candidates did not include

Devon, where I then lived. The Party collapsed, and I returned smartly to what remained of the Labour Party as a middle-of-the-road democrat.

My interest in transport owes almost nothing to the motor car, though in my first university year Farrant and I bought a Citroën Cloverleaf (an open two-seater with a commode behind, outside the hood) for £10. We used it to run round Oxford. It was an odd car, which used little petrol but enormous amounts of oil. On steep hills we had to walk beside it, while it went up by itself on the hand throttle. On my first vacation a back wheel came off and rolled through a field gate to find rest against a cud-chewing cow, and later its driving shaft collapsed. I pushed it into the ditch and sold it to the first garage I came to for £2.

Having joined the university branch of the Royal Aeronautical Society in order to take part in organised visits, on 3 June 1929 I went to the Royal Airship Works at Cardington to see R101, then being built. I had never before handled balsa, the very light wood being used for passenger accommodation. We were also taken some way up the mooring mast to see how the passenger gangway would be used, an American friend Teddy Welles (later a bishop) and I alone volunteering, in the high wind blowing that day, to climb to the mast's top, 200 ft above the ground, to see how the airship's nose would fit into the mooring cone. Sixteen months later, on 5 October 1930, R101 passed over my Oxford lodgings before crashing at Beauvais on her way to India.

During my third year I took *Modern Transport*, then an excellent weekly newspaper, and read some elementary books on railways. Having decided to become a railwayman, I applied for one of the two annual traffic apprentice jobs offered by the old LNER to university people. In February of my last year, 1932, I went to the smoky caverns of Liverpool Street station to be interviewed by a row of elderly gentlemen. I aired my hard-won knowledge, and then came an unexpected question: 'Why, Mr Hadfield, are you interested in railways?' I said the first thing that came into my head: 'Because I had a model railway as a boy, sir.' The board laughed and laughed. I got the job, perhaps on that answer.

It was not until a fortnight before I was due to leave Oxford that I was summoned to my medical, whereupon I was told my eyesight was not good enough for the apprenticeship course, which involved putting trainees through all sorts of practical jobs. So I was out, with no job, only a few pounds in hand, in the middle of the Great Slump, when two million were unemployed and there was no social security. I also wished to get married to Violet, for marriage was now to take priority over transport, politics, economic organisation, and the reading, writing, publishing and speaking of 'our sweet English tongue' in my life's concerns.

So ended youth. Now succeeded years of adventure that, as I look back, must have owed something to my courageous mother, something to my slightly rakish father; something, too, to great-grandfather Joseph.

I found myself a partner in a tiny mainly second-hand bookshop in Soho, then a larger one in St Martin's Lane. Both were hopeless earners because my partner, as I soon discovered, knew far less about the book trade than he had pretended.

Quickly I forgot I was an Oxford graduate. I learned something of the book trade from the bottom up, for instance by going round publishers' trade counters with a sack over my shoulder to order and collect single copies of new books bought at a discount. One day in 1935 the Bodley Head traveller showed me the first ten Penguin paperbacks at sixpence each, bound in bright orange, green or blue. Daringly, I ordered ten of each. Delivered, we put them in the stall outside; by evening all had been sold.

In 1936 I discovered that my partner was also running a clandestine pornographic business in our basement, and decided to get out before I found myself sharing a police-court dock. I therefore obtained an introduction to Kenneth Sisam, secretary of the Clarendon Press at Oxford. He sent me to Sir Humphrey Milford, head of the London branch of the Oxford University Press who offered me a job. Unknown to me, the Press then began to train me for a senior post.

Meanwhile, Violet and I were living in a basement flat at 175 Sutherland Avenue, Maida Vale. I there joined the local Labour Party only a year after its electoral defeat in 1931, when it consisted largely of old stalwarts like Mr Featherstone. He was a big elderly man with sandy hair and a walrus moustache, who had been a building worker until he became a full-time union official. He was garrulous to boredom but he was true, honest and good, and spent all his spare time and money in working for the Party, willing to turn his hand to anything.

In summer 1934 I was asked to stand for the Paddington Borough Council, upon which Labour held one seat, as a candidate for Harrow Road ward, considered to be a hopeless proposition. As my book collecting sack had taught me something of the working book trade, so did that election of working politics. Our main platform was an attack on Paddington's infantile mortality rate, at that time the highest in London. It was a good line, but it was helped by the experience of one of our candidates, an elderly ex-Liberal election agent called Tom Turner. He suggested one day that three or four of the nine candidates for Harrow Road ward, as well as some fighting hopeless wards, should between them write a signed personal letter in their own handwriting to every married couple in the ward. My share came to 1,600 letters, each written out in full and put into an addressed envelope. They ran as follows:

Dear Mr & Mrs Bloggs,
    I hope that you will both vote for the other Labour candidates and myself on Thursday, 1st November between 8 a.m. and 9 p.m.
                                        Yours sincerely,

I spent every spare moment in the bookshop and at home writing and signing those letters, and got them done in time for delivery on the evening before polling day, too late for our opponents to counteract them. I fancy they were effective. It was a change for the electors to receive something personal, and they probably thought they knew me. To our astonishment we carried Harrow Road ward by a majority of 1,000 and altogether won 21 seats out of 60. I was twenty-five, I think the second youngest councillor in London, and felt very inexperienced in the problems of governing a population of 140,000. At the Party meeting of Labour councillors I was elected deputy whip, youngest of the four officers of the Party group. Within a year I had become whip, an office which I held for ten years, my new deputy being Sid Greene, later Sir Sidney Greene, general secretary of the National Union of Railwaymen. We then had the curious situation in the Council that the Labour Party had a leader (James MacColl, later MP and parliamentary under-secretary at the Ministry of Housing and Local Government in the 1964 and 1966 Labour Governments), and whip who were both under thirty and both Oxford 'intellectuals'.[1]

I liked the red leather seats stamped with the Council's arms and the sight of the mace being carried before the Mayor in his robes, and enjoyed the debates. Speeches were limited to five minutes; thus were we trained in conciseness.

At Amen House, the London offices of the Oxford University Press, my publishing training began with days in the showroom (where I read the Biggles books for boys and the Dimsie books for girls, which we published), and continued with days in the library, learning the books, reading, and talking (on the rare occasions when someone else was not doing so) with the tall, good-looking, red-haired, dauntingly intelligent librarian, Alice Mary Smyth. Into the library, to sit in her chairs or walk declaiming poetry, arguing, questioning, came the great ones of the press: Sir Humphrey Milford himself, slight, with inscrutable parchment face and still ways; Charles Williams, editor, poet, dramatist, essayist, critic, novelist, biographer, theologian – grey-haired, spectacled, quick, exciting, with high-pitched voice, jerky movements and words that always seemed to suggest more than they said, a man who continually made the ordinary extraordinary; or Gerard Hopkins, in charge of publicity, novelist, superb translator, nephew of the poet Gerard Manley Hopkins. These amazing figures, and others, came and talked and went, she the magnet, they the filings, and so did I.

Then I started on instalment selling of the great Oxford Dictionary in 13 volumes, and sold quite a number. With a colleague, I also started a general scheme to sell any OUP books to a minimum value then of, I think, 40s, on revolving credit terms. This also worked, and continued for many years. I was prevented from becoming a hire-purchase tycoon by a brief interview with Sir Humphrey in the autumn of 1938. He told me that on 1 April 1939 I would take charge of the Juvenile Department in succession to Mr L'Estrange, then better known, jointly with Mr Ely, as juvenile author Herbert (or Mrs Herbert) Strang. As I remember, it did not occur to him to ask me whether I'd like the job, or to tell me how much I should be paid, or to me to wonder whether I should take it.

'Juvenile' was a sizeable organisation. It had been built up by L'Estrange mainly on the Oxford Annuals. We produced (I think) four each year, but this was only the beginning. The stories, line drawings, and coloured pictures being our copyright, each year we reshuffled the texts and blocks of past years to make Grand Books, Big Books, Little Big Books, Big Little Books, Little Books, and every other conceivable kind of Book. Some blocks were thirty years old, but still they got shuffled, added to, and dealt out again as Christmas came around. Annuals and their progeny had made the firm a great deal of money, oddly perhaps for a university press. But now their day was over, as I realised with a shock when I looked at the accounts, and I was clearly expected, as soon as L'Estrange had gone, to end one era and begin another.

I walked up to the top floor of the new building, where I was now to work with *de facto*, though not yet *de jure*, authority. 'Juvenile' was in one way a misnomer, for I found myself the youngest (I was then twenty-nine) of the staff of seven. I got a foretaste of my reforming job when I saw the filing system for 'Juvenile' correspondence: a pile of letters and flimsies in date order in a corner of my future secretary's office. I invented a new filing system on the spot, much to the consternation of the elderly lady who presided over it, was asked by L'Estrange to shorten *Bevis* for the Herbert Strang Library of boys' and girls' books, and retired after an exciting day to think out a new policy for a kind of publishing about which I knew nothing whatever.

In my six months of apprenticeship and five of authority before the war began I could only make a start upon the changes that were necessary. I at once shut down all the Annuals and their derivatives, to the horror of the staff, then created some new series as the quickest way of giving Oxford Juveniles a new image with booksellers and the public, and because inclusion in a series makes it easier to sell each book. I started a children's series called Chameleon Books, each jacket to vary in two colours, but with a common format and price. They began at 1s 6d and ran for many years. Another then called Meridian, later Compass, Books covered interests and hobbies, for which I commissioned books on *Codes and Ciphers* and *Secret Societies*. Another was a group of painting books. Previously these had been made up from uncoloured illustrations in old Annuals. I thought them cluttered, and commissioned a series of new ones using bold, plain outlines and bright simple colours. They sold well.

My fourth series was the 'Oxford Novels for Children'. Most of our travellers thought 5s to be the highest safe price for children's fiction. Dent's were, however, publishing really good well-illustrated stories at a higher price, so I decided that what they could do, we could also, a decision practically simultaneous with the unannounced arrival in the office one day of Hilda Lewis with *The Magic Ship*.[1] She came before I was formally in charge, but I had to see her, woefully ignorant as I still was of dealing with authors experienced in seeking good terms. I tottered from the interview having learned a lot quickly about author–publisher relations, but having got the book. It became the first in my new series, was successful, and remained in print for many years.

Though the Oxford Annuals had been closed down, I felt there could be a sale for similar books tied to a person or subject. Arthur Askey was then well known on the radio for his comic programmes, which included humorous songs with catchy tunes. We therefore did an *Arthur Askey Annual* which was written, illustrated and sent for setting in a fortnight. Sir Humphrey, so I was told, had been heard asking who Arthur Askey was. The book was published just after war had been declared, and sold out easily enough.

Most Londoners were beginning to think about what they would do if war broke out. I wanted to remain in London, so I borrowed an Auxiliary Fire Service recruiting booklet. A spectacle-wearer, I found myself a low form of life; I could not be a proper fireman at the front end of a hose, but only a Class B pump-operator. This would have wounded my pride, had I not noted that in the River Service, where firemen worked on boats, there was no such distinction, and proper firemen could wear glasses. I knew one end of a boat from another, so I decided to join. A few days later I was passing the headquarters of the London Fire Brigade at Lambeth, and saw the boats of the river station. I hurried down the gangway. The station officer produced a form, asked me what I knew about boats, paid no attention to my answer, and in a minute, subject to medical examination, I was a fireman.

Between April and September 1939 I did some desultory training, but there was much else to think of. [By this time Charles's relationship with Alice Mary was developing, and she was at her parents' house in South Cerney, Gloucestershire.] I got a day's leave from Amen House, and on the Thursday I went down to South Cerney; on the Friday I learned that Germany had invaded Poland. Sure that London would be bombed the moment war was declared, and that successful defence was not possible without me, I caught the afternoon train to London.

CHAPTER TEN

THE FIRE SERVICE AND WARTIME

As the train to London drew into Swindon, there on the opposite platform stood a long line of children, divided into sections marked by a letter on a stick. Each small citizen of England had a gasmask and a parcel. As I watched, it began to rain lightly from a grey sky, and the evacuees huddled together.

At Paddington I bought a paper, and learned that the AFS had been mobilised. Thinking that war would hold off till the morning, I went to my lodgings to pack and make a list of my needs. We had been told to bring enough food for 24 hours, cutlery, blankets, and spare clothes, as well as the dungarees, rubber boots and cap that had been issued to recruits. I could not guess how long it would be before I saw my room again, and took no chances. The next morning I bought a stock of tinned food, which I packed up with several changes of clothes, three blankets and a pillow, a tin plate, mug, cutlery, a *Collected Shakespeare* and a book by Charles Williams. It did not seem excessive for a long war. Then I took a taxi.

I wondered on the way whether a taxi was the right conveyance in which to arrive at Battersea river fire station, but in the yard were two rows of expensive cars, so I withdrew my doubts. Having taken my baggage to the top floor and put it in a room with no furniture or bedding, but only other bundles around the walls, I reported at the office. To be asked my religion gave me a turn; to be handed an asbestos identity disc gave me a worse one. There was such a very broad hint about asbestos.

We slept in our blankets on the floor, after a canteen supper of our amalgamated rations. We settled down to work 48 hours on duty, 24 hours off; so every third night was spent off the fire station. In the morning – Sunday – I was sent home for 24 hours, and went to bed to finish my night's rest. Air-raid sirens woke me. I jumped out of bed, dressed, sat in a corner out of the way of the window, and began to read Collingwood's *England under the Romans* in an effort to persuade myself that England would not suddenly cease to be. There was silence. The all-clear sounded, and I went to sleep again. England was at war.

After a week of pub dinners, with breakfasts and suppers being taken in the crowded canteen, word went round that a new station was to be opened up-river, at Putney, and that men were to be transferred, together with *EFB* (Emergency Fire Boat) *1*. The list was posted, and my name was there. The next day seventeen of us piled into the boat, cast off, and started upstream. The power station, factories and wharves of Battersea, Fulham and Wandsworth slipped by; I watched gloomily the fire risk they represented, and wondered how much longer the bombs would hold off.

We took over Vesta rowing club on Putney Embankment. On the ground-floor a boathouse full of racing craft, upstairs a recreation room, hall and kitchen, bar, office, locker room and shower room. We dumped our gear, and were introduced to Tommy Ball, the ex-steward of the club, who had been enrolled in the AFS by Arthur, the section officer in charge of us, a few minutes after we had arrived. Arthur lined us up, told us he aimed to make the station just like home, and led us to the bar, where we drank the whole remaining stock of the club's bottled beer. Then, while two began to cook food for supper, the rest of us fell to sandbagging a garage on the opposite side of the road to be our air-raid shelter.

We soon found that we had struck a good station. While others slept on boards, we had stretcher beds belonging to the club, hot water laid on to the showers, a twopence-in-the-slot telephone, and the bar, arrangements for replenishing which we made immediately. The office became the watchroom, continuously manned.

Drills began. I learned for the first time how to handle a boat. The *EFB 1* was a broad-beamed pinnace some 40 feet long fitted with two heavy pumps amidships and, forward on the half-deck, a monitor or water-gun that could be connected to the pumps by short lengths of hose. If the monitor was not to be used, then hose could be rowed ashore in a skiff, and water pumped ashore for delivery to land firemen whose supply from the mains might be insufficient through bombing.

Rowing hose ashore, we discovered, was not as easy as it looked. The lengths are flaked or folded into the sternsheets of the skiff, which is then rowed towards the shore by two men, while the third pays out the hose over the stern. The difficulty comes from the tide. The skiff itself must be steered diagonally, so that it does not get broadside on to the movement of the water, and so be carried downstream. The hose lies on the surface of the water, and takes up a semi-circular shape between the fireboat and the skiff. The oarsmen, if they have far to go, must row fast enough to get to the shore before the tide can pull the bight of hose tight, while the man at the stern sees to it that the hose couplings do not catch and that the hose runs freely, and the man on the pump puts water into the hose to sink it behind the skiff. If once the tide begins to drag at the stern of the skiff the men have failed. Ignominiously they drift downstream while they throw the rest of the hose overboard. It is pulled back on board the fireboat, and the operation begins again. If they have succeeded, water continues to be pumped through the hose, which then disappears from the surface to lie on the river bed.

The river fireman's life and work was very different from that of a landsman. He was concerned with handling his fireboat at all conditions of tide, in knowing the depth of water up and down the river, the position of buoys and barge roads and wrecks, and the names of wharves. He learned the lights carried by different types of craft, the mysteries of splicing ropes, and he learned signalling.

Chas was our electrician. A big, cheerful man who drove an MG Magma car, he had been the manager of an electrical company, and soon he fixed up wires between the recreation and locker rooms, with a lamp and a key at each end. We became known as the best station on the river for signalling, and later it came in useful.

Chas, the Major and Shappy and I were good friends. Chas and the Major were public school men. The latter had a bright red face, obtained in Persia from experiences in oil, above a stout body. He was older than we others, and had a liking for whisky and a dislike for manual work. He was often seen neighbouring a broom and a bucket, but seldom using them. Shappy was an academic, who reckoned to pass the time by learning a fresh language every six months. He had mastered Provençal and was well advanced in Arabic when he was moved from our station.

The winter of 1939/40 came; blocks of ice floated past our windows, and bumped against the fireboat's stem. By day we handled frozen mooring ropes, started and ran the pumps and the propelling engine that were kept warm by paraffin heater lamps beneath their canvas covers, and chipped ice. In the evenings after supper half a dozen would settle down to cards.

Attached to our station was a motor cruiser manned by four men belonging to the River Patrol. These men were auxiliary firemen, and their job was to look after the needs of the larger fireboats for petrol and food and to patrol the river to observe fires. After six months they were disbanded, and the men transferred to us, and badly we missed the boats during the Blitz, when so often petrol or food was not to be had upon the river. Meanwhile the crews came ashore every evening, and played darts, table tennis and cards with us. One dark night when the crew were ashore we heard a crash from the river. Shouts, and an investigation by the crew of the skiff, showed that a tug with its load of barges, navigating without lights as was then the rule, had overrun the patrol boat which was nowhere to be seen. The then superintendent of the river earned our gratitude that evening by coming up to ask anxiously whether any lives had been lost.

The inactivity of the early weeks of the war sent many men into the armed forces, or back to their civilian occupations. AFS men could then give a week's notice and leave, for it was not until a short time before the Blitz that it was made impossible to leave the service without special permission. It was a short-sighted policy to allow the men to leave, because training expensive in time and money was lost, and much potential officer material disappeared.

Many of the men felt that they could be more useful to the country elsewhere. In this they were encouraged by the newspapers and the general public. The former took the view that London would never be bombed, and attacked the blackout and the evacuation of London business houses, while the latter saw AFS men walking about, knew they were earning £3 a week, and accused them of being slackers and army dodgers. We became ashamed of our uniform, and never wore it in the street. The government appeared to agree, for whereas the men of the AFS were allowed to resign, the 3,000 women of the WAFS in London were dismissed: later they had to be re-recruited and retrained.

Another reason was the attitude of the regulars of the LFB and of the London County Council. At the beginning of the war we were under an AFS officer, Arthur, while two LFB men were attached to our station as instructors. After a few months an encroachment clearly authorised from above, but never explained to the men, began, and slowly the ordering of drills and the life of the station came under the regulars, who became sub-officers. Endless rows went on between Arthur and Bob, till Arthur gave a month's notice and entered the Navy, and we were left with Bob.

Bob was a good seaman and fireman, but he was incapable of authority. He was also a boaster, especially about women. When not in the boathouse he was often in one of the private houses round the station, and should he be wanted on the telephone we pacified the enquirer while a messenger ran for Bob, who came lumbering down the road to explain to the telephone that he had been out on the boat. 'Work never stops here, mate,' he would say.

For a time Bob did not take part in our mess. Instead, he bought his own food. When we were in the middle of dinner he would come in and spread a newspaper full of fish and chips out on the tablecloth. Then with oil-grimed fingers he would search in his jacket pocket till he drew out and placed in his mouth his set of false teeth, to which were sticking matches, shreds of tobacco, and anything else his pocket contained. Then, ignoring knife and fork, he ate his dinner.

His conceit was armour-plated. During one of our rows I gave my opinion of Bob as an officer in terms which, as I cooled down, seemed to be stronger than I had intended. So I sought him out.

'I'm afraid I said a bit too much, Bob,' I said.

'That's all right, mate,' he replied, 'I knew you didn't mean *any* of it'.

We were a happy crowd at Putney, and not a man left for five months after the beginning of the war, long after other stations had begun to lessen in numbers. Then Mac went, then others, then Chas and the Major, especially after the days [in August 1940] when we watched a stream of small boats pass our station going down river on their way to evacuate troops from Dunkirk. We applied to take our boat too, but were refused. By the beginning of the Blitz only half a dozen of the original seventeen were left. All the others had returned to civil life or joined the Forces. I tried for the Air Force, but my eyesight was too poor for flying duties and I was too young for administration. I also tried to enter the Inland Waterways section of the Royal Engineers. The interviewing officer said that they could only take men with practical knowledge, however, and I had to confess I had never worked a lock in my life.

Numbers fell until the Police and Firemen's Order froze the Service. At the beginning of the Blitz [in September 1940] we had roughly one-third of the men who had answered the mobilisation order. We had, however, boats. From November [1939] onwards these were delivered, till now the position of the beginning of war was reversed, and we had more boats than we could man. Crews of ten dwindled, till when the Blitz began we went away with an officer and four men. These new 'Thames'-class boats were good. Fifty feet long and broad in the beam, they were driven by two Ford V8 engines enclosed in a cabin, and carried two extra heavy pumps giving a total output of 2,800 gpm: we envied the stations that had them. We, as the station furthest from trouble, had the *EFB 2* which had replaced the *1*, a single-screw boat with no cabin, driven by a very reliable Thorneycroft engine that required to be swung left-handed. I usually acted as motorman, and that engine and I came to understand each other.

My Blitz experience was unrepresentative of that of London firemen generally, for I was stationed on the outskirts of the London Fire Brigade area, manning a boat maintained to guard property from Putney Bridge to Chiswick. Only on the worst occasions were we called downriver. It was late in August [1940] that I heard my first bomb, one afternoon while an Alert was on. A single bomber came over and dropped two HE and an oil bomb two streets away. The dust fell in clouds from the roof as we streamed out, seized hose, a branch and a key and bar which we had laid ready (though we were not supposed to fight land fires, or to leave our station), and ran to where the bombs had fallen. The broken glass, the smell of explosive, were new, but Bob and an AFS man, Frank, who had land experience, took the lead and we followed. A house was burning, but we quickly put it out, and behaved in a lofty way to the pump's crew from the land station when it arrived two or three minutes later. Our stock went up in the neighbourhood.

A fortnight later, on the evening of the first Saturday in September, George, two new men and I sat in the boathouse beneath the station. The sirens sounded, and suddenly a passer-by called to us: 'Come and have a look at this!' We came. Over the docks, several miles downriver from us, there hung a great cloud of smoke. We left our mattresses, put on our firegear, stowed supplies of petrol and food in the skiff, and waited. The telephone rang. We were ordered to Acorn Yard. No one knew where Acorn Yard was, but we could see the fire. The four of us had a regular, B—— in charge, who was standing in for Bob.

We chugged along in the evening light, past Wandsworth and Battersea and Chelsea and Vauxhall and Westminster. It might have been a pleasure trip, if not for the great plume of smoke, and now the sight of flames above the buildings. Once through Tower Bridge we began to pass burning buildings, and then, as the water whipped up with the in-draught of the great fire that was burning in the Surrey Commercial Docks, we came to a bank of smoke thick across the river, carried there by the south-westerly wind. It was so thick that we could get no further, though we knew from the map we had looked at on the way down that Acorn Yard was a quarter of a mile further on. Alongside the river stacks of timber were blazing, while the banks were lined with burning barges. Now and then one, its mooring ropes burned, would drift downriver on the tide, and opposite us a blazing wreck was being methodically rammed by a tug till it sank at the edge of the fairway. The roar of the fire, the whistle of bombs, the crack of an opening Molotov cocktail, the falling of incendiaries, created a noise above which rose the roar of our pumps, as we started work with our monitor upon a blazing barge tier.

B—— was horrified, and indeed the first days of the Blitz were worse for the regulars. For years they had fought chimney, shop and house fires, with a conflagration such as that of Wood Street, Carron Wharf, or Colonial Wharf so rare as to be a topic of conversation for years afterwards. Colonial Wharf stories were told to us long after the Blitz was over, by men upon whose minds the great fires of the war had not impressed themselves with the same force as had the lesser ones of peace. In addition, their fire experience had taught them the dangers that lie in the fighting of even a small fire by inexperienced firemen, and they were appalled by the magnitude of the dangers that presented themselves to regulars and auxiliaries alike.

We, on the other hand, had seen no fires of importance before, and a hundred acres of fire seemed to us the sort of wartime blaze to fight which the AFS had been recruited. Of dangers other than those from falling bombs we were quite unaware.

After we had put out our barges, we lay alongside another fireboat which was engaged on water relay, while B—— began a long talk to the other officer on what we should do next. We suggested that we should cross the river to several small fires that were starting, but he insisted that he had been ordered to the south side of the river and there he was going to stay. In the excitement of our first Blitz both we and the crew of the boat next to us forgot the ebbing tide, and found ourselves aground. B——'s agitation now reached fever heat. In the middle of the river lay *Gamma*, one of the pre-war regular fireboats, water relaying, and to it B—— was rowed, while we stayed behind to watch the flames approaching the riverside. The skiff returned with an order for me as a signalman to go aboard the regular boat. I was soon afterwards followed by the whole crew.

In the cabin, built to seat eight, there were some twenty-five firemen: members of the *Gamma*'s crew, of our two boats, and men from a land pump who had been cut off by the fire, and were rescued from the end of the pier by the *Gamma*'s tender.

Hour after hour the *Gamma*'s pumps roared, almost overcoming the great roar of the fire, and only allowing a bomb to be heard a moment before it hit the banks or fell into the water. In the early hours of the morning we regained our own boat, and as the tide floated her we moved into the bank and began to pump water ashore to the land crews fighting the timber fires. There we stayed for six hours.

It was mid-morning when we received orders to make up and go home. We chugged upstream, while wondering passers-by on the bridges peered at dirty oil-stained men and wet hose heaped on the foredeck. They waved, we thumbed back, and then the crew lay on the deck and slept, while I nodded over my engine. Our boat was always the last home because of the distance we had to travel, and it was one o'clock when we arrived. A few of the locals were on the bank to welcome us. The men who had come on duty that morning cleaned the boat, changed the hose and serviced the engines, while we went ashore to hot showers and food. Then we fell asleep for four hours. Wakened for tea, and having been told all leave had been cancelled, we ate quickly to the siren's sound, listening for the telephone. It came: 'Take the fireboat to Tower Bridge.' Oilskins and boots again.

So it was through those September days. The river was then a strange highway, as we moved down between the fires. I once counted over fifty between Tower Bridge and Greenwich, all on the river banks. It was as if we were the heroes of a torchlight procession. The whole panorama of a burning city was shown to us, the tongues of flame from unknown streets, the great blanket of smoke, the glittering incendiaries reflected in the broad water. That water became treacherous with strange passengers. Great baulks of wood from wharves, sacks of wool, crates, rolls of paper, blocks of wax, bodies, all floated up and down on the tides, at night invisible to anyone on a hurrying fireboat. A bump, push the controls to neutral, and hope that the obstruction would not take a propellor off.

One other picture of the Blitz, and that is all.

It was two o'clock in the morning when the bell was sounded by the duty man. We huddled in the skiff on the dark foreshore, dressed in oilskins, clutching our haversacks full of anti-gas clothing, spare tins of petrol, loaves of bread, bottles of milk, and all the accompaniments of a voyage on a fireboat. As we passed between the dark banks and beneath the crossing searchlights, the flames of a great fire lit up the sky ahead. The bridges were dark bars between us and it. Dock warehouses were burning; we moored to the river wall while Bob went ashore for orders, and the flames roared up over our heads and bannered out across the river. We felt a little happier for the sound of the all-clear. Bob returned, and we entered St Katharine's Dock. The gates shut behind us, the water rose, the gates opened, the lock keeper seeming quite unperturbed. We passed into a basin, swung to starboard, and entered a rectangle of water, three sides of which were ablaze. Only on the side by which we had entered was the fire being held back by water streams. In the centre two fireboats were already moored, their monitors playing into the mass of flames that roared within the seven-storey warehouses. The floors had already fallen in and only the walls remained, those facing us balanced upon the stout stone pillars of the ground floor. We too began to throw our 1,500 gallons a minute into the fire, which for hour after hour did not allow one drop to fall back into the dock. We seemed to have no effect at all.

The force of the monitor so swung the boat about, however, that we had to take a mooring line to the dock wall. In the skiff we rowed through a film of wax that had solidified on the water, thick enough to make it difficult to put the oar blades in the water. Immediately above us towered the wall of fire. The line was made fast, we now rode steady, and once more the monitor took up its work. This great water gun has a power behind its jet that can knock down a brick wall without difficulty. Many of us were frightened of a steep sliver of wall balanced upon two pillars which faced us, so Joe, our second regular, turned the monitor upon it to reassure us as to its strength. It did not move, and we took confidence. The heat mounted; the wood of the boat was hot; our tin hats were hot; and a steady rain of soot fell upon us all, and lay upon the cups of tea we made ourselves.

All day we worked, going ashore to a pub for lunch, and now and then for petrol. On one of these trips George and I, waiting outside the dock gate with our rows of empty cans for the petrol lorry to arrive, watched a Salvation Army canteen van drive up. It was the first food I had ever been given by charity, and it tasted good.

The afternoon wore on, the evening came. We were sadly aware that our fire must be visible thirty miles away, and that we were in the middle of it. Then, as darkness came, we were relieved by another boat, and ordered home. As we moved upriver the sirens sounded, and we drew into a riverside fire station to report.

It was the evening of the barrage, the night when first the guns of London spoke. The whole of London was enheartened, symbolic as was their early effect. We waited for orders. They came. We were to return to our dock because the relieving boat had broken down. This time we berthed in a different corner of the dock. I took over the monitor and the care of the pumps, while the rest of the crew, except one, tried to get some sleep.

The one was needed to bail, for the glands of the monitor leaked, and a stream of water entered the bilges. We had among the crew that night an ex-pavement artist, an elderly man totally unused to manual work, who had joined the AFS a few weeks before the Blitz. I cannot think how he survived the land training course, but he was then passed, understandably, to the river, and appeared at our station. Since we had nowhere to pass him to, we had to keep him. Useless for most jobs, we set him to bail. He worked through the night, steadily scooping water out of the bilge and throwing it into the dock. Meanwhile I operated the monitor, and concentrated upon one corner of the warehousing, steadily working over a limited area till the water stream began to better the fire. I awoke two of our men, and sent them in the skiff for petrol. While they were gone two bombs fell with a howl that could be heard above the roar of the flames and the pumps. One fell on the dock wall by the entrance, and luckily penetrated a considerable distance before it exploded. If it had not, it would probably have sealed the dock. The second fell in the street behind the spot where our monitor was playing, and killed an AFS pump's crew working there. The men in our skiff had the fright of their lives.

Soon after this we went ashore and, standing in a City street in oilskins and lifebelts, drank lukewarm but welcome cocoa served to us by two AFS girls from a double-decker London bus in temporary use as a canteen van. Those girls had all our admiration.

Later I slept in the two-foot space between the roaring pumps, while George took over the monitor and Joe the bailing. At dawn when I woke George had put out my corner and widened the area, while Joe was fast asleep, lying in a pool of water that was well over the floorboards. At ten o'clock we were ordered home, and at eleven, after thirty-three hours with no meal, we tied up to our home buoy and went ashore. We slept all day, and that night we were not ordered out.

During raids, people thought company preferable to safety. All the houses round the station had Anderson shelters, but many were unused, while instead twenty or thirty people, all sexes and ages, would come every evening to the public house on the corner and sleep in the cellar. Round the walls there would be arranged the beds. In the centre stood the barrels of beer, from some of which ran tubes to the beer engines on the floor above. The cellar had no real protection, and everyone there would have been much safer in their own Anderson shelters, but at least they were in company. For a short time our station telephones were out of order, and we used that of the public house. The man on duty by the telephone had all the comfort of a coal fire in a warm snuggery beside the bar, but often he would pull the instrument out on to the bar floor, and be found sitting on the cellar steps, where he could hear the small movement of the other human beings. Such actions were, perhaps, natural reactions to the inhumanity, the mechanised nature, of bombing, the coming together of human beings against the sub-human.

After weeks of continuous raiding, there came a night of wind and storm. Ten o'clock came, and George and I walked over from the pontoon game in the shelter to make some tea. The sirens had not sounded, we made the tea, and general indecision settled on the station. Should we sleep in the station? Could we risk undressing? Some did one, some did another, but we stayed up late, and the absence of sirens worried everyone. We all slept badly.

In December [1940] I exchanged leave days until I got four together and went to Oxford. It was the first time I had slept off the station, or in a bed, since the Blitz had started. I had taken the holiday just in time, for the inevitability of the siren was beginning to get on my nerves, especially as I then saw no reason why nightly raiding should not continue till the end of the war. I spent the first night, twisting, turning and bouncing in bed for the sheer pleasure of not lying on boat planks or a stretcher bed.

Although I had had something to do with trade unions before the war as secretary of the Paddington Borough Labour Party and Trades Council, I had not joined one. I was, however, soon known on my station as the political bloke; when therefore, in April 1940, literature arrived addressed to the secretary, AFS Section, Fire Brigades Union, it was handed to me. I had never heard of the Fire Brigades Union. The literature told us that we could join for 3d a week; though our station was a good one, we had plenty of complaints about our conditions of service, and the whole station joined. I was appointed secretary.

A week later we were told to send a delegate to an FBU conference of AFS men from the whole country. I went, and found 200 men representing 15,000 AFS men who had been added to the small pre-war membership of regulars. I found two other river men and we formed a bloc.

The conference was called to approve a ten-point list of demands. They included a second uniform, injury pay beyond a fortnight (after which a fireman currently only got the civilian rate of 30s), and sick pay beyond three weeks in the year. The delegates interested me, for my experience of politics was inside one London borough, but here were men from all over the country. The speeches reflected nine months of phoney war, during which firemen had tried to show pride in a service no one regarded, were doubtful of the objects of the war, and saw few signs of equality of sacrifice. Many had left jobs at £5, £8 or £10 a week to earn £3 putting out wartime fires. There had been no fires, but instead acres of floors to scrub, public sneers, and the sight of careful types who had stayed in their jobs now getting rises. The men were bitter. When the time came to elect a Management Committee, we found that each of the six districts of the London Fire Brigade had been given one member, the river having been joined to 'F' district. The three of us thereupon asserted that the problems of the water were quite different from those of the land, and fireboat men from all over the country were at once given their own seat. The other two moved and seconded my election, and a fortnight after having first heard of the FBU, I was on the Management Committee of its AFS section.

The small pre-war Fire Brigades Union (it dated from 1887) had been founded to press for the abolition of the continuous duty system in London, by which a fireman had virtually no free time away from the station, and had built up a membership of two thousand or so among the men of the country's regular brigades. A few months before the war a new union secretary had been appointed, a young fireman and ex-merchant sailor of twenty-seven called John Horner.

Soon after the war began the Union decided to admit AFS men. This problem of wartime temporaries was one which later the big industrial unions had to solve, but the FBU was probably the first to encounter it. Its regular members acted with extraordinary comradeship and generosity, for outside the Union the regulars regarded the amateurs as a threat to jobs and hard-won standards of service and wages. Yet they put up money to organise the AFS, and suggested a dual system of representation. The sections for regulars and AFS were kept separate: each had its Management Committee, and each its own set of paid officials and organisers, with John Horner as secretary of both sections. At first the Executive Council, the final authority of the Union, was composed only of regulars, but soon after AFS men were given a third of the seats, and later half. Later again the president of the whole Union was to be a former AFS man. I doubt if there existed another example of such wholehearted cooperation between old hands of a craft union and dilutees.

The first meeting of the Management Committee of the AFS Section, with some 17,000 members, introduced me to W——, the chairman, and his henchman J——. I was astonished at his chairmanship, for he entered lengthily into every discussion and hardly allowed adequate expression to views different from his. The meeting, which had begun at 11 a.m. ended around 8 p.m. with the agenda unfinished. The minutes, of the type where a resumé is given of each man's arguments, ran to over forty pages. I had been used to orderly borough council committees, where an able chairman can dispose of a long agenda in about two hours, and to political party committees. Clearly there were new factors at work.

Most of the AFS Committee had never been members of such a body before. Thus was raw material thrust into the machinery of a modern union. In most committees an inefficient chairman is assisted by the good sense and orderly minds of the members, but in those early days the other members of the Management Committee evidently thought that W——'s manner of conducting affairs was normal. I was horrified.

It was obvious that W—— was anti-regular, and that he and Horner were at loggerheads. For four or five months the endless quarrels went on. W—— was eventually voted out of the chair, and Ken Baker, a man of solid ability, took his place. Then J—— made a mistake. He approached the Transport & General Workers to see whether they would form an AFS Section. If so, he would bring over most of the FBU's AFS members. Unfortunately, the official he interviewed was a friend of mine on the borough council, who took the correct line of notifying Horner, as secretary of the FBU, of the advance that had been made to him, and also spoke to me on the subject. J——, when asked to explain his action, produced an unconvincing story, and was expelled, followed by W——. For a time meetings were punctuated by the entrance of one or other of the pair to protest; then they formed their own union. For a short time an embarrassment, it was refused TUC recognition, and settled back to be small and uninfluential.

Meanwhile I had been trying to organise the London River Service by establishing union branches at each station spread over nearly a hundred miles of river, getting a committee going, and arranging for representation with the superintendent. We were lucky to have him. A forty-year-old former seaman, Mr King loved boats, and under his control a feeling of belonging to a special and good service began to grow up.

As a result of my dealing with the superintendent I began to understand more fully what the function of a trade union should be, whether in a uniformed service or industry. That we were uniformed seemed to many people a reason why we should not have a union at all: it was, they said, incompatible with discipline. Properly run, and accepted by the authorities, it can be the reverse. Trade unions are, in the mind of the public, associated with the right to strike, and it is true enough that to withdraw his labour is the last resort of an injured man. Yet firemen, who had their union, then understood well enough that the theoretical strike weapon they possessed could never be used. Fires, peacetime or wartime, had to be put out, though action could be taken if the worst came to the worst against station duties, and in all the angry discussions I heard on the methods to be chosen for forcing redress of grievances such as the level of injury pay, no one, however militant, suggested that we should not put out fires.

Almost my last act as district representative was to start a small duplicated paper for union members, *The River Service Bulletin*. It was the first means of bringing fireboat men throughout Britain to a common pride in their particular branch of the service. Throughout the country there were then over 300 fireboats and firefighting craft, their crews held together by a common love for boats. But whereas we of London's River Thames Formation had some 2,000 men, in a small provincial port or river town there might be one fireboat with a crew of half a dozen.

These new experiences were to prove most useful when, some years later, I found myself operationally responsible for a large staff, and sitting on the employers' side of the negotiating table.

I had also been elected to the union's Executive Council, and made a member of two or three sub-committees. Union work took two or three full days a week. Special leave was given me, under arrangements made between the union and the London Fire Brigade.

Much happened: the bombing of our head office and the loss of all our records; the starting of a benefit fund; efforts to organise munitions work at the stations. They all widened my experience.

I enjoyed sitting on the Executive. Several members were Communists, the rest assorted left-wingers, I alone a right-winger, often therefore unable to find a seconder for a mild political motion. Personally, however, all were pleasant colleagues: I remember Sidney Darke, a former busman, who later left the Communist Party; John Horner, the union's secretary, is still a good friend. I had many an argument with him – then a convinced Communist and atheist – and his charming wife Pat, on both politics and religion. Just before the 1945 election I told him that the fairly numerous Communist candidates would poll few votes, and he told me to be a realist. I was right. Much later, John left the Communists over the issue of Hungary, and became a left-wing Labour MP.

One day a circular reached my station seeking applications for a post as assistant editor of the *Manual of Firemanship*, to be attached to the Home Office Fire Staff. I had never, I fear, heard of the *Manual*, but I knew something of editing. I applied, was interviewed, and got the job, moving from being a leading fireman to the chairborne officer class as company officer, later as senior company officer.

The *Manual* staff, housed in one room in London's Horseferry House, were three: V.J. Wilmoth, peacetime editor of the magazine *Fire Protection* and author of a handbook for auxiliary firemen; Frank Eyre, former racing motorist (Brooklands had done his front teeth no good), yachtsman, white-water canoeist, writer for a research agency, and NFS officer (on 18 August 1941 the former auxiliaries and regular brigades had been amalgamated into the single National Fire Service), and me.

The original idea of the *Manual* – planned as a seven-volume encyclopaedia of peace and wartime firefighting – had been that experts should write on their specialities. It was soon found that firemen, however expert, could not write well, and a new beginning was made with those who could. We were to pick the brains of the experts, and distil their knowledge into pages that would lucidly convey it to the trainee and the promotee. That policy worked well, and the volumes I helped to write between 1942 and 1945 remained textbooks for many years thereafter.

I had a deal to learn. Wilmoth had been in the world of firefighting before the war; Eyre had been a successful Blitz fire officer and, like Wilmoth, had a technical bent. I was a river man, whose experience of land firefighting was limited to one short and terrifying training course, at which I had been sent climbing with hook ladders up the outside of the four-storey drill tower at Lambeth. Neither had I any technical inclination. However, there is no simpler place at which to begin than the beginning, and there I began.

I came later to the work than the others, when the early volumes were under way, Part I indeed printing. We worked by each taking certain chapters to research, write and illustrate. Research was partly from written sources, mostly technical, and partly by going out to look and to question. Having done basic research for a chapter, we would then write a first draft, which was widely circulated to experts for comment. After about three drafts, we had a text ready to print. Meanwhile we would have been getting illustrative drawings done in the Fire Staff studio. With Gordon Logie, later a distinguished LCC architect, in charge, the staff included the painter Leonard Rosoman. All three of us worked on each final draft and set of proofs, to make sure no mistakes crept in. Few did. I found myself getting absorbed not only in the subject-matter of the chapters I had to write, but in the fireman's life and the organisation of the service. So did Frank Eyre. Together we also tried to interest Collins in a Fire Service volume in the wartime 'Britain in Pictures' series: they refused, but we did one on *English Rivers and Canals* instead. We also collaborated on *The Fire Service Today* in the 'Pageant of Progress' series of my own OUP Juvenile Department, which sold well for many years.

The job's interest lay in learning a new subject, then setting it out clearly and readably for ordinary recruits. To write a chapter on 'Fires in Crashed Aircraft', for instance, I not only studied the construction of operational aircraft, but visited many East Anglian fire stations to talk to men who had fought fires in bombers returning from Germany. Indeed one night I cruised in a dimly lit car along Fenland roads looking for a crash so that I could watch firemen at work. We found one: I still remember the fair handle-bar moustache of a dead officer I found flung a hundred yards from his plane.

I wrote chapters such as those on fires in oil installations and in ships; one too on fires in rural areas, which included thatch, ricks, crops and forests. I was gratified when a senior officer returned my draft of that one with the comment that it could only have been written by a fireman of long experience. In fact, I had never seen a single one of the fires I had written about. But I had talked to dozens of men who had.

In the last year of the war I did a tremendous amount of work for a volume on *Special Fires*. I visited every kind of textile mill and works, and a wide range of other industries – oil-cake mills, cork processors, starch works, furniture makers, shipyards, match-manufacturers and many more. The work gave me an insight into the processes, working conditions and efficiency of a wide range of industry: later it was to serve me well in the Central Office of Information. I was disappointed when the end of the war in Europe came with the *Special Fires* volume still incomplete.

One memory comes back: of the only time I have ever been so drunk that I've had to be put to bed, all because of interviewing the retired chief of Bradford fire brigade, expert in fires in woollen mills, in the Old Star. As one fireman to another, we pledged each other in pints of old and mild. He told me much about woollen fires as we drank the evening away: next morning my notebook was illegible, my memory vague, my head painful.

Frank Eyre and I were demobilised at the end of July 1945. In the rather over three years since I had joined the Fire Staff, we had published seven volumes totalling 1,264 printed pages, and containing over 600,000 words. I reckoned at the time that I had written about half a million words each year, including all the drafts. It was absorbing work. Maybe I have been lucky, but I have found interest in whatever I have found it necessary to do. And finding interest, one gets on top of, and to some extent shapes, the job, instead of allowing it to take charge.

CHAPTER ELEVEN

LOVE IN PEACE AND WAR

Back in university days at St Edmund Hall, I had once seen in the quad a tall, red-headed, lively girl, and again on the Cherwell I once saw her punting left-handed, attractively and efficiently.

I joined OUP in October 1936, and not long afterwards was put to share a little room with Theodor Schuller. It was on the ground floor off a short passage that joined the front hall of Amen House to the library, and one wall was filled with rows of index cards on shelves. Now and then a tall girl with deep red hair, eyes that were blue when they were not green, usually wearing a dark blue dress embroidered with gold or swags of flowers, would invade us to consult the cards: enquiry from Schuller told me that this was Alice Mary Smyth the librarian, whose married name was Miller, and who was also editing *The Oxford Book of Quotations*, then being prepared.

It was my red-head of the quad and punt.

She was born at South Cerney, Gloucestershire, on 14 December 1908, her father being an army officer. She went to Cheltenham Ladies' College from 1922 to 1928, to St Hilda's College, Oxford, until 1931, then for a post-graduate year to Mount Holyoke College, Massachusetts. In 1935 she married Peter Miller, Oxford friend and later barrister, an early enthusiast for the Territorial Army.

In spring 1938 Alice Mary was twenty-nine, I, Charles, seven months younger. I too was married, my wife being twenty years older. Nevertheless, I regarded myself as happy, and did not regret my marriage, odd though I know it looked. I had no idea how shallow my experience so far had been, nor how shifting were the sands upon which I had built my house.

Before long Alice Mary and I had got to know each other as agreeable companions. A poem of hers suggested more:

> Now say, as far as you can see
> is this a bargain true
> that you shall say nice things to me
> and I'll read Donne to you?
>
> So if the South Downs wait for us
> and still we have not been
> by train, or car, by bike or bus
> to Oxford, nor have seen

the imagined counties spread below
Bredon's enchanted hill
where eye and mind reach out to know
past Wales and further still

and if in no long summer twilight
we lean on Ludlow bridge
and watch the swallows' swirling flight
below the Castle ridge

if field and river, town and sea
never can be true,
still you shall say nice things to me
and I'll read Donne to you.

One omission was rectified in that spring of 1938. On Saturday 14 May we went to Oxford to hire a punt on the Cherwell at Magdalen Bridge and take it over the rollers and on to the Victoria Arms at Marston Ferry. My contemporary notebook records:[1]

A mass of white may on the bank, and in front Beatrice upright on the front of the punt. Her red hair was haloed with white. We walked over the wet fields from the punt, hand in hand, and in the little pub ordered our beer. I gave Beatrice the first poem I had ever written her, and while she read it I looked with embarrassment at a brewers' calendar which showed with woodcuts the seasons of the year. Beatrice having read it came up behind me and put her arms around me and we stood until the barmaid disturbed us.

We walked back across the fields, and at the last stile we kissed: twice, and then I broke away, for I had that day found passion, and I could not then think it good.

References to Beatrice were because we had been attending Charles Williams's lectures on Dante.[2] Was not her – and indeed my – whole remaining life balanced on the fulcrum of the hours until a day or two after the Victoria Arms, she sent me the first love poem I received from her, the last verses of which run:

Did we kiss once, or did we kiss for ever?
The moment's worth what every moment vows,
there is no more, or less; your one, my other endeavour
seek but the treasures which each one allows.

You have possession, therefore desire is trouble,
and at this opening of a different way
all thought and action hold themselves as double,
in your right and in your left hand's balanced obscure sway

> Did we kiss once, and did we kiss for ever
> will you not shrink so hardily to invoke on you
> the long compressed and perilous passion of this heart and liver
> searching through word and line to love and to be true?

The phrase 'did we kiss for ever' and the last two lines show her need and longing to love and to be true for ever, and 'all thought and action hold themselves as double' the choices balanced on the moment's fulcrum.

A few days later, on 23 May 1938, Heinemann published Charles Williams's *He Came Down From Heaven*. In it, Williams expounded the doctrine that owed its beginning to his own married love. Alice Mary must have known about his ideas, but nevertheless I suspect that when she first read the book's last three chapters, 'The Theology of Romantic Love', 'The Practice of Substituted Love' and 'The City', perhaps in an advance copy, she suddenly saw love differently. Her use of the word 'liver' suggests that. Here is Williams, following Dante: 'The first appearance of Beatrice produces three separate effects: it moves the heart as the scene of spiritual emotions, the brain as the centre of perception, and the liver as the place of corporeal states – what . . . we might call the spiritual and the spatial heaven of romantic love.'

Love, I realised, is not only a state; it is, as Williams later calls it, a Way, one susceptible to labour and fruition. This appealed to me, by nature one who tries to act upon my beliefs and experiences.

I arranged to stay in town. We went first to hear a lecture on part of Dante's *Purgatorio* by Williams, then on to the Victoria Palace to see and hear Lupino Lane in *Me and My Girl*. There, in the circle bar during the interval, Love chose me. I put it like that because it seemed like that. I did not choose it, expect it, even welcome it. It chose me. After the show we walked together (one could in safe pre-war London) from Victoria up Park Lane, past Marble Arch and along the Bayswater Road to her front door in Peel Street, off Church Street, Kensington. In a daze, we did not speak a word the whole time, and only exchanged one gentle kiss at parting. In my notebook I wrote: 'It is from this evening that my new life begins,' a phrase taken from Dante's early book, *The New Life (La vita Nuova)* and Charles Williams's phrase 'The new life on the new way'.

Some three weeks later, on Monday 13 June [1938], I being with Alice Mary, I had the kind of experience Dante had had with Beatrice. I knew intuitively in the flash of a second, that I would belong to this woman, whom I hardly knew, for the rest of my life and – my intuition firmly told me – eternity. So it happened. From that day I belonged to her, and as I wait I still do.

Long afterwards, in 1966, recalling her early life, she was to write:

> I suppose the story of our own marriage begins with the day when Charles told me he had left his wife, and taken a single room, and would never live in his old home again, because he had learnt what love and marriage ought to be, and would not keep up a mistake. Nothing but the real thing was marriage. I felt,

with him, that marriage was involved in a moral value that sustained our whole nature, even if my particular experience of it had not been of that kind. I did not see, as he had 'got on' to learn, that an outward ceremony and arrangement might only be an imitation of marriage, and involve very little moral value.

After weeks of indecision, I left my wife in February 1939, moving to a bed-sitting room in Elgin Crescent, London. My action seems to have decided Alice Mary, for she wrote on the 21st: 'we cannot be parted now. Even if we may not always like it, I think Love has taken us and will not let us go, and while we are each with Love we must be with each other, in presence or absence.'

She wrote later that

The war approached. I stayed at home with my husband and child. What changed me was the fact of change in him. Charles lived as married to me but temporarily staying in another house. War broke out, and my husband was called up. Charles joined the Fire Service and was stationed in London, so that we could telephone and sometimes see each other.[3]

On Vesta river fire station on Putney Embankment, life had still to be lived in the early months of war. There Chas and I found that we shared an interest in canals, started to collect books about them, and planned to buy and convert a narrow boat. However, he left the AFS for the RAF, and thus ended our plans. Nevertheless he, and the books we bought, had revived a latent interest.

Then came Hitler's invasion of northern France in early summer 1940, and soon afterwards a telegram to Alice Mary to say that her husband Peter had been killed [in the Dunkirk retreat]. A few weeks later she told me she had agreed to her parents' wish that she should take her daughter Laura to Bermuda, where her naval brother was stationed. I had underestimated the effect that Peter's death would have on her; the desire many people then had to send their children out of beleaguered Britain; and the determination of her parents to get her away from me. I had begun to think that marriage would be in sight once Alice Mary's distress had lessened, for Violet would now see a different situation.

I was bitterly disappointed. However, I had chosen to love, and could not complain when love in absence was substituted for love in presence. I met her in Oxford for a last day together; she was standing in a white coat on the station platform as my train pulled out for London in that late August of 1940. I was not to see her again until January 1944. A few days later her ship sailed in convoy; though some units were sunk, she and Laura reached Bermuda safely. For a time she stayed with her brother and his family; thereafter she had her own little house by the sea, and worked in the Admiralty and in a bookshop.

I learned to live with the situation: by writing part of an airmail letter almost every day and posting it every week (about one in four failed to arrive, as did hers to me: when they did, the censor had sometimes removed a chunk or two); by reading intellectually and emotionally solid books, Shakespeare, Dante,

Wordsworth, Aquinas among them, by considering the applicability of what I read to the state of love in absence that I had to maintain; and by wearing always a band of her red hair around my arm. As Donne did in *The Funeral* I would have bid

> Who ever comes to shroud me, do not harm
> Nor question much
> That subtle wreath of hair, which crowns my arm;
> The mystery, the sign you must not touch,
> For 'tis my outward Soul . . .

Alice Mary having left England, and I in lodgings, such spare time as I had at Vesta came from duty in the watchroom, which had to be manned continuously. I used it to clear my mind on what I believed about the theory and practice of romantic love, in the light of what I had learned from Charles Williams's books, and my love for Alice Mary.

The result was *Strange Fidelity*, its text supplemented by quotations from all manner of writers about love. Finished in 1942, I showed it to Charles Williams, who sent it to T.S. Eliot of Faber's and the publishers Geoffrey Bles. The former said he would prefer a similar book written by Williams himself, the latter turned it down. Rewritten, [Williams] approved it, writing on 6 January 1944: 'I think it is a very good and useful book, and much more valuable than most which try to help our poor lovers.' Six days later Alice Mary was back in England, and wedding time could be foreseen. The manuscript was laid aside, and there it remained until 1992, when a few copies of the original typescript were made available to friends of Charles Williams.

While in OUP's Juvenile Department I had collaborated with C. Hamilton Ellis in *The Young Collector's Handbook*, published in 1940. I took indoor collections, Ellis outdoor. In my boyhood I had enjoyed most of them, to the dismay of my parents, who thought it was unhealthy to be shut up with stamps, coins, tickets, birds' eggs, shells and cigarette cards when I might be playing with other boys. I did not like most other boys and most certainly they did not like me, whereas my collections were good friends in their day. It is a convenience to the budding author if he is also a publisher, as I was, because he can then consider his own manuscript, find himself persuaded of its excellence, and publish it. The *Handbook* was a potboiler, but I earned £20 from the outright sale of my half, and the firm broke even. I only heard of two people who had read it. Much later, I saw it on a second-hand stall, its dust jacket tattered, its price no longer 4s 6d but 1s. I went back every day for a week to see if an unknown friend had bought it. At last it went, I hope to the hands of a boy and not a pulping mill. A delicate emotion hangs around one's first book. So young, so immature, so foolish, and yet a necessary beginning.

Soon after the Blitz began, a friend in the English Universities Press rang me at my fire station to ask if I would write a simple handbook on firefighting for volunteer fire watchers, to be ready in a fortnight. I made a deal with the men on the station that they would do my station housework in exchange for drinks at the bar, went on my next leave day to the Home Office to collect all available literature, consulted one or two regulars, and retired to our air-raid shelter with my portable. Two weeks later I emerged with the manuscript. *Civilian Fire Fighter* sold, as I remember, about 30,000 copies at a shilling in the few weeks before official instructions were available. It was amateurish but cheap, and probably served its ephemeral purpose. A juvenile book, *Maps*, followed in collaboration; I wrote on their history, my collaborator on how they are made. It sold until about 1970. I also unsuccessfully tried my hand at boys' adventure stories, which were followed by *The Fire Service Today* and *English Rivers and Canals*, both with Frank Eyre.

Without Alice Mary, my leave days needed filling. I filled them with theatre-going and canal history research.

A few theatres kept open during the worst of the bombing: others opened later. With Violet I had seen my first ballet, *Job* with Anton Dolin, at the Old Vic before the war. Later I took especially to ballet. I then belonged to the Arts Theatre Club, which often put on an hour at lunchtime; so did the Ambassadors' Theatre: Harold Turner in the Blue-bird *pas de deux* from *The Sleeping Princess*, and Peggy van Praagh in *Peter and the Wolf*. Better were evenings at Sadlers Wells: there I absorbed into myself the dancing of Margot Fonteyn and Robert Helpmann and Frederick Ashton's choreography, watching everything from *Swan Lake* through *Facade* and *The Wise Virgins* to *The Rake's Progress*. Ballet helped me to keep a quiet mind through war and loneliness. Canal history research went on mainly behind the sand-bagged library windows of the Institution of Civil Engineers.

My religious past had been erratic: enthusiasm at confirmation had given way to indifference; at Oxford, three of my closest friends were religious, and for a very short time I became high church. Finding the atmosphere too rarefied, I became a lowish church attender at college chapel until I backslid into agnosticism. Alice Mary stopped all that. So I sought some religious education, in a small India-paper Bible I used on the fire station, in Aquinas and Mother Julian and *The Cloud of Unknowing*.

Most raids stopped in 1942: in the following year, flying bombs (V1s) began, and later rockets (V2s). I had heard no gossip about the V1s, and when my first came over, cut out, and exploded, I thought a plane had crashed. Not long afterwards Tommy Ball from my old station was on a crew that found an unexploded one. I dined out for months on his remark when he returned: 'Blimey, Lofty, it was numbered 136,245. Do you think they've got all that lot?'

I didn't like flying bombs, and saw no reason to be brave on leave nights, for I wanted to be a live man and not a dead hero when Alice Mary came home. However, on one occasion I was brave. In my Fire Service officer's uniform, I was waiting on a Waterloo platform for the last train to Stoneleigh, reading the evening paper. Near me, doing the same, were a British naval and an American army officer. A few yards from us was an air-raid shelter. A flying bomb droningly approached: I thought of all that blacked-out glass overhead, but kept on reading;

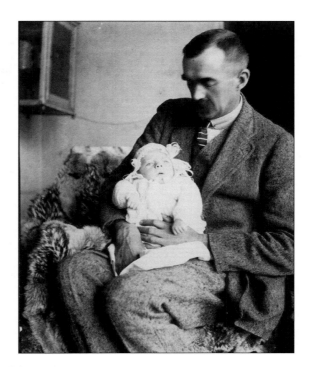

Newly born, with his father
Alexander. As Charles himself
commented, both look nervous.

Charles, aged three months, with
his mother Marion.

Charles with his father at Mountain View, in
October 1910.

Charles with his South African nurse, 'My
beloved Esther', probably in October 1910.

Charles and his parents on board *Dover
Castle*, on his first voyage to England, in
October 1911.

Charles with his mother Marion, around 1915, when he was aged six.

At Park Town School, near Johannesburg. The adults are the headmaster and his wife 'Fishy'. The children are unidentified.

Charles, aged about eleven.

Charles rowing at Plettenberg Bay.

A typical 'dorp', probably Wolmaransstad.

Charles's father, Alexander, when he was a magistrate at Wolmaransstad, about 1920.

Charles as, in his own words, 'mainstay of the Officers Training Corps' at Blundells School, Tiverton.

Rock House, Halberton, next to the Grand Western Canal, where Charles and his mother lived in 1927–8.

St Edmund Hall, Oxford, which Charles attended between 1928 and 1932. Charles's room was in the top dormer on the right.

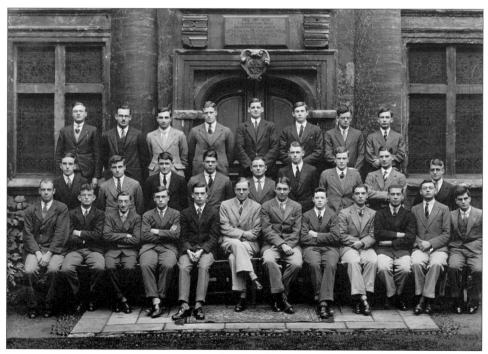

At St Edmund Hall in October 1928, newly arrived. Charles is in the light suit in the front row.

Manual of Firemanship staff, 1945. On the front row, left to right: Charles; V.J. Wilmoth; Commander Aylmer Firebrace, Chief of Staff; Frank Eyre, co-founder of the Inland Waterways Association; and Gordon Logie.

28 Newton Road, Paddington, where Charles and Alice Mary lived between 1946 and 1962.

Choosing the site for the UK pavilion at the Brussels Exhibition, 1954. Charles is slightly hidden in the centre; on his left is Howard V. Lobb, one of the architects who designed the pavilion.

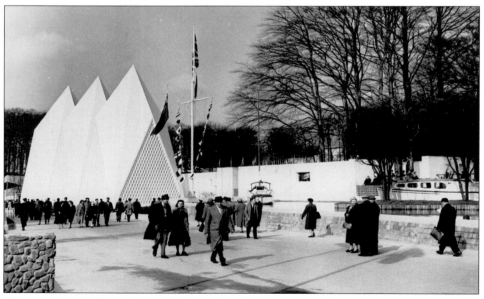

The three-spired UK pavilion, seen from the side. Note the modern pleasure boat in the right background.

At Charles's retirement party from the Central Office of Information, 1962. Alice Mary is sitting talking to Ben Thomas, another COI Controller. Held aloft is the extended retirement card showing Charles steering a narrow boat while reading a book.

Charles and Alice Mary on holiday in Devon in 1954.

Silver Street House, where the Hadfields would live between 1962 and 1972, in summer 1954, when they were using it as a holiday home.

Silver Street House in 1962.

Charles and Alice Mary, 1950s.

Charles and Alice Mary in the late 1960s.

One of Charles and Alice Mary's last canal engagements, on the RCHS visit to the Midlands on 19 May 1984. They are standing on the Engine Arm aqueduct, overlooking the Birmingham Canal New Main Line at Smethwick. (John Horsley Denton)

Charles, Alice Mary and Marty Seymour of the West London Industrial Archaeological Society, outside the Eliot Arms in South Cerney. (Marty Seymour)

Charles Hadfield in his prime. This appears to be a passport photograph, probably taken for his COI trip to Africa in 1960. Charles intensely disliked having his photograph taken, and this is perhaps the best portrait from this period.

so did they. The bomb cut out. We all kept on reading. The explosion came. We all let out our breaths, and kept on reading. Three service honours had been saved.

I was clear about my love for Alice Mary, but her regular and loving letters could not entirely reassure me that she would not marry in Bermuda, and never come back. She was free to remarry; I was not. And to return to me she had to cross the submarine-threatened Atlantic, for air flights were for those with a very special reason for return. However, late in 1943 a great friend of hers, Joan Bordewich, wife of an RAF officer, with a little boy, decided to return, and asked Alice Mary to accompany her. Joan had priority, returning to her husband, and rightly thought the authorities would not separate her from Alice Mary once they had started.

Ronnie, Joan's husband, hinted to me that her convoy was expected. I did not dare leave the big Fire Staff office in Horseferry House in case the telephone call for which I had waited for over three years should come while I was out. It came [on 13 January 1944]: I was at the other end of the room, and hurtled past desks and cabinets to take it while the others, well knowing my romance, listened with held breath. Alice Mary had arrived at Liverpool in an air-raid, had spent the night in a transit hostel, and was going to South Cerney.

We arranged a few days together at Ludlow. [On 26 January] I went down by train, which she would join at Kemble station, nearest to South Cerney. There she was on the platform with Laura, and we were reunited in a crowded Great Western third-class compartment. I then started my first lessons in getting on with a child, for Laura, not quite then five, was disinclined to share her mother. I was still not free to marry, but with Alice Mary home, I could once more press my wife for a divorce. It took eighteen months.

In time not spent in fire stations, I lived in lodgings; finally with James MacColl, leader of the Labour group in the Paddington Council, of which I was still a member, though during the war the main work had been done by a small emergency committee. James, with whom I later collaborated on two books on local government, leased a delightful two-storey house, The White Cottage, 21 Randolph Road, Little Venice, only a few yards from the canal. Much later, it was to become a much-loved home to Alice Mary and me.

Rockets, though more devastating [than flying bombs], were less worrying, for one did not hear them coming. Yet one of the last rocket-bombs to be fired [in January 1945], caused my only war wound. Breakfasting with MacColl, I was lifting a cup of coffee to my mouth when the bomb fell some way away. I jumped, and the cup cracked a front tooth.

I returned to Oxford University Press in September 1945 again to head Juvenile Department. While waiting for [my] divorce to be made absolute, we house-hunted in London. Meanwhile, Ronnie and Joan Bordewich had bought a small six-roomed semi-detached early nineteenth-century house at 28 Newton Road, off Westbourne Grove, Paddington. They were ready to move in – Ronnie had already stripped the wallpaper ready for redecoration – when, within a few days of first becoming ill, Joan died of cancer. Stricken, he offered us the house at what he had paid for it. Alice Mary had collected from country sales furniture and linen, for those were the days of 'points' rationing for all new curtains, sheets or other textiles. She found enough; more we bought over the months from second-hand shops in London. In any case we were too excited to notice much.

We married on 20 October, the day after my divorce had been made absolute. Inwardly we were at Heaven's threshold, accompanied by choirs of angels. Outwardly it was Paddington Register Office in the Harrow Road, before a kindly registrar. Once the ring (Bravington's jewellers, Charing Cross, £1 5s, all we could afford) was on her finger, I was occupied in holding tightly on to her hand, wondering what I was going to say when our healths were proposed at the rationed lunch the Cafe Royal had provided for the dozen guests that we could afford. In reality all went well, and in late afternoon we were able to dispose of our relations, and turn the key of our little house with only ourselves and my newly gained step-daughter Laura, inside. Alice Mary was rising thirty-seven, I seven months younger. It was a moment of joy and fright. For 7½ years we had worked doggedly in presence and absence for this moment.

An early discard was prudence. As the war had drawn to an end there had grown in Alice Mary and me an urgency to start real life again; family life, a job, ideas, books, pictures, music. Laura needed a home, Alice Mary and I a home and a baby. So, with the minimum of furniture and no wallpaper, we ate our first meal in our own home, put Laura to bed, and gave ourselves to completing our initial programme on the floor, for the railway, with clear grasp of essentials, had delivered the centre of the bed but not the headboards or the legs. Just under a year later Alec was born.

CHAPTER TWELVE

COI, AFRICA AND BRUSSELS

Almost nine months after our wedding, I doubled my salary. I was reading *The Times* at breakfast. The previous day I had been made furious by my boss's (Sir Humphrey Milford had by now retired) removal, without consultation, of part of my precious allocation for Juvenile books of then tightly rationed printing paper in the interests of other parts of Oxford's list. I turned to the 'Situations Vacant' column: 'Central Office of Information', I read, 'Vacancies for a Director of Publications Division and a Chief Books Editor.' The advertised salary of the first post was twice what I was earning; of the second, one and a half times. I showed Alice Mary the advertisement. 'I might try for Chief Books Editor.' 'Try for both,' she insisted.

That evening I typed out two applications. They disguised, I hope, the fact that I had been in publishing for less than four years, with my own department for only eighteen months. I posted them; on my way a thought occurred to me: 'What is the Central Office of Information?' I looked it up in *Whitaker*. Ministry of Information, yes, but no Central Office (it had only been set up in April). Odd. What had I done?

I soon found out. A letter summoned me to a Board. Behind a table sat a darkish young man; in a corner huddled others, wreathed in smoke, anonymous. The dark man asked question after question. No one else spoke. Then he turned to me and asked 'Why do you think the Ministry of Information wartime illustrated books – *Battle of Britain*, *Bomber Command* and so on – were so successful?' For nine months I had struggled with one overwhelming problem, that of paper on which to print books, any books, for my stock shelves were empty. Before me rose an image of the bright piles of *Bomber Command* on the railway bookstalls. 'Plenty of paper,' I said. The dark man sat quietly, but beyond the smoke in the huddled corner I heard a chuckle. I was shown out.

I did not then know who the interviewer was. Robert Fraser had been a journalist before he joined the Ministry, where he had risen to be director of publications. He it was who had been responsible for producing *Battle of Britain* and the others, masterpieces of popular presentation, each picture, each caption lovingly considered and thoughtfully put just so; their combined sales exceeded thirty million. Now he was director-general of the Central Office of Information, and I had told him their sales were due to the paper on which they were printed. Not many men would have given me their own old job after that, but Bob Fraser did.

On 2 September 1946 I arrived to take over the job of director of publications. I had by then established COI as a common-service government department without policy responsibilities, producing all kinds of publicity material for home and overseas use, which I assumed my new division was busily preparing to produce for Britons once again at peace. My experience was, I thought, up to that. Fifteen minutes later I had a nasty shock. I discovered first, that 'Publications' meant far more, and that my responsibilities covered some dozen monthly magazines and hardly any books, because the wartime ones had ended and no one had thought what peacetime ones would be needed; worse, almost all the magazines were in foreign languages, and went to the four corners of the world. No one had even mentioned them. I knew nothing whatever about magazines, and since my boyhood my only overseas experience was of a boarding house in Brittany. After that it was a minor shock to find that I had a staff of about sixty. If I had had any idea of where to walk to, I would have walked out. Instead, I sat at my desk and wondered where to start. I pressed the bell for my secretary, and asked her what she advised. 'Send for your section heads,' she said. I hadn't been used to sending for people at Oxford – I had just got up and put my head round their door. 'Hadn't I better go and see them?' I countered. 'Certainly not. Send for them. You must begin right,' she replied; 'start with John McMillan'. I sent for him. He came. I was launched.

The next eighteen months were glorious. John McMillan, an old Heinemann man who had gone to the Foreign Office during the war to run propaganda magazines, and now found himself in COI, was head of the magazine side, managing a group of British and foreign-born editors who combined eccentricity with brilliance. At that time we were selling in European countries, most just liberated, a series of 128-page monthly digests under the name *Echo*, published each month in French, German, Dutch, Italian, Greek and Finnish in collaboration with local publishing firms, their purpose being to bring populations up to date on world events and thinking. To these, he and I added at Foreign Office request four more digests for Asian countries, partly in English and partly in their own languages; having looked everywhere in England for Chinese type and finding none, we had to get the language pages of the Chinese edition done by calligraphy. Total circulation of the ten digests was some 760,000, of which the German version took 550,000.

We also produced two picture magazines, *Blick in der Welt*, a 56-page monthly selling some half a million, and *Today*, for free distribution by the Colonial Office, to tell inhabitants of the colonies about Britain and each other. It was produced every six weeks in English and Swahili.

We also started a 32-page monthly picture paper called *Coal* for circulation to the miners, then just nationalised. By guess and by God we worked with the Ministry of Fuel and Power to get material, design, edit, produce and sell 100,000 copies of the first issue all in a few months. Later we handed it over to the National Coal Board.

I had few worries on the magazine side, but plenty on that of books. No Chief Book Editor had been found, and for a year I had to do two jobs. The demand for COI booklets mainly for use within the United Kingdom also rose rapidly. In this post-war phase, the government wanted economic information widely spread, so we had to produce for sale (but not write) simple booklets on the economic facts of life illustrated with charts.

Then came the proposed National Insurance and National Health schemes, both to start on the same day in 1948, and both requiring explanatory pamphlets with household distribution. This meant the printing of some fourteen million copies of each. To print two such pamphlets together meant occupying batches of printing machines for months on end at a time when everyone wanted print, and when the government, contrary to popular belief, had no compulsory power to get it done.

The Ministry of Health, the Ministry of National Insurance and I were responsible for the texts. The health pamphlet was a short, simple job, on which Tom Fife Clark, then Chief Information Officer of that Ministry, did most of the work. That on insurance was very different. *The Family Guide to National Insurance* was a 32-page booklet which had to explain the new benefits and how to claim them, as well as the new contributions and what they were for. The text had no force in law, but it had to be accurate and at the same time simple enough to be understood by the man or woman behind the letterbox. So day after day I sat beside Matthew Crosse, Chief Information Officer of National Insurance. The first draft from the administrators was fine, except that neither he nor I could understand it, so we worked over it line by line. When we got a paragraph to read clearly we would ring up the expert to know if it was still correct. Often it wasn't, and we had to try again. In the end we were reasonably satisfied.

Because we felt 32 pages of small print needed some illustrations, we put in some humorous drawings of little owls. The result as far as I was concerned was to get half a dozen abusive letters and some anonymous ones. Some complained of the owls and some of the government. I replied to the abusive ones thanking the writers for their interesting comments, which I said I would circulate to my staff for their instructions. One writer apologised. I tried not to remember the wording of the anonymous ones. This was the only occasion in my life when I have had any such, and I was horrified by their virulence and by the effect, when anonymous, that they had on me.

By June 1948, twenty months after leaving my quiet Oxford room with its filed rows of Biggles and Dimsie, I had a staff of over a hundred and was madly but happily coping with household distributions in Britain, British Book Export schemes in Europe, and magazines selling in Indonesia and China. Outsiders refer to the civil servant as sheltered. In fact, there are few occupations more hazardous than the public service. A civil servant, in those circumstances, had to work very fast within properly granted financial authorities that could not be exceeded without permission, while being completely accurate. These points escape many.

One morning in June 1948, Robert Fraser offered me the post of controller (overseas), in charge of my own division and four others which mainly produced material for use by information officers overseas. At that time the COI was a big office, with some 1,700 staff. Under the director-general, there were four controllers; I was in charge of material used overseas. Under us were the directors of divisions. Later, the number of controllers was reduced to two, home and overseas. A Films division was then added to my five existing divisions. Yet I was still a temporary civil servant, pensionless and removable at a month's notice.

We were then in a thoroughly difficult position. COI was suspected by the public of being a vast propaganda organisation which wasted quantities of money, and by the Conservative opposition as likely at any time to show political bias towards the Labour Government. It was therefore difficult to recruit staff. War having ended, many of the best people in the Ministry of Information had returned to their old jobs, and the ebbing tide had not been followed by a flood of the same quality. Only those of strong public spirit or very hard up for a job were willing to work as unestablished civil servants in an organisation so little regarded.

Because of the staff difficulty, and because we were all new to the job of peacetime government information work since it was itself new, what we did was patchy. Worse, our relations with our client departments, those that wanted books, films, exhibitions or whatnot from us, were poor, exasperation leading by many lengths from satisfaction. Admiration was to most of us an unknown feeling.

It was clear that if the climate did not quickly change the COI would cease to exist as soon as the Conservatives got into power, and a potentially good activity would end. My job as controller was to change it on the overseas side – and quickly.

Among so much to be done, one action stood out. I could no longer go on calling myself controller (overseas) until I had taken myself abroad to visit countries administered by the three departments to whom I was then responsible, to learn for myself what the information officers who used our material thought of its utility (its policy content was of course not our business), and what improvements they could suggest. Thus I returned to Africa early in 1951.

I was away from home for almost three months, and visited (I use the old names) Italy, Cyprus, Egypt, Uganda, Kenya, Northern and Southern Rhodesia [Zambia and Zimbabwe], the Union of South Africa, Swaziland and Portuguese East Africa [Mozambique]. I wrote to Alice Mary almost every day. In retrospect these letters have some historical value because of their immediacy. Written with no purpose other than love's, they tell what I saw and thought.

From all the countries I visited I have space only for some glimpses of one, Uganda. I had flown there from Cairo, with a refuelling stop at Khartoum, in a Hermes forty-seater, to fly in over Lake Victoria Nyanza to land at Entebbe.

Monday 29 January, 3 pm, Lake Victoria Hotel, Entebbe
This is ideal Africa! From my window: green meadow and parkland, a few flowering shrubs, a bed of red hot pokers and canna lilies, clumps of trees, and Lake Victoria Nyanza, soft blue to the horizon, with a little green island in the foreground and two or three in the distance. . . . The sun shining out of a clear sky, and a slight heat haze and shimmer over the ground. Entebbe is almost on the equator, 3,700 feet up on Lake Victoria.

A pretty two-storey cream hotel with red tiles built in a square round a green courtyard. My room – twin beds – has dark polished wood furniture, local I should think, red and blue native cloth, and a polished red floor. . . . I go to Kampala tomorrow . . . It is the business town while Entebbe has the government offices, and then off into the interior. . . .

Monday 29 January, 9 pm, Lake Victoria Hotel, Entebbe
Palled up with an elderly Scottish railway engineer, out to survey a new line. We had drinks and dinner together, and have just come back from a walk. The nice lake breeze has died away, it is rather stuffy and hot, and a little summer lightning in the distance. The grasshoppers chirruping away like anything, sky bright with stars. . . .

Tuesday 30 January, 10.15 pm, Imperial Hotel, Kampala
. . . I spent the morning and part of the afternoon here in the Inf[ormation] Office here, after a 20 mile car run from Entebbe. Press Officer called Parry, and the PRO and Social Welfare Officer, Gayer, who is over him, both nice. Tea with Gayer and his wife, and a Colonial Office man called Chinn who is here studying social welfare. . . . The plan is to go out looking at Uganda from Thursday to Saturday and from Monday to Wednesday. . . .

The Africans I have seen along the roads look strong and healthy – the women especially tall and well-built, dressed in a sort of sari of one bright colour or a Paisley kind of pattern. Many of them have bicycles: small-holdings all over the hills. Banana-trees along the roads (most bearing a local type of hard green banana which is cooked), mealies [maize] here and there. In the town bougainvillaeas and other flowering shrubs, the better buildings cream with red tiles. The Gayers had a lovely African house – one-storey, big rooms, dark and cool inside, big garden all around. Kampala is growing quickly, and some of the new houses are quite a long way out, but his is a new one near the centre. . . .

Wednesday 31 January, 5 pm, Imperial Hotel, Kampala
. . . Uganda seems to have no noticeable colour bar – all races scrum in the shops and the Post Office, and Indians come into the hotel, though I do not know if Africans ever do. An Indian is Mayor of Kampala. Uganda is a protectorate with a number of native governments, the biggest being the province of Buganda, under the Kabaka . . . who has his palace a few miles from here.

I went out to Entebbe after lunch to see the Director of Agriculture and the Secretary for African Affairs – the second a courtesy call, the first to see whether COI could produce any instructional material on such subjects as soil erosion. It is possible, but I think better if it is done locally, as conditions vary so much from place to place . . .

Thursday 1 February, 9.15 pm, Mountains of the Moon Hotel, Fort Portal
We got here at 7, to find that Chinn, the Colonial Office man, who was the centre-piece of the trip, was ill. He went to bed, the proprietress of the hotel

took his temperature, and it is 105 [degrees], so we have sent for a doctor – luckily there is one. . . . I am going to deputise for him tomorrow – no one will know the difference. . . .

. . . The distance from here to Kampala is 205 miles. . . . Very pretty run. First through hilly country, rather like the lowlands of Scotland, strips of woodland along the valleys that weren't so different from English woods except that they were thicker, because of the creepers. . . . Then over the hills, and down here through thick forest, but we didn't see much of that as we ran into a heavy storm. Uganda hasn't many villages. Each farmer lives in a little house (mud and wattle, rising to mud and wattle with corrugated iron roof, rising to brick with a tile roof) in the middle of his own smallholding of 20 acres or so. Usually it is the middle of a banana plantation, and looks very snug. Often a bright shrub outside the door. We saw cotton growing, and near here the tea plantations. . . .

You would love the space. . . . the bright colours, the hills, and so much else. It is a prosperous place – partly owing to producing needed raw materials like cotton, sugar and tea – partly also to having a good deal of spare land, so that anyone can buy a little plot for a small sum and become a farmer. So there cannot be unemployment or a floating population. Masses of Africans have bicycles, and some have cars, and their clothes are quite good. Their shops are full of good quality food, and cheap coloured clothes.

Saturday 3 February. Mountains of the Moon Hotel, Fort Portal
. . . I haven't explained about the mountains. The range is called Ruwenzori (which does not mean Mountains of the Moon). It is about 20 miles long, and for part of its length forms the boundary between Uganda and the Belgian Congo. The hotel faces one end of the range – the mountains are about 20 miles away – but up the other end the highest peaks, over 17,000 feet, are snow-clad and provide Alpine climbing. They are nearly always in cloud, but at sunset last night we got a glimpse of them. When Stanley passed to the south of here he was told that there was a range of mountains to the north with salt on the top, which he disbelieved. It did not occur to him that it might be snow on the Equator.

Chinn had a touch of the sun through not wearing his hat – he stayed in bed yesterday, but is all right today . . . You would have laughed . . . at me yesterday deputising for Chinn. They are trying to get what we would call Women's Institutes going in these little places in order to provide some interests for the women and also on the one hand to make them a little less dependent on their husbands, and on the other to prevent the younger ones from being attracted by the bright lights of Kampala. So about six women's clubs have been got going by African women with some encouragement from Government, and a club house built here – like a village hall with a stage and dressing rooms. Yesterday the six clubs were joining in a sale of work at the club house, so in the morning we drove 8 miles to one of the clubs to meet the members and look at the work they were sending. It was run by the Chief's wife, and had about sixty members. No one spoke English . . . I made a few flowery remarks, and we piled the work into the car together with the two leading ladies, and came back to Fort Portal . . .

. . . Then to the sale of work, which was exactly like a similar affair in England. The grand lady who opened it (the Queen . . . very well dressed, who arrived in a large car and presented the prizes, and walked round to talk to the stallholders); the clergyman (the Rural Dean, black); the leading ladies (mostly chiefs' wives); the cups of tea and buns; the efforts to earmark the best things before the opening, the gathering on the platform for the opening, and so on. . . .

In the evening, we went up to see the R.C. Mission which has been here since 1895 – there is also a CMS [Church Missionary Society] one. Fathers of all nationalities – about a dozen – with an American in charge. They showed me the church – a large one with quite a good interior in spite of the corrugated iron roof. It holds about 2,000. There is a school and a technical school attached to the mission. Nearly all education here is done by the missions, who get a government grant.

Then we went to the village dance in the same hall. . . . The dancing was western, with a very energetic band conducted by a gentleman in tails. . . . Just like a village dance – few good couples and the rest hopeless. . . .

I ran across one of the settlers this morning – there are very few here, because land purchase by Europeans was stopped in 1910. He was a big tea planter who is said to be wealthy. He said to me: 'The Government makes too much of these paramount chiefs,' when he saw the Mukama's car going by. It is not difficult for people out here in the Government service, who have no personal interest involved, to maintain what is a very altruistic and high-minded attitude towards the African's future – I'm sure the right one. But it is not so easy for settlers or merchants, who have a stake in the land. . . .

I suppose the position will be reached in twenty or thirty years when all the West and East African colonies will be more or less self-governing with African majorities. [In fact, Uganda became independent in 1962.]

This is a really lovely place. I'm sitting on the (single-storey) hotel verandah. In front, green lawns, masses of bright flowers in beds, one or two poplar trees, a row of a sort of palm, a jacaranda tree (blue) and a pink flowering tree beyond, then glimpses of big banana groves and the village, beyond a row of conical hills that were once volcanoes, and then the mountains, 10,000 feet opposite us, but as we are 5,000 here they are 5,000 above the hotel . . . It is cool today, with a breeze and white clouds, though we are almost on the Equator. . . .

During my three years-odd as controller (overseas) before the 1951 election brought in a government with a Conservative majority of sixteen, the staff under me worked hard to turn us round, from a group of divisions with a negative to one with a positive reputation. Those on the Home side were doing the same. We just made it. The COI was cut to half its size; active information work within the UK nearly ended, and overseas reduced. But we survived. Till 1954 we continued to be cut; thence to Suez we ran level, and from Suez until 1961 we expanded in money and activity well past the point from which we had started, though in staff smaller, because of higher productivity. The curve was levelling out when I left COI in 1962.

I soon found out that if one had energy and good temper and could bide one's time, the scope for creative enterprise in the public service was great, while the ends one served were usually worthwhile, and seldom worse than harmless. The last word is not denigratory. In many occupations of the modern world a man will do well to be able to say to St Peter 'I did no harm.' Here COI was fortunate, for many of its Divisions were headed by outstanding men and women who would never normally have entered the service but having joined the wartime Ministry, some quite low down like Fraser himself, had stayed after the war because they enjoyed the work; him I especially liked for his humanity and admired for his powers of thought and expression.

It was then the civil service view – as it was also in industry and commerce – that compulsory internal common services, whether within one department or the service as a whole, increase efficiency. That was not my view. Therefore, a senior officer in a common service department myself, I considered that COI could only succeed if it became so efficient that our clients would feel it a pleasure and not an irritation to come to us.

Government information work overseas is now a recognised activity of many countries, its purpose being to support the policies of the government and the interests of the nation, by informing others of facts upon which to judge and act, and by persuading them to accept our policies as sensible and constructive. Therefore it then seemed to me necessary to provide reliable services on facts, and clear guidance on policy. Underlying the heavy stuff, however, there should be a flow of material which presented the country as interesting, lively and stimulating and its people as thoughtful, enjoying themselves, getting on in life, helping others – human and preferably likeable. This because few are prepared to listen sympathetically to arguments or persuasion from those they dislike or find unsympathetic.

It was not difficult to send out correct facts. COI's Reference Division did so. It was relatively easy, too, to explain and support policy once Ministers had decided what it was. But the presentation of 'The British, Are They Human?' was full of pitfalls. If one presented one's countrymen and women without their warts, the percipient foreigner, who had met them in the flesh, became incredulous. If one showed them as one thinks they really are, foreigners are favourably impressed by one's honesty (their own people are much the same), but one's own countrymen overseas write excited letters to Ministers about the picture of Britain being put out at public cost. Fortunately, being in foreign languages and placed in foreign newspapers or radio or television, they didn't often recognise that it was information material.

Within my own department there was scope for as much energy and ability as I had, and as much responsibility as I cared to take. My experience almost exactly reversed the popular idea of the buck-passing, uncreative, committee-ridden civil servant faced with responsible, creative individualists in private enterprise. This remark is not lightly tossed off. COI spent much time seeking the cooperation and help of firms in publicising British exports overseas, and one of my duties was to look after parties of businessmen who spent a day at the office at the rate of two or three hundred a year. I always enjoyed doing it, and I learned much. But I did not have cause to be ashamed of my colleagues or the organisation to which I belonged.

Late in 1953, I was told that I was to be awarded a CMG. A holder of the CMG is a Companion of the Most Distinguished Order of Saint Michael and Saint George, an Order originally created in 1818 as an award for those who had served well while the Ionian Islands, off the coast of Greece, were a British Protectorate. It was later recreated as an award for those whose service to the State had mainly been overseas. The choice of St George, who is patron saint of Greece as well as England, is a reminder of its origin. I have to relate that within the civil service its initials are said to stand for 'Call Me God'.

My other main excitement of this period had an African flavour of its own. The Belgians decided to stage outside Brussels in 1958 the first full-scale international exhibition to be held since the Second World War, to commemorate the fiftieth anniversary of the Belgian Congo. Visitors to Brussels can still see the Atomium, built as the central feature of 'The Brussels Universal and International Exhibition'. Exhibitions Division of the COI were given the job of planning a British pavilion, and just enough money to do it. There was also to be an industrial pavilion, the responsibility of the Federation of British Industries and the Board of Trade.

We began planning in 1954. Such jamborees had been held regularly before the war, and we had to design, build and operate for some six months, a pavilion which would do Britain credit. Pre-war British efforts had not done that. Legends of walls decorated with fishing rods and hunting horns were still strong. COI was a professional department, with the brilliant Cecil Cooke as director of exhibitions, and he determined to do much better.

He roughed out the design – I still remember it – on the back of an envelope for the first planning meeting. He then employed an excellent pair of architects, Howard V. Lobb and John Ratcliff, to build it and James Gardner as interior designer to interpret our ideas. My role was almost nominal on the creative side. I was, however, the character with whom the buck would stop should we fail to open on time, or exceed our financial allocation from the Treasury. Happily we opened with about ten minutes to spare, Cecil telling me later that the last stretch of carpet was being nailed down at one end as he was preparing to open the doors at the other, unlike some of our rivals, who opened weeks late. Happily also we kept to our money limits.

A few days before the exhibition opened on 17 April 1958, some British newspapers were making fun of the exterior of our pavilion, with its three spires, flat roofed continuation, and no windows. But from the moment of opening a queue waited to get in. In conception it was simple, and in execution cheap; it had to be. First, no windows, and lighting placed to illuminate only what we wished the visitor to see. When walking through many of our glass-walled rivals, spectators spent more time looking out of the windows than they gave to the exhibits. Second, controlled circulation, a single passage through the pavilion, which ensured that [the viewer] passed what we wanted him to pass. Third, surprises.

As he entered, we gave the visitor the traditional Britain he expected to see – dimly-lit, cathedral-like, hung with banners, lined with spotlighted figures in ceremonial dress, the floor richly carpeted; at the far end an enlargement of the Annigoni portrait of the Queen, then newly painted. At the far end the queue moved through a low tunnel from Britain past to Britain present – to a lit transparency of Dounreay atomic research station and then a roomful of animated models of our latest inventions, some done by back-projection film, some actually working. One of the most successful was a film from the cockpit showing an aeroplane making a blind landing. This gallery fascinated visitors, and we had to enlarge it. Then into open courts, where people could browse, with music, books, or variegated lists of things Britain had invented, from international exhibitions to bottled beer.

Some hundreds of thousands passed through the UK pavilion in the six months of the exhibition, and a jury awarded us third prize. I was proud of COI when the award came through, for the days of sneers were over. Cecil Cooke indeed deserved the CMG he was later awarded.

Long-stop for COI's own work was, however, only one of my two Brussels responsibilities. There was also an administrative organising job to be done with the Belgian exhibition authorities on behalf of the whole British participation, from choosing our site to arrangements for the open day. It must have looked easy to the outsider, but we inside remembered what seemed endless Anglo-Belgian meetings and correspondence, and much hard bargaining with tough businesslike Belgians.

I began to feel I should stand back from Brussels and put my job into perspective. Moreover, with our West African colonies moving towards independence, it was then considered a British interest that text and reference books in English should continue to be bought and used. The question was whether government assistance was needed. With some book trade experience and contacts behind me, I was asked to visit West Africa to investigate this question in particular. So, early in 1960, I flew to Paris and on across the Sahara to Dakar to begin another African visit; and another series of letters to Alice Mary.

My journey took me across Africa from west to east, from Senegal to the Belgian Congo, visiting French-speaking countries, and then back by way of Nigeria, Ghana, Liberia and Sierra Leone, whence I returned by sea on Elder Dempster's *Accra*. I have chosen the Western Region of Nigeria as representative of my double task, to study the effect of COI's information material in use, and also the local trade in British books. I begin in Western Region's Ibadan.

3 February, 2.20 pm in the plane Kaduna–Ibadan
. . . A lazy morning – wrote up some notes before breakfast in my room at 9, then visited some bookshops, had a talk to the Governor, an early lunch, caught the plane, and here I am, soon to cross over the River Niger on my way to the Deputy-Governor's cocktail party. Oh dear, these parties! . . . 100 people at Lagos and Enugu, 150 at Kaduna, probably a thousand tonight if Billy Graham [the American evangelist] does not prove a counter-attraction. You'd laugh to see me as the guest of honour, wringing everyone by the hand as they come in, and trying to look intelligent.

11.30 pm
. . . a short note . . . to report that I have experienced a sherry party and a dinner party that included Billy Graham. I was impressed, as was the Deputy-Governor, Murphy, with whom I am staying. Not perhaps a man of very great brain, but I would say both a sincere and a good man. Considering his eminence, I thought he talked with considerable modesty. . . .

Thursday 4 February, 7.50 am
Just a few minutes waiting for breakfast in my room. I stepped out of the plane yesterday into the coastal heat, in which I shall now stay till I leave Africa. Porter met me, acting IO [Information Officer] come up from Lagos because the local man is away, ex-COI Reference Division. I'm staying two nights with the Deputy-Governor, a quiet bachelor.

Ibadan is built on hills – the biggest town south of the Sahara, bigger than Johannesburg or Leopoldville, I'm told – and I'm looking from my window across a lawn and past a tree brilliant with red flowers to a valley and a long range of hills. . . . The town itself is sprawling and, as far as I have seen, quite undistinguished, but I saw the tremendous University as we came in on the plane, and there are other institutions connected with it, such as a big teaching hospital. . . . back here to dinner, half African and half European, the Europeans being Murphy, Graham, the US Consul and his wife, and the Porters. . . .

The habit of sitting round in a large circle in drawing room or on lawn makes any general conversation impossible, and one is stuck with one's immediate neighbours. If they are Africans, they don't necessarily feel the need to talk at all, and many just sit. I don't feel it is a practice high in the social arts. Now off for much talking.

2.30 pm
. . . A round of talks this morning, with the CMS [Church Missionary Society], the Ministry of Education, and the University. The University is very impressive, though I only really saw the bookshop and library. One doesn't easily grasp the isolation of such a University – that if something that one wants to consult is not in the library, it may take months to borrow it from England, if it can be borrowed at all. Everyone mistakes me for John Hadfield, and they apologise because copies of *Love on a Branch Line* have not yet arrived. . . .

Friday 5 February, 7.30 am Ibadan

. . . I am waiting for the car to take me to Porter's house, where I shall be staying tonight . . . I spent yesterday afternoon visiting bookshops in the African streets, including one African tycoon who has a business with about twenty branches. One curious fact is that the African here speaks English much worse than in French territories he speaks French. That is apparently because in most of Nigeria he is taught by African teachers – only in the North, where African teachers are scarce, has he been taught by English people, and then the difference is startling, and often one finds perfect English spoken. I say this because it was quite difficult for the tycoon and me to understand each other. Afterwards we climbed a tower at the highest point round about to see this formless, sprawling city of tin roofs, and then back to Porter's house to talk further.

5.10 pm Porter's House, Ibadan

. . . Today we did a long drive of about 200 miles. First to Ede, where we visited a big girls' boarding school, to talk to the librarian, who was a very nice and intelligent person from Trinidad. The headmistress was an elderly African who was a perfect dear – she gave us coffee, and had been educated at St Andrews University in Scotland. Then on a short distance to Oshogbo, where we had lunch in the Rest House and visited the local library and reading room. Each fair-sized town has a local library as in England, which is financed by the local authority. . . . Then to Ife, the old religious centre of the region.

We saw the courthouse in the local ruler's residence, a curious blend of fluorescent lighting and elephant tusks. There were two tall wooden poles – maybe staves of office – with native carvings of white man in topees, one on a bicycle and one on a horse. Not all that flattering. Then to the Museum, where they have a collection of twenty bronze heads supposed to be about 500 years old that were dug up near Ife, and also some terracotta figures and various pots and whatnot. . . . from Ife we motored back to Ibadan, much of the car run being taken with discussions between Porter and myself on COI material.

Near Ibadan there was pretty thick forest, which thinned out as we got further north-east. The villages are less picturesque here than in the other regions, most of the houses being mud with tin roofs – no thatch. In the towns the older houses are usually two-storey, with balconies and a good deal of openwork decoration and pillars under the balcony and on each side of the door. They may have been built by early traders . . . most are now pretty dilapidated.

So I left Western Region for Lagos. I had arranged to return to England by sea from Sierra Leone on board the *Accra*, so that I could draft my report and recommendations on British books before I got home. I set out my observations on the trade in English language books, and then stated my conclusion, that no government financial help was needed, and my reasons for reaching it. My report was accepted with relief by the three departments.

I was back with Alice Mary and the family, back also with COI and at work. Yet before long I found myself becoming restless, and wondering whether I should retire before long, now that I had reached fifty. I had been controller (overseas) since 1948, one of the top three of the Department. I enjoyed the job, got on reasonably well with those in COI's client departments whose policy wishes we were there to execute, was liked by my own personal staff, and was well paid. Perhaps I needed more challenge than I was getting from a smooth-running operation.

My restlessness was increased by some difficulty in getting on with Fife Clark. I recognised his experience and ability – both greater than mine – but he was damnably tactless. An unlucky remark of his reflecting on the efficiency of my personal staff finished it. I went home to consult Alice Mary. We agreed to retire to our house in South Cerney in six months' time. A day or two later I put in a note to Fife Clark giving five months' warning of one month's notice, and left on 27 July 1962, a few days short of my fifty-third birthday.

I still look back to my farewell party in COI's top floor canteen. It was packed with friends. Fife made a generous, Ben Thomas the Controller (Home) a delightful speech. Alice Mary was given an enormous bouquet, myself a bicycle, a leather briefcase, and a coloured extending card (Reggie Mount of our Studio designed it) showing me taking my ease on a canal boat, feet sticking out in front, my nose in a book, negligently steering. On the back was the long typeset list of those who had subscribed to my presents. Framed, it hangs in my study.

So I left my familiar room with its three telephones, its display racks of COI products, and its big wallboard covered with tables of figures, the most important being the monthly forecasts that kept me up to date upon how much expenditure was going for each of our vote subheads, so that I should never be caught short of money.

When I chose self-employment, I did not realise how much I should miss that office: the bustle of business, the friendships made in sharing ideals and objectives, the pleasures, achievements and excitements of crisis; the quiet of one's own desk and the efficiency of one's secretary; the pleasure of chairing a meeting to a good end; the door-keepers' 'good morning' and 'good night'. I never regretted my decision, but I did greatly miss COI. I have only been back three times: it is not wise to return, except very transiently, to where one has been happy. I hope the public got value for its gifts to me.

CHAPTER THIRTEEN

IN THE END IS MY BEGINNING

A few days after I had left COI, we moved to Silver Street House at South Cerney. Alice Mary's brother-in-law, Kenneth Miller, a brilliant architect, was hurriedly called in to plan necessary alterations, to be carried out by our local builder, who found a disused well under the spot where she (and our tenants) were accustomed to stand to cook! Most important to me, a converted outhouse gave me a big study lined with bookshelves, while she had another study at the other end of the house.

At the turn of the year 1962 I looked forward to working for David & Charles, and joining the British Waterways Board. I did not foresee the coldest winter for 200 years; the frost came down on 17 January and did not once lift until early April. Oddities I remember; coming down to my study on the 17th and finding it in darkness, for snow had covered the windows; the curious sensation of learning that the village had been cut off by snow, with no letters, newspapers, milk, or new stock for shops. The frost gave me one bonus: in a car I was driven on the ice across the Stratford-upon-Avon Canal.

We survived the winter well enough, but other changes caused more upset than I could have believed possible. It was long before I accustomed myself to working at home. To leave home for work, to arrive back, had been unremarked habits since university days. Similarly, Alice Mary and the children (except Laura, now married) had to cope with my continuing presence on the one hand, and erratic absences on the other.

We also lost London pleasures we had taken for granted: opera, ballet, most theatre-going; shopping in Regents, Oxford or Kensington High Streets; second-hand bookshops and the pleasures of the ever changing Thames. The result was stretches of grumpiness in us both. As well, I had to work very hard if I was to plug the huge gap in our finances caused by my retirement without pension until 1969. For years 'work' at COI had meant 'take responsibility'; now it meant 'do it yourself', the reality of self-employment.

I filled the gap to some extent with work for David & Charles and the British Waterways Board, and with income from my books. Alice Mary had her own writing, and lots of gardening in our huge garden, divided into three: flowers, vegetables and 'wild part'.

Other occupations soon found us. Alice Mary started the South Cerney Trust, not for village preservation but rather to influence inevitable village development and pursue 'all activities which will increase the pleasure of living in South Cerney and Cerney Wick'. The Trust committee worked out where housing and industrial developments should not be sited, and where they might. Having done so, we met the county planners regularly, to show them our maps and explain our reasoning. So doing, the Trust was remarkably successful. Later we supported the first publicly agreed village plan in Gloucestershire. The work we did still determines the shape of today's greatly enlarged village.

We also battled with the highways department to get a stream of full and empty gravel lorries out of the village. We suggested a short by-pass road. The county assured us it was impracticable, then three years later began a far more extensive one than we had dreamed of.

We waymarked footpaths, defined areas of common land, planted trees and flowers, helped to start or restart village activities (the Cricket Club and the Arts Group were two), organised a village directory, and lectures and exhibitions on the old canal and railway, of the work of a popular village artist . . . and so on. As I write the Trust is still active.

As for me, a Londoner destined to be village committee fodder, within months I was jockeyed into the chairmanship of the Village Hall Committee. I soon found out why. The only thing not needing urgent attention was the thatch. The committee room was falling down, the toilets were indescribable, and the heating system didn't. With an excellent secretary and treasurer to work with, we raised and were granted the necessary money in seven years. I have seldom enjoyed a part-time job more.

From Alice Mary came three children's books published by Chatto & Windus, collectively called 'The Williver Chronicles', successful attempts to introduce children to industrial and social history by following the adventures of a single South Cerney family at intervals, 1788, 1814 and 1848. She was a good story-teller, and the books sold well.

Meanwhile, we [were asked to write] a book on the Cotswolds for Batsford. It seemed a natural for Alice Mary, but not for me, but Batsford answered that my name was better known, and must be added to hers. So *The Cotswolds* appeared in 1966 in the Batsford's 'Britain' series. She felt that just as canals were my subject, the Cotswolds were hers. So the text was written throughout by 'I', never by we. Yet I much enjoyed map-reading so that she could concentrate on making notes, and so the character of the Cotswolds grew upon me. We learned one lesson from that book: never to mention an unspoiled pub. We ruined at least two by publicising them.

Soon afterwards she read an article about a Chartist Land Company's cottage estate near Rickmansworth. She had never heard of either, but her historical curiosity had been aroused. The result was *The Chartist Land Company*, published by David & Charles in 1970. To my mind it is her best book, a masterpiece of detailed research and moving narrative. I played only a small part. She had by now moved out of a difficult time into one constructive and loving.

Then David Thomas suggested that we edit (and contribute to) a symposium on the Cotswolds similar to David & Charles's successful *Dartmoor: a New Study*. *The Cotswolds: a New Study* was published in 1973. It sold well.

I had enjoyed being a manager, variously expressed in the OUP, COI, David & Charles and British Waterways Board. By [1968] I had left them all, and felt restless for some such activity outside the village. So I went to our bank manager and asked him whether he knew of a small business with which I could involve myself in exchange for a little financial backing. So I became a fencing contractor, an occupation of which I had previously never heard.

Peter managed fencing and allied businesses in Surrey for his father, but wanted one of his own. He heard of one at Cirencester; we met, talked, and liked each other. I offered a bank guarantee in exchange for a directorship. Peter, John, an excellent accountant friend of his, and I formed the board; in nearly four years before I left South Cerney and so resigned, we had quadrupled the turnover, were paying nominal directors' fees and making modest profits. In a corner of the garden of 'The White Cottage', to which we moved in 1972, [was placed] a wrought-iron gate, carrying the initials CH and AMH: Stamford Fencing's parting gift to a most improbable director.

Fun and full of interest as our South Cerney life was, nevertheless I became restless for London: red buses, theatres, shop windows, my many friends or acquaintances, and new activities beckoning. Alice Mary, however, had become more and more emotionally involved in whatever was happening in the quickly growing village. Too involved, as I realised when our doctor found that she had developed high blood pressure; fortunately, it had done no harm.

The choice was made for us by the death of my bachelor old friend James MacColl, with whom I had lodged at the White Cottage, only a few hundred yards from the Regents Canal by Little Venice. We went to his funeral; afterwards, I sought out his cousin and executor, and enquired what was to happen to the house. A few days later he offered it to us at a very reasonable price. Alice Mary agreed, and so we went ahead with her brother-in-law in charge of necessary alterations. Here is [part of] a letter of hers which accepts what had been my decision in words so loving that they still move me to tears. It was written in the spring of 1972, shortly before our move to the White Cottage:

When you are away and I have the house and village without you I realise clearly that you are the basis of all. Sometimes you say I would be happy here on my own, but these short times of your absence make clear that this is NOT true. You are my base and my centre and no one and nothing else. My dear love, we have had a good life in London, and in Glos, and shall find it again in London, being together and me not so busy. . . . Dear heart, how good you have been these 10 years. Some you enjoyed, some of the time, but how much of it was alien to you. I have been very neglectful of this. Now we go back to our canalside house and buffet suppers and as much idleness as we can force in, and to great freedom and expansion, I'm sure.

In 1972 we left South Cerney in style, with a three-evening party for 200 of our friends and even our non-admirers, which also enabled us to announce the engagement of our eldest son Alec to delightful Ann Altmayer. As our taxi left we guessed the villagers would heave a huge sigh of relief: at last that energetic couple, full of ideas that meant work for others as well as themselves, had gone.

So we moved to our lovely White Cottage. We gained all that London had to offer, most of all its theatres, for Alice Mary much enjoyed opera and concerts, I the ballet, both of us good plays, restaurants and pubs. Yet we took the Cotswolds with us. Before leaving, she had agreed to do another general book, *Introducing the Cotswolds*. Its writing enabled us to revisit this much-loved area, she again doing all the writing, I the planning and navigating. Published in 1976, it was a much better book than its predecessor from Batsford.

Charles Williams had very greatly influenced Alice Mary since their first encounter in January 1933. He continued to do so throughout his life, and indeed hers. I had known him in life as a colleague in the Oxford University Press, as a friend, and as one influenced by his books. After his death in May 1945, a few of us kept memory of him alive by meeting to read from his writings. Then came a conference, and out of that the founding of the Charles Williams Society in 1976. Her knowledge of him and his work and my experience of organisation brought the Society into being, and it flourishes as I write.

[Alice Mary had written] *An Introduction to Charles Williams* in 1959, when he was beginning to be forgotten. It is a very personal book, and one which well fulfils the claim of its title, 'An Introduction'. With *Introducing the Cotswolds* published, she now turned back to her knowledge of Williams. She decided to create a volume of extracts from his letters, [and] wrote to as many of his correspondents as were still alive. She completed a specimen section of the book, but much to her disappointment, it did not take, I judge because Williams was not a natural letter writer.

The New York branch of the Oxford University Press [then wrote to say] that her friend Humphrey Carpenter, at that time writing a biography of Tolkien, had suggested Alice Mary for a new and enlarged biography. She was of course delighted, realising that she could use the letters she had collected as quite new material to add to the product of her greater knowledge since 1959. Later I tidied up her drafts.

She at once began work on the biography, and had completed a rough of the whole book before our final move back to South Cerney. She sent it to OUP (NY), telling them that she would prepare it for publication after we had moved house. As it happened it was fortunate that I had worked closely with her to get the job done in time, and knew the text nearly as well as she did.

[Charles's account now moves to the point at which they left London to return to South Cerney; partly prompted by financial and practical motives, this was partly to please Alice Mary. Both seemed to have anticipated a form of retirement, if a very active one; sadly, for Alice Mary, this was not to be. Undoubtedly, he had regrets.]

We felt bereaved as we looked round the empty rooms of our White Cottage, the long-grown beauty of its garden, with its Italian spring fountain that played outside my study window, our 200-year-old mulberry and leaning pear tree, and the more distant full-sized trees along the boundary of our internal square. Our furniture had gone earlier in the day, and now our old friend and taxi-driver Eric Poole was waiting for us. Out of the familiar Randolph Road, along beside the canal, and so to Westway and the A40.

The furniture was for store in Cirencester, and we for a temporary stay at our South Cerney pub, the Eliot Arms. Then off to Canada, to explore more waterways for *World Canals*, and stay with [Alec] and his family, now in Saint John, New Brunswick.

[Our return from Canada was] not, however, to our new house at 13 Meadow Way, alterations to which were not quite finished, but for a month to the Eliot Arms until 22 July 1981, when at last it was ready. We also started to explore again our old rambles, especially an old favourite circle round a yachting lake, once a gravel pit, and back by the old railway line. We lay in the grass side by side, and were satisfied that our decision to come back had been right.

About now Peter Maguire, chairman of the South Cerney Trust, asked Alice Mary to give a public talk in the village hall on her memories of the village in girlhood. She drafted it to the exact length of an hour. She was an excellent public speaker – able to make herself clearly heard in the back row, and when the talk was given in February [1982], every one of the hundred seats was taken. (The talk was published in 1991 by the Trust under the title *Cerney Sixty Years Ago*, and proved popular.) It was to be her last public appearance.

Our small house, enlarged to our requirements, was ready, and we moved in. We had to leave book-arranging, drawer-filling and filing cabinet-sorting to fulfil a booking with an [IWA] party of a few days in Belgium in the last week of September, to see some rather special canal sights. On the trip we renewed acquaintance with a canal couple: perhaps the last semi-strangers to talk to her as she then was: 'We keep a sharp and joyous memory of her, a graceful, friendly, enthusiastic, erudite person such as one seldom has the pleasure to meet.'

Back at 13 Meadow Way, Alice Mary waited for an answer from OUP (New York) on the outline manuscript she had sent them a fortnight before we left the White Cottage. I find in her publishing file [a letter commenting on OUP's provisional interest and their appointment of Peter Sutcliffe as their editor at Oxford]: 'Thank you for your letter of 26 October. Of course I will cooperate with OUP Oxford and as far as possible revise three chapters according to their specification. I have telephoned Peter Sutcliffe and . . . he will come over here on 11 November. I'm glad to have things moving.' Nothing could be more normal. She was back at work in her specially built study at the opposite side of the house from me, and eager to start work. Domestic help arranged, garden begun, house becoming organised, all seemed set fair.

I have spent many wretched years puzzling over happenings between 29 October, when she wrote that letter, and 11 November, when Peter Sutcliffe came.

The date of the first is conjectural, because it was unnoted. We were returning along School Lane from a walk through the old part of the village, which must have included Silver Street, where stood our former house. I was a few yards in front when she called urgently, agitatedly, to me: 'Big, get me out of here!' Our house was only five minutes away, so I took her there, sat her down and asked her to tell me her trouble. As I remember, she said that she wanted to go back to London. I wondered wildly what to say. I must have tried to mitigate what I am sure was my careful financial reasoning by suggesting a day visit back to the area round our first house at 28 Newton Road, for later we did indeed do so, and enjoyed it. By then, however, it was too late.

Preliminary unpacking of our books showed that we had brought more than our new built-in bookcases would hold. I started to weed my share, and asked Alice Mary to see what she could spare. [She] brought from her study and laid out on our sofa a large part – maybe a third, of her collection of poetry. Poetry had always been her love, and over the years, she had built up a fine collection of, perhaps, 800 volumes. They had had pride of place in our sitting room at the White Cottage, and she or I often used it for reference, or as a quarry for reading aloud to each other in the evenings. I was horrified, and protested that I'd only asked her to see whether some could be spared. But she was firm – she didn't want them any more. So they were sold early in November. This action of hers seemed out of character, and I felt uneasy. It represented something I did not understand.

Then came Peter Sutcliffe's visit which I left entirely to her. She took him into her study to talk. Later I heard him go. Then she came into my study, holding her first draft chapters, and put them down in front of me. I turned and said that I hoped that the draft had been accepted. She replied, 'He wants me to do more work on the manuscript (which we knew already), but I didn't quite understand what it was he wanted me to do. So I asked him to pencil in his suggestions for the first paragraph.' There they were. I read them again and again. Sutcliffe had done perfectly straight-forward editorial work to tidy up the wording, the kind of thing any trained editor – as she was – could do in her sleep, and which she would have done if our move had not intervened.

We talked, and over perhaps half an hour I realised the truth: she no longer knew *how* to edit. Something was gone from her brain.

> Let me not to the marriage of true minds
> Add impediments

Now she no longer had a true mind, though

> Love is not love
> Which alters when it alteration finds
> or bends with the remover to remove
> Love alters not with his brief hours and weeks
> But bears it out even to the edge of doom.

It was a long time before I admitted the truth to myself; though still we loved, our relationship of husband and wife had become one of carer and cared-for.

The cause? I thought at first she had gone stale, as writers do, took over the editing of her manuscript (*Charles Williams: an exploration of his life and work*, published in 1983), and tried to interest her in different kinds of writing. No success. Then I threshed around trying to find an outside cause: something in the water . . . ? I was sure that if only I could find the cause, say the operative word, press the right button – work a miracle if you like – she would be restored to the vivid person she had been such a short time ago. I did not then, of course, understand that man cannot restore what has been physically destroyed.

One of the worst results was to inhibit laughter. We had always laughed together, for we shared a sense of the comic and the ridiculous. Laughter had been a part of our daily lives. Dementia ended that. Yet to laugh together gives each a sense of proportion: lose it, as I did, and judgements become less and less reliable as mental loneliness increases.

Yet so much remained. Her love of travel took us several times to Devon, to Ironbridge and our beloved Ludlow; abroad, to Italy, especially Venice, to Switzerland, Majorca, Canada again and twice to South Africa, the last only eight months before she died, yet during which she had happily been up Table Mountain in the cable-car. Her ability to play and enjoy the piano and to sing remained, to cook well, and deeply to enjoy the countryside.

Yet all were old experiences, even in new form, and all with me as companion. By herself, she could do nothing that was not habitual. Activities that required original thought, however small, such as deciding upon a walk or an outing, no, the saddest being the ending of her favourite activity, gardening, for she could no longer create, only weed and potter.

The cause? I am still not sure, but the most likely explanation seems a bruised blood vessel, perhaps caused by an unremarked bump on the head added to existent high blood pressure, [which] then gave way, probably at her cry of 'get me out of here', and then began to leak more blood into her brain than the natural drainage system could remove. Much later I realised that her mother's death had been accelerated by something similar.

So slowly, very slowly, over seven-and-a-half long years (the exact period between our falling in love and our wedding so long before), a pool of blood must have spread over the whole brain, eliminating her faculties one by one, until the last went a few days before she died. Marriage had gone with one urgent cry, but love remained to the end. She died peacefully and imperceptibly, holding my hand; it could not have been otherwise.

During the previous two or three years she underwent increasing misery because of my behaviour. I did not understand until far too late that her inabilities were not because she wouldn't, but because she couldn't. So I nagged her, did everything I could to restore what I still thought of as sloth. She, poor darling, knew only that the man she loved was becoming more and more cross and complaining – except, mercifully, when we were on holiday. By now she knew that she couldn't do as I asked. One day she wrote over and over again in her shaky handwriting: 'May the light of Christ rising in glory scatter the darkness of our hearts and minds.' She must have realised then the darkness of her own mind and the despair of her heart.

My behaviour can, I suppose, be slightly excused as I became more and more tired. As her brain ceased to be so active, so her body began to fail. My love very nearly failed as hope lessened daily and weariness increased. Hers did not. The last verse of the first poem she had given me in May 1938 began: 'Did we kiss once, and did we kiss for ever?' and ended 'searching through word and line to be true?' She had kissed for ever, she did love, and she had been true. Almost at the end, bearing my despairing efforts to achieve something, she wrote on a slip of paper I was later to find on her desk: 'Get my love up again.' She had always maintained that between lovers there is no question of forgiveness; one starts again, over and over. So I believe she knows I have started again on a new life without her, and loves me. Indeed, I know it, for she and I are still close to one another, still communicate, and soon will be together in the next world as we shall be in our village churchyard.

In the end is my beginning.

NOTES

Unless otherwise indicated, all letters cited are to or from Charles Hadfield, and works cited are by Charles Hadfield.

CHAPTER ONE

1. See page 175.
2. Foreword to Helen Harris, *The Grand Western Canal*, David & Charles, Newton Abbot, 1973, p. 9
3. *Round Africa in Eighty Years*, unpublished MS, 1988, p. 31
4. Ibid.
5. W.T. Jackman, *The Development of Transportation in Modern England*, Cambridge University Press, Cambridge, 1916, p. xxxi
6. Ibid., p. xxxii
7. C.E.R. Sherrington, *100 Years of Inland Transport, 1830–1933*, Second impression, Frank Cass, London, p. 8
8. T.S. Willan, *River Navigation in England*, Oxford University Press, London, 1936, p. 15
9. Obituary, T.S. Willan, *Independent*, 22 June 1994
10. D.C. Coleman, *History and the Economic Past*, Clarendon Press, Oxford, 1987, p. 87
11. 'Sources for the History of British Canals', *Journal of Transport History*, vol. II no. 2, November 1955, p. 84
12. Frank Eyre and Charles Hadfield, *English Rivers and Canals*, Collins, 1946, p. 16
13. Letters to Alice Mary Miller, 14 and 26 September 1944
14. Foreword to L.T.C. Rolt, *Narrow Boat*, Alan Sutton Publishing Ltd, Stroud, 1994
15. Ibid., p. 13
16. Ibid., Foreword
17. Ibid., pp. 194–5
18. Ibid., Foreword
19. L.T.C. Rolt, *Landscape with Canals*, Allen Lane, 1977, p. 170
20. Letter from Tom Rolt, 23 January 1946
21. Letter from Tom Rolt, 28 January 1946
22. PRO30/82/2: Letter from Robert Aickman to Tom Rolt, 12 July 1946
23. Letter from Tom Rolt, 24 October 1946
24. Letter from Robert Aickman, 9 December 1946
25. Charles Hadfield, Introduction to Eily Gayford, *The Amateur Boatwomen*, M. & M. Baldwin, Cleobury Mortimer, 1996
26. Letter to Alice Mary, n.d. (October 1946)
27. *Waterways Tales to Tell*, unpublished MS, 1995
28. 'L.T.C. Rolt – An Obituary', *Waterways World*, vol. 3 no. 6, June 1974, p. 29
29. Letter to Alice Mary, n.d. (October 1946)
30. Jack Simmons, 'Review', *British Railways* and *English Rivers and Canals*, in *Time and Tide*, 17 May 1946, p. 50
31. Letter to Alice Mary, 7 August 1947
32. Letter to Alice Mary, 10 August 1947
33. From a draft for *Our Love*, related in a letter to JB, 24 December 1993
34. Letter from Tom Rolt, 16 March 1950
35. Ibid.

CHAPTER TWO

1. 'Talk given on canal experiences, 1975–6', unpublished notes
2. Letter from Tom Rolt, 20 March 1950
3. Letter to IWA honorary secretary, 6 April 1951
4. Letter to IWA honorary secretary, 10 June 1951
5. *The Canals of Southern England*, Phoenix House, 1955, pp. 335–6
6. Derek H. Aldcroft, *Studies in British Transport History 1870–1970*, David & Charles, Newton Abbot, 1974, p. 1

7. Kenneth Hudson, *Industrial Archaeology: a New Introduction*, John Baker, London, 3rd edition, 1976, p. 21

8. Editorial, *Journal of Transport History*, vol. 1 no. 1, May 1953, p. 1

9. Ibid., p. 2

10. 'Sources for the History of British Canals', *Journal of Transport History*, vol. II no. 2, November 1955, p. 80

11. Ibid., p. 81

12. Ibid., pp. 80–1

13. Ibid., p. 89

14. C.R. Clinker, Preface to E.T. MacDermot, *A History of the Great Western Railway*, vol. 1, revised edition, Ian Allan, 1964, p. xi

15. Letter to JB, 30 June 1994

16. Ibid.

17. *Introducing Canals*, Ernest Benn, 1955, p. vi

18. 'Out and Back', *Waterways World*, vol. 13 no. 8, August 1984, p. 31

19. *Introducing Canals*, p. 86

20. Ibid., p. 56

21. Ibid.

22. Ibid., p. 59

23. Ibid., p. 137

24. Ibid., p. 146

25. Ibid., p. 153

26. Letter, *Railway World*, July 1954

27. This and later extracts are from the Minutes of Council Meetings of the RCHS, kindly provided by leave of the Society's Council

28. Review, in *Journal of the Railway and Canal Historical Society*, vol. 1 no. 4, October 1955, pp. 34–5

29. 'An approach to canal research', *Journal of the Railway and Canal Historical Society*, vol. 1 no. 3, July 1955, pp. 23–4

30. 'Report on visit to the Grand Junction Canal', *Journal of the Railway and Canal Historical Society*, vol. 1 no. 2, April 1955, p. 9

31. *Youth Shows But Half*, unpublished MS, 1974, p. 215

CHAPTER THREE

1. Letter to Howard Williams, 5 July 1955

2. Foreword to David Bick, *The Hereford & Gloucester Canal*, Oakwood Press, Headington, 1994, p. 5

3. *Waterways Tales to Tell*, unpublished draft, 1995

4. Letter from H.D. Emmanuel, 7 December 1957

5. Letter to Charles Clinker, 23 March 1958

6. Unattributed quotations from letters in the next section are from a series of letters written to Alice Mary in May 1958

7. T.S. Willan, Review, in *History*, 1961, p. 65

8. Charles Hadfield and Michael Streat, *Holiday Cruising on Inland Waterways*, David & Charles, Newton Abbot, 1968, p. 13

9. Ibid.

10. This and all unattributed excerpts about canal boat trips are taken from Alice Mary's unpublished logs

11. *Holiday Cruising*, p. 14

12. Ibid.

13. Letter to R.L. Jones, 22 August 1990

14. T.C. Barker, 'Too Much Over-Specialisation?', *Journal of the Railway and Canal Historical Society*, vol. 6 no. 5, September 1960, p. 96

15. David St John Thomas, 'Why we're here', in *Good Books Come From Devon*, David & Charles, Newton Abbot, 1981, p. 12

16. Letter to David St John Thomas, 31 October 1960

17. Letter to Peter Lead, 17 February 1984

18. Letter to Alice Mary, 1 March 1963

19. Letter to Gordon Biddle, 26 July 1965

20. PRO MT124/569: File on Appointment of Members of British Waterways Board. Memorandum prepared for John Hay MP, 30 January 1962

21. Ibid, Note from David Serpell, 12 October 1962

22. *Round Africa in 80 Years*, unpublished MS, 1988, pp. 265–6

23. PRO MT124/291: File on Transport Bill – Inland Waterway Authority. Note by J.E. Sanderson, 16 November 1961

24. PRO 30/82/117: Letter from Robert Aickman to Lionel Munk, 18 December 1962

25. IWA *Bulletin* 67, November 1962, p. 91

CHAPTER FOUR

1. *Youth Shows But Half*, pp. 221–2

2. BWB 26, February 1964. This refers to Paper no. 26 put to the BWB. Further references in this chapter are similarly abbreviated

3. Robert Legget, *Rideau Waterway*, University of Toronto Press, Toronto, 1955, p. 98

4. Ibid.

5. BWB 31, 25 March 1963
6. BWB 76, 30 January 1964
7. Ibid.
8. Ibid.
9. PRO30/82/118: Letter from Robert Aickman to Lionel Munk, 29 January 1963
10. PRO30/82/122: Letter from Robert Aickman to Lionel Munk, 6 May 1963
11. Letter to Sir John Hawton, 25 March 1963. All unattributed quotations here are from this letter
12. Letter from Sir John Hawton to SWCS, quoted in *Broadsheet*, 54, August 1963, p. 4
13. Euan Corrie, 'Time on the Board', *Waterways World*, vol. 17 no. 9, September 1988, p. 45
14. David Tomlinson, in *Broadsheet*, 83, January 1966
15. BWB 51, September 1963
16. 'Talk given on canal experiences, 1975–6', p. 77
17. BWB 123, 14 October 1964
18. Comments on BWB 157, 30 December 1965. All unattributed references in this section are to this paper
19. BWB 160, 28 January 1966
20. Charles Hadfield, 'What should British Waterways policy be? 1 – Pleasure cruising', *Modern Transport*, March 1967, p. 29
21. Ibid., p. 30
22. Ibid., p. 30
23. Barbara Castle, *Fighting All The Way*, Macmillan, 1993, p. 396
24. British Waterways Board, *The Future of the Waterways*, HMSO, London, 1964, p. 24
25. Quoted in IWA *Bulletin* 68, May 1963, pp. 15–16
26. BWB 26, February 1963. Unattributed quotations below are from this paper
27. Ibid., p. 2
28. BWB 76, 30 January 1964
29. 'What should British Waterways policy be? 2 – Commercial Transport', *Modern Transport*, May 1967, p. 46
30. Ibid., p. 47
31 Letter from David St John Thomas, May 1962
32. O.S. Nock, *One Facet of an Autobiography*, Pentland Press Ltd, Durham, 1992, p. 70
33. Letter to David Thomas, 9 September 1964
34. Letter to David Thomas, 20 August 1997
35. Letter to Gordon Biddle, 2 January 1963
36. Letter to Gordon Biddle, 26 July 1965
37. Review, 'The Canals of the East Midlands', *Journal of the Railway and Canal Historical Society*, vol. XII no. 3, July 1966, p. 50
38. Letter to John James, 4 April 1993

CHAPTER FIVE

1. Review, *Transport History*, vol. 4 no. 2, July 1971, p. 199
2. Foreword to Helen Harris, *The Grand Western Canal*, David & Charles, Newton Abbot, 1973, p. 10
3. David St John Thomas, 'Seventeen Eventful Years', *The Bookseller*, 16 April 1977
4. Private correspondence
5. Letter to Alan Faulkner, 28 April 1976
6. Letter to Alice Mary, 30 November 1970
7. Review, *Waterways World*, vol. 2 no. 6, June 1973, pp. 34–5
8. Letter to John Gagg, 24 January 1977
9. Letter to Alan Rowe, 13 June 1976
10. Letter to Robert Legget, 17 May 1979
11. Letter from Brian and Marty Seymour to JB, 20 July 1997
12. Minutes of the Eighth AGM of the RCHS, 26 June 1976, p. 3
13. Ibid., p. 4
14. Jack Simmons, *Parish and Empire*, Collins, 1952, pp. 147–8
15. 'Telford, Jessop and Pontcysyllte', *Journal of the Railway and Canal Historical Society*, vol. XV no. 4, October 1969, p. 74
16. Letter to A.W. Skempton, 9 May 1974
17. Letter from David St John Thomas, 10 June 1974
18. Letter from A.W. Skempton, 26 September 1974
19. Letter to A.W. Skempton, 9 November 1975
20. Letter to A.W. Skempton, 29 October 1976
21. Letter to D.R. Symes, 3 July 1987
22. Review, *The Newcomen Bulletin*, 113, April 1979, p. 15
23. Letter to A.W. Skempton, 16 April 1979
24. 'L.T.C. Rolt – An Obituary', *Waterways World*, vol. 3 no. 6, June 1974, p. 29
25. Quoted in Canal Transport Marketing Board *Newsletter*, August 1972
26. 'Trade and Navigation', IWA *Bulletin*, 100, March 1972, p. 43
27. *Youth Shows But Half*, 1974, p. 239

28. *The Canal Age*, David & Charles, Newton Abbot, 1968, p. 13
29. H.J. Dyos and D.H. Aldcroft, *British Transport*, Pelican Books, Harmondsworth, 1974, p. 441
30. These are extracts transcribed from Alice Mary's notebook; she made notes as the journey through the Gorge was under way. I have amalgamated separate sections where the sense is clear, but the order remains that in the notebook
31. 'IWA Continental Visit – It was a huge success', IWA *Bulletin*, 115, December 1975, pp. 27–9. All unattributed quotations above this reference are from this article
32. Letter to Philip Weaver, 12 July 1978
33. Ibid.

CHAPTER SIX

1. Letter to Stanley Holland, 30 September 1981
2. This account is amalgamated from letters to David Tew, 10 August 1988, to Neil Pitts, 10 March 1989, from Charles's original autobiography manuscript, *c.* 1995, and from *Waterways Tales to Tell*
3. Charles's original manuscript for this book, *c.* 1995
4. *World Canals*, David & Charles, Newton Abbot, 1986, p. 51
5. Ibid., p. 13
6. Letter to Robert Legget, 29 August 1986
7. Letter to John Gagg, 3 September 1986
8. Book Review, *IWA Waterways*, 146, April 1986, p. 27
9. Ibid.
10. Review, *American Canals*, no. 57, May 1986
11. Letter to David Blagrove, 9 April 1980
12. *Canals of the West Midlands*, 3rd edition, 1985, p. 12
13. Letter from John Horseley Denton to JB, 18 January 1996
14. Speech to Shakespeare Memorial Trust, unpublished, 11 July 1989
15. *British Canals*, 7th edition, 1984, p. 336
16. Ibid.
17. Letter to Harry Grafton, 22 December 1982
18. Letter to John Gagg, 28 November 1984
19. Letter to R.A. Buchanan, 18 October 1984
20. Letter to R.A. Buchanan, 3 September 1986
21. Letter to A.D. Cameron, 12 July 1989
22. Letter to R.A. Buchanan, 4 August 1989
23. Sonia Rolt, contribution to 'Charles Hadfield Remembered', *Waterways World*, vol. 25 no. 10, October 1996, p. 33
24. Letter to Robert Legget, 29 August 1986
25. Letter from Maurice Barbey, 31 March 1987
26. Letter from Jack Simmons, 16 March 1993
27. John Liley, Review, 'Race Against Time', *Waterways World*, vol. 19 no. 8, August 1990, p. 86
28. Letter to Jean Lindsay, 17 February 1989
29. Letter to Harry Arnold, 16 October 1991
30. Letter to Joan Heap, 2 September 1992
31. Letter from David Hilling to JB, 26 September 1996
32. *World Canals*, p. 16

CHAPTER SEVEN

1. Text of speech by Charles Hadfield at WLIAS annual dinner, 17 March 1978. Unattributed quotations below are taken from the same speech
2. Speech to WLIAS annual dinner, 17 March 1978
3. 'The Dangers of Industrial Archaeology', WLIAS *Journal*, vol. 10 no. 1, 1980
4. Jack Simmons, *The Railway in Town and Country, 1830–1914*, David & Charles, Newton Abbot, 1986, p. 11
5. Letter from Jack Simmons, 11 April 1983. The book was not published until 1986
6. 'The Dangers of Industrial Archaeology'. op. cit.
7. Ibid.
8. Ibid.
9. Interview with Charles Hadfield, 1992. John Horseley Denton kindly supplied me with a copy of the tape from which this statement has been transcribed
10. Gerard Turnbull, 'From Thames to Titicata: an appreciation of Charles Hadfield', *Journal of Transport History*, Third Series, vol. 8 no. 1, March 1987, p. 98
11. Ibid., p. 99
12. Ibid.
13. Christine Richardson, contribution to 'Charles Hadfield Remembered', *Waterways World*, vol. 25 no. 10, October 1996, p. 33
14. Foreword to L.T.C. Rolt, *Narrow Boat*, Alan Sutton Publishing Ltd, Stroud, 1994 edition

15. WLIAS *Journal*, May 1977
16. Letter from Jack Simmons, 25 April 1983
17. Letter to the Chartered Institute of Transport, 10 May 1990
18. Letter to John Taunton, 13 May 1992
19. Letter from Sir Frank Price, 16 February 1984
20. Andrew Ross, *The Chicago Gangster Theory of Life: Nature's Debt to Society*, Verso, London, 1994, p. 2
21. Inland Shipping Group, *UK Freight Waterways: A Blueprint for the Future*, Inland Waterways Association, London, 1996

CHAPTER EIGHT

1. My entertaining ancestor's travels were published as *An Englishman in America*, ed. Douglas S. Robertson, The Humber-Rose Co., Toronto, 1933

2. Barbara Macmorran, *Octavius Hadfield*, Wellington, privately printed, 1969

CHAPTER NINE

1. This appears to be an error on Charles's part; the book referred to is *The Ship that Flew*, published in 1939

CHAPTER ELEVEN

1. These words have been added from one of Charles's earlier drafts
2. This sentence has been added from one of Charles's earlier drafts
3. Alice Mary and Charles Hadfield, 'Marriage à La Maison', unpublished MS, 1966. These words are by Alice Mary

SELECT BIBLIOGRAPHY

This bibliography is a shortened and updated version of that produced for *Canals – A New Look* by Dr Mark Baldwin, whose permission is gratefully acknowledged.

WATERWAYS BOOKS AND BOOKLETS

(With Frank EYRE) *English rivers and canals*. London: Collins, 1945. (Britain in Pictures Series No. 84) 2nd impression 1947.

British canals: an illustrated history. London: Phoenix House, 1950. Republished by Readers' Union 1952. 2nd edn. 1959; 2nd impression 1962. 3rd edn. 1966, incorrectly described on title page as 3rd impression of 2nd edn. 3rd to 7th editions published by David & Charles, Newton Abbot. 4th edn. 1969; 2nd impression 1972. 5th edn. 1974. 6th edn. 1979. 7th edn. 1983. 5th, 6th and 7th edns include Ireland. 4th, 5th, 6th and 7th edns also published in paperback. 2nd and 4th edns republished by A.M. Kelley (New York) in 1968 and 1969.

Introducing canals: a guide to British waterways today. London: Benn, 1955.

The canals of Southern England. London: Phoenix House, 1955. Later expanded into two separate volumes.

The canals of South Wales and the Border. Cardiff: University of Wales Press; London: Phoenix House, 1960. 2nd impression 1960. 2nd edn. published by David & Charles (Newton Abbot) 1967, in conjunction with University of Wales Press; 2nd impression 1977.

(With John NORRIS) *Waterways to Stratford*. Dawlish: David & Charles; London: Phoenix House, 1962. 2nd edn. 1968.

Canals of the world. Oxford: Blackwell, 1964.

Canals and waterways. Newton Abbot: Raleigh Press, 1966. (Raleigh Press Brief Guide No. 22).

The canals of the East Midlands (including part of London). Newton Abbot: David & Charles, 1966. 2nd edn. 1970.

The canals of the West Midlands. Newton Abbot: David & Charles, 1966. 2nd edn. 1969. 3rd edn. 1985. 2nd edn. republished by A.M. Kelley (New York) 1969.

The canals of South West England. Newton Abbot: David & Charles, 1967. 2nd edn. 1985. Republished by A.M. Kelley (New York) 1968.

The canal age. Newton Abbot: David & Charles, 1968. 2nd impression 1969. Paperback edn. published by Pan Books, 1971. 1st edn. republished by F.A. Praeger (New York) 1969. Readers' Union edn. 1969. 2nd edn. 1981.

(With Michael STREAT) *Holiday cruising on inland waterways*. Newton Abbot: David & Charles, 1968. 2nd edn. 1971, also published as paperback by Pan Books (London), 1972.

The canals of South and South East England. Newton Abbot: David & Charles, 1969. Republished by A.M. Kelley (New York) 1969.

(With Gordon BIDDLE) *The canals of North West England* (2 vols.). Newton Abbot: David & Charles, 1970.

Canal enthusiasts' handbook 1970–71 (ed.). Newton Abbot: David & Charles, 1970.

The canals of Yorkshire and North East England (2 vols.). Newton Abbot: David & Charles, 1972–3.

Canal enthusiasts' handbook No. 2 (ed.). Newton Abbot: David & Charles, 1973.

Introducing inland waterways. Newton Abbot: David & Charles, 1973. Paperback edn. 1973.

(With F. DOERFLINGER *et al.*) *Barges or juggernauts? A national commercial waterways development projection.* London: Inland Waterways Association, 1974. 2nd edn. 1974; 2nd impression 1975.

Waterways sights to see. Newton Abbot: David & Charles, 1976.

(With C.R. CLINKER) *The Ashby-de-la-Zouch Canal and its railways.* Bristol: Avon–Anglia, 1978. Reprint.

Inland Waterways. Newton Abbot: David & Charles, n.d. [1978].

(With Alice Mary HADFIELD) *Afloat in America.* Newton Abbot: David & Charles, 1979.

(With A.W. SKEMPTON) *William Jessop, engineer.* Newton Abbot: David & Charles, 1979.

World Canals: Inland Navigation Past and Present. Newton Abbot: David & Charles, 1986.

Thomas Telford's Temptation. Cleobury Mortimer: M. & M. Baldwin, 1993.

(With Joseph BOUGHEY) *Hadfield's British Canals*, 1994. Stroud: Sutton Publishing Ltd. 2nd impression 1998. Rewritten 8th edition of *British Canals.*

WATERWAYS PAPERS, ARTICLES AND OTHER SHORT CONTRIBUTIONS

Canals between the English and the Bristol Channels. *Economic History Review.* 12 (1) and (2). 1942. 59–67.

The Thames Navigation and the canals, 1770–1830. *Economic History Review.* 14 (2). 1944. 172–9.

James Green as canal engineer. *Jnl. Transport Hist.* 1 (1). 1953. 44–56.

(With C.R. CLINKER) The Ashby Canal: importance of its tramroads. *Modern Transport.* 7 August 1954. 5.

Report on visit to the Grand Junction Canal. *Jnl. Rly. Canal Hist. Soc.* 1 (2). April 1955. 8–9.

An approach to canal research. *Jnl. Rly. Canal Hist. Soc.* 1 (3). July 1955. 23–6.

Sources for the history of British canals. *Jnl. Transport Hist.* 2. 1955–56. 80–9.

Passenger boats on the Chester Canal 1775–1806. *Jnl. Rly. Canal Hist. Soc.* 2 (3). May 1956. 34–6.

The Cromford Canal. *Jnl. Rly. Canal Hist. Soc.* 3 (3). May 1957. 49–51.

(With C.R. CLINKER) The Ashby-de-la-Zouch Canal and its railways. *Trans. Leics. Archaeol. Hist. Soc.* 34. 1958. 53–76. Later reprinted as a booklet.

Canals: Inland waterways of the British Isles. Article in *A History of Technology.* Vol. IV. Oxford: Clarendon Press, 1958. 563–73.

Canals. Article in *Victoria County History of Wiltshire.* Vol. 4. London: Oxford University Press, 1959. 272–9.

The Grand Junction Canal. *Jnl. Transport Hist.* 4 (2). 1959. 96–112.

Writing railway and canal history. *Jnl. Rly. Canal Hist. Soc.* 8 (6). November 1962. 91–5.

Britische Kanal- und Fluss-schiffahrt. *Wasser und Boden.* Hamburg. March 1964. 83–7.

Water transport, Inland. Article in *Encyclopaedia Britannica.* 14th edn., 1966. Sections I, IV, V, VI and VIII. Reprinted, with revisions, up to 1973.

What should British Waterways policy be? 1 – Pleasure cruising. *Modern Transport.* 97. No. 2462. March 1967. 29–31.

What should British Waterways policy be? 2 – Commercial Transport. *Modern Transport.* 97. No. 2464. May 1967. 44, 46–7.

Cruising on the Llangollen Canal. *Country Life*, 2 May 1968. 1136, 1139.

Telford, Jessop and Pontcysyllte. *Jnl. Rly. Canal Hist. Soc.* 15 (4). October 1969. 69–74.

Commercial transport: some possibilities. Chapter V in *Canal enthusiasts' handbook 1970–71.* Newton Abbot: David & Charles, 1970.

Canals. Article in Georgano, G.N. (ed.). *A history of transport.* London: Dent, 1972. 197–214.

Trade and navigation. *IWA Bulletin.* 100. March 1972. 38–47.

Canal. Article in *Children's Britannica.* 3rd edn., 1973.

Transport. Article in *Children's Britannica.* 3rd edn., 1973. Section on Inland Waterways only.

The basic points [of IWA policy on commercial waterways]. *IWA Bulletin.* 104. March 1973. 44–7.

IWA's first Secretary – a tribute to Mr L.T.C. Rolt. *IWA Bulletin*. 110. September 1974. 6–7.

IWA Continental visit – it was a huge success. *IWA Bulletin*. 115. December 1975. 27–9.

Lionel Munk – a distinguished IWA campaigner. *IWA Waterways*. 117. August 1976. 8–9.

Charles Hadfield records Fred's role [Fred Doerflinger as ISG chairman]. *IWA Waterways*. 121. December 1977. 21.

The evolution of the canal inclined plane. *Jnl. Rly. Canal Hist. Soc.* 25 (3). September 1979. 94–101.

Glimpses of the North American waterways. *IWA Waterways*. 127. Winter 1979. 16–17.

Rivers and canals. Chapter V in Skempton, A.W. (ed.). *John Smeaton FRS*. London: Thomas Telford, 1981.

Recipe for a Vice-President. *IWA Waterways*. 140. April 1984. 10–11.

Out and Back. *Waterways World*. Vol 13 No. 8. August 1984, 31–2.

Evolution of the Canal Inclined Plane. *American Canals*. 58. August 1986, 4–7.

Obituaries. Frederic Doerflinger. *IWA Waterways*. 164. April 1992, 37.

Canals and river navigations: The Canal Era; and William Jessop. Contributions to J. Simmons and G. Biddle (eds) *The Oxford Companion to British Railway History*. Oxford University Press: Oxford, 1997.

OTHER BOOKS AND BOOKLETS

(With C. Hamilton ELLIS) *The young collector's handbook*. London: Oxford University Press, 1940. 2nd edn., entitled *The collector's handbook*, ed. by Charles J. Kaberry, 1951.

Civilian fire fighter. London: English Universities Press, 1941. 2nd edn. 1941.

(With Alexander D'AGAPEYEFF) *Maps*. London: Oxford University Press, 1942. (Meridian Book Series); 2nd impression 1945; 2nd edn. 1950 (Compass Book Series No. 3).

WILMOTH, V.J. (Ed.) *Manual of firemanship* (7 vols. in 8). London: HMSO, 1943–8. Charles Hadfield wrote a significant proportion of this, but is not credited with the authorship.

(With Frank EYRE) *The fire service to-day*. London: Oxford University Press, n.d. [1944]. 2nd edn. 1953.

(With James MacCOLL) *Pilot guide to political London*. London: Pilot Press, 1945.

(With James MacCOLL) *British local government*. London: Hutchinson's University Library, n.d. [1948]. (Hutchinson's University Library No. 14).

As ALEXANDER, Charles. [Nom de plume]. *The Church's Year*. London: Oxford University Press, 1950. 2nd edn. 1956 (described as 2nd impression); 2nd impression 1959; 3rd impression *c.* 1963.

Quaker Publicity. London: Friends Home Service Committee. 1959. 2nd edn. 1962.

(With Alice Mary HADFIELD)

The Cotswolds. London: Batsford, 1966. 2nd edn. 1967 (described as 2nd impression).

Atmospheric railways: a Victorian venture in silent speed. Newton Abbot: David & Charles, 1967.

(With Alice Mary HADFIELD) (eds. and contributors).

The Cotswolds: a new study. Newton Abbot: David & Charles, 1973. Paperback edn. 1981.

(With Alice Mary HADFIELD)

Introducing the Cotswolds. Newton Abbot: David & Charles, 1976.

Strange Fidelity. South Cerney: Alice Mary Books, 1992.

Soren Kierkegaard. South Cerney: Alice Mary Books, 1992.

UNPUBLISHED WORKS

(With Alice Mary HADFIELD) *Marriage à La Maison*, 1966 (submitted for publication)

Youth Shows But Half, 1974 (privately circulated)

Round Africa in Eighty Years, 1988 (submitted for publication)

(With Alice Mary HADFIELD) *Love Poems*, 1991 (privately circulated)

Our Love, 1990–4 (incomplete drafts)
Waterways Tales to Tell, 1995 (incomplete drafts)

A Note on Collections

Charles Hadfield's two main collections are housed as follows:

British Canals files and BWB files: British Library of Political and Economic Science, London School of Economics, Portugal Street, London

World Canals files and photographs: Boat Museum, South Pier Road, Ellesmere Port, South Wirral

Further items will be archived after publication of this book.

INDEX

This index excludes reference to Charles Hadfield himself. Dates of birth and/or death of selected figures are included, whether or not these are referred to in the text. Where dates are uncertain, this is indicated by *c*.